Prem Rawat and Counterculture

Also available from Bloomsbury:

Hinduism and the 1960s, Paul Oliver
Islam and Britain, Ron Geaves
UFOs, Conspiracy Theories and the New Age, David G. Robertson
The Pop Festival: History, Music, Media, Culture, ed. George McKay

Prem Rawat and Counterculture

Glastonbury and New Spiritualities

Ron Geaves

High Culture : Global
of the Hippie Trail : An History

BLOOMSBURY ACADEMIC
LONDON • NEW YORK • OXFORD • NEW DELHI • SYDNEY

BLOOMSBURY ACADEMIC
Bloomsbury Publishing Plc
50 Bedford Square, London, WC1B 3DP, UK
1385 Broadway, New York, NY 10018, USA
29 Earlsfort Terrace, Dublin 2, Ireland

BLOOMSBURY, BLOOMSBURY ACADEMIC and the Diana logo are trademarks of
Bloomsbury Publishing Plc

First published in Great Britain 2020
This paperback edition published in 2021

Copyright © Ron Geaves, 2020

Ron Geaves has asserted his right under the Copyright, Designs and Patents Act,
1988, to be identified as Author of this work.

Cover design by Maria Rajka
Cover image: June 1971, the second annual Glastonbury music festival, which saw the first
use of a pyramid stage. (© Ian Tyas/Keystone Features/Getty Images)

For legal purposes the Acknowledgements on p. vii constitute an extension
of this copyright page.

A catalogue record for this book is available from the British Library.

Library of Congress Control Number: 2019949115

ISBN: HB: 978-1-3500-9087-3
PB: 978-1-3502-6544-8
ePDF: 978-1-3500-9088-0
eBook: 978-1-3500-9089-7

Typeset by Newgen KnowledgeWorks Pvt. Ltd., Chennai, India

To find out more about our authors and books visit www.bloomsbury.com
and sign up for our newsletters.

Contents

Figures

Acknowledgements

This book could not have been written without Prem Rawat who permitted me to accompany him to Glastonbury in 1971 and stand on the first pyramid stage with him as he addressed the crowd. I also acknowledge the precious friendships which developed at that time and have outlasted time and circumstances. Some I carry within me as death has separated us in recent years. We are a generation on our way out. Special thanks are due to Chris Partridge for the work he has done on counterculture and his interest in this work. I acknowledge my debt to the counterculture for helping me frame my life. As always, I thank my wife Catherine and my son Dominic for their patience and assistance when I am working on a project as lengthy as this one. A final acknowledgement has to be offered to Prem Rawat. I apologize if the various representations I have made do not in any way meet his recognition of himself. These are my academic deliberations and in no way function in the same world as the gratitude I feel for the way he has enhanced my life over the five decades I have known him. In all the contacts I have had with him, he has always remained gracious.

Note on quotations and spellings

In most cases, there are not any issues regarding spellings as in the most part the contents deal with contemporary religious manifestations in Britain and North America. However, on occasion, backgrounds of various figures that originate in India require an exploration of Hindu or Muslim doctrines or practices. In such cases where Hindi, Sanskrit or Urdu terminology are utilized, the work does not use diacritics and the conventions of anthropological fieldwork, wherever possible, are followed. There are exceptions. Quoting from sources, I have followed the spelling used in the quotation or citation. Thus, it is possible for the same terms to be spelled differently throughout the book. Titles of works that are transliterated from Hindi, Sanskrit or Urdu precisely follow the variant used in the original. There is an issue of names of Indian masters (gurus). These are often titles utilized in India, where it is considered disrespectful to use a given name(s). However, Prem Rawat prefers his given name to be used. This has not always been the case. I have decided to use Prem Rawat throughout except where writings of the period refer to him as Guru Maharaj Ji or Maharaji. I am aware that Andrew Kerr, the primary organizer of Glastonbury Festival in 1971, preferred 'Fair' as opposed to 'Fayre'. Andrew considered 'Fayre' to be pretentious. I have, after consideration, decided to use 'Fayre' as it was used in the publicity for the event and speaks of the neo-Romantic desire to return to nature and old Albion.

Abbreviations

DLM	Divine Light Mission
DUO	Divine United Organization
HHH	(3HO) Healthy, Happiness, Holy Organization
HPM	Human Potential Movement
ISKCON	International Society of Krishna Consciousness
LSD	(Acid) Lysergic acid diethylamide
NRM	New Religious Movements
PEP	Peace Education Programme
RILKO	Research into Lost Knowledge Organization
RPFS	Renaissance Pleasure Faire of Southern California
TM	Transcendental Meditation
TPRF	The Prem Rawat Foundation

Preface

'Mr. Geard has the idea', John went on, addressing himself now to Sam Dekker alone, 'of holding a sort of Pageant. A sort of Religious Fair at Midsummer. ... I believe he has the 24th June in his mind, ... In the Tor Fair-field, eh, Sir? His idea is to make this such an event, that people will come to it from France and Germany, as well as from all over England. It will, of course, be entirely friendly to all religious bodies. It won't be a church affair. It won't be a non-conformist affair. It'll be ... I'm right in this, aren't I, Mr Geard? ... A Glastonbury Revival, absolutely independent of the Churches. ... '.

Powys, 1933: 161

Cottage industry of ageing hippies

The British novelist and esotericist John Cooper Powys, writing in 1933, was almost prophetic speaking through the mouth of his character, Mr Geard, the mayor of Glastonbury. Andrew Kerr, the main inspiration for Glastonbury Fayre in 1971, would bring the idea of a 'sort of Religious Fair ... at Midsummer' to fulfilment. Glastonbury Festival has gone on to become an event that is known by just about everyone in Britain and remains the foremost rock festival in the world. My interest in writing this book arose from my attending the Fayre in 1971 not in the crowd but standing on the famed Pyramid Stage as Prem Rawat addressed the attendees. I looked down on a large number of freaks, many completely high on various substances, as they chanted 'Hare Krishna' and wondered what was about to happen. At the time, I no longer felt that I was one of them. My life had been transformed in India on meeting Prem Rawat, and I no longer participated in psychedelic or opiate use. I was healthy in body, mind and spirit, vegetarian and considered myself a lifetime resident of the ashram established in Britain in early 1970. Many of the audience would, although they did not know it at the time, experience similar life-changing epiphanies over the next two years.

My journey with Prem Rawat began in India in the summer of 1969. I had travelled overland and encountered the Indian organization, Divine Light Mission, established by Prem Rawat's father. I didn't like it much. I had been an active anarchist for several years and had an issue with organizations. I left for Varanasi where I became a sadhu, living on the streets to the detriment of my health. I returned and met Prem Rawat in the town of Ghaziabad where he addressed a crowd of around ten thousand. In our meeting, the 11-year-old boy would hold a short conversation with me. He asked me, 'What are you looking for?' I replied, 'Peace'. After all, I considered myself a peace movement activist. Instead of accepting my answer, he asked again, 'What kind of peace are you looking for?' I floundered. He went on to explain that peace could not be achieved in the world unless it was found within the heart of each individual. He asked me if I had found such peace. I knew the answer was 'No!' He then requested me to search throughout the length and breadth of India, meeting the countless religious and spiritual paths on offer and to return to him if I could not be satisfied. He grinned and said, 'I am young. You have time.' More than his words, I was struck by the enigma of an 11-year-old playing with a tape recorder, whose countenance shone, whose eyes radiated authority and whose atmosphere was one of profound stillness. I stayed.

With these words, I ceased to search for peace in political activism and dismissed the drug experiences I had relied upon for spiritual enlightenment. I find myself at odds with Stephen Kent, whose excellent book *From Slogans to Mantras* (2001), I have drawn upon extensively. Kent too was inspired to write his book after an encounter with Prem Rawat in 1974 while a 'hippie'. Like me, he went on to become a professor in religion. He considered Prem Rawat's examples to be 'banal' and unlike his companions dismissed the guru (p. xvi). Even so, the encounter led him to 'ponder this mystery for years'. The riddle would lead him to recall that 'disorientating night' and be motivated to 'interpret the crucial experiences of my generation'.

They were my generation too, and although I have never found Prem Rawat's discourse 'banal', I also find myself motivated to address the same question. Kent's moment would arise from the encounter in Philadelphia, mine would be the Pyramid Stage at Glastonbury Fayre. He would go on to write a number of articles on the counterculture whereas I would get there more slowly. My interest as an academic was in the transmigration of South Asian religions to Britain after the Second World War. I focused on the migrants and their children rather than the Indian gurus who influenced the lives of so many of my generation. Like many in the Study of Religion, I would be drawn to theorize as a result of my empirical work. I would be surprised to the degree at which academics essentialized religions, preferring text to lived experience. This would lead me to write 'The Borders between Religions: The Challenge to the World Religions' Approach to Religious Education', *British Journal of Religious Education*, 21 (1), pp. 20–31, in Autumn 1998, and 'The Dangers of Essentialism: South Asian

Communities in Britain and the 'World Religions' Approach to the Study of Religion', *Contemporary South Asia* 14 (1), pp. 75–90, in 2005.

I would be distracted for many years and remain so by the global crisis of values impacting on Muslims in Britain but would be compelled to write on Prem Rawat as I noticed the lacuna in the literature written from the Study of Religion, and where such literature existed, the number of factual errors concerning his life and teachings. A number of interventions would result between 2004 and 2013, including 'From Divine Light Mission to Elan Vital and Beyond: An Exploration of Change and Adaptation', *Nova Religio*, 7 (3), pp. 45–62, in March 2004; 'Globalisation, Charisma, Innovation, and Tradition: An Exploration of the Transformations in the Organisational Vehicles for the Transmission of the Teachings of Maharaji', *Journal of Alternative Spirituality and New Age Studies*, 2, in April 2006 and in the same year, 'From Guru Maharaj Ji to Prem Rawat: Paradigm Shifts over the Period of Forty Years as a "Master" (1966–2006)', *New and Alternative Religions in the US*, 4, Asian Traditions, Eugene Gallagher and William Ashcroft, eds. Westport: Greenwood. In 2007, I continued with 'From Totapuri to Maharaji: Reflections on a (Lineage) Parampara', in *Indian Religions: Renaissance and Revival*, Anna King, ed. London: Equinox, and in January 2009, 'Forget Transmitted Memory: The De-Traditionalized "Religion" of Prem Rawat', *Journal of Contemporary Religion*, 24 (1), 19–33. The last piece was written in 2013 entitled, 'Hans Ji Maharaj and the Divya Sandesh Parishad', in *Handbook of Oriental Studies*, Section 2, India, *Brill Encyclopedia of Hinduism*, J. Bronkhorst and A. Milinar, eds, 22 (5), Knut Jacobsen et al., eds, 470–5. Leiden: Brill.

 As with many scholars, the tendency is to write a monograph after several articles. I have decided to write it now because ⌈Prem Rawat's arrival in the West and Glastonbury Fayre in June 1971 were only four days apart.⌋ Each will celebrate fifty-year anniversaries in 2021. As with Stephen Kent, I can say, I have decided to 'set theory aside and allowed the very colourful material to speak for itself' (p. xvii). At least, that was the intention but I began to realize that the concepts of Easternization and the Western esotericism explored so ably by my friend and colleague Professor Chris Partridge, and considered to form the bricolage that came to known as 'New Age', were often too essentialized to form an accurate picture of events in that period of 'peace and love'. Therefore I set out to discover the theorists who were writing on these topics. ⌈Inwardly, I seethed at descriptions of Prem Rawat as 'New Age'. I knew that he profoundly drew upon a tradition that predated new spiritualities in the Western world by centuries.⌋ He might agree with New Age practitioners that experience is paramount but the experience he refers to was most vividly portrayed by what Gold (1987) and Vaudeville (1987) call the sant phenomenon. So, theoretical frameworks had to re-emerge and inform my interpretations of events.

Finally, I had to undertake some interviews with those who were around at that time. I call them 'conversations' rather than interviews as they were undertaken in 2018 with people I regard as friends rather than informants. The best part of such conversations was seeing them again, in some cases after several decades had passed. I thank them for the love that has lasted throughout most of my adult life and wish them well.

1

Introduction

The contents of this book revolve around a little-known encounter between Prem Rawat (Guru Maharaj Ji) and the British counterculture gathered at Glastonbury Fayre in June 1971. Although Prem Rawat was only a child and attended the festival for little more than one hour, his short speech to the gathered 'hippies' would have a dramatic impact on his life and the direction of the late-1960s counterculture on both sides of the Atlantic. The events leading up to the encounter and its aftereffects reveal elements of counterculture spirituality that throw light on the important scholarly theories of occulture and Easternization in the study of contemporary spiritualities.

On 17 June 1971, the 13-year-old Prem Rawat, known in his native India, or at least the Hindi-speaking northern states, as Balyogeshwar, loosely translated as 'the born Lord of Yogis', and called by his Indian devotees as 'Guru Maharaj Ji',[1] arrived at Heathrow Airport. He was greeted by a motley crowd of counterculture flower children who covered him in garlands, to a degree that he could hardly see over the top. He was led through a VIP tunnel to a Rolls Royce equally bedecked in flowers and whisked away up the M4 to a small street off the King's Road where he stayed for the next two weeks. Some of those who greeted him were dressed in white saris (if female) or white Indian pyjamas (if male). Others were in the more well-known and varied garb of the late 'flower-power' era. They held flowers or incense sticks or stood with folded hands and bowed their heads as if in prayer. The British media had a field day covering the event with photographs. Typical of the tongue-in-cheek tone of the national newspaper coverage, the *Daily Mirror* on 18 June sported the headline 'Worshippers greet the boy guru straight from Heaven' and went on to state, 'They fell in homage at his feet. They threw garlands of carnations round his neck. They smothered him with petals taken from a massive sack.' Those who had come to greet the guru didn't help matters with comments quoted by the reporter; for example, 'a white-robed Indian, said that the Guru came from Heaven although the youngster's body,

Figure 1 Prem Rawat arrives at Heathrow, 17 June 1971. Copyright RKV Delhi.

he admitted, came in fact from the Himalayas'.[2] In other respects the article was informative, stating that the guru would stay in Britain for thirteen days and 'make appearances in London, Leicester, Exeter and Glastonbury, Somerset'.

On 20 June, three days later, Glastonbury Fayre began on the land belonging to Worthy Farm in Somerset. The free festival would last until 24 June and would include Midsummer's Day on 23 June. Even today, for all of the success of the Glastonbury Festival, attracting the biggest stars in popular music globally, and attendances well over one hundred thousand and worldwide media coverage, Glastonbury Fayre in 1971 is considered iconic—'the Legendary One' (McKay, 2000: 96). On the evening of 23 June, the young guru spoke from the Pyramid Stage to the assembled crowd of around twelve thousand, many of whom were 'high' on cannabis or LSD, breaking into the set of Brinsley Schwartz, whose lead singer was Nick Lowe. This event is documented in a variety of media outlets, most of them highly subjective.[3] Confirming the truism that 'if you remembered the '60s, you probably were not there', very few in the crowd can recall the guru's actual words. His twenty-minute speech has however been documented. Nick Lowe thought that he was 'touting' for money;[4] others thought that he was proclaiming a world without sex. Thomas Crimble, one of the co-organizers and member of Hawkwind (1969–70) and Skin Alley (1970–72), noted that 'the thing that freaked everyone out was when he said there would be no more "sex" in the world. His English wasn't quite perfect and what he meant to say was there would be no more "sects" ' (Crimble, 2004: 33). The combination of a poor sound system, Prem Rawat's command of English and his thick Indian accent, and the crowd's level of a hold on reality led to these misunderstandings, and Nick Lowe was justifiably angered after having his set interrupted by overzealous followers ('The Best of Glastonbury Moments'). All in all, the hype was tremendous. Underlying the various narratives of the occasion is an interesting story of how a 13-year-old boy attending St. Joseph's Academy in Dehradun, where he was taught by Benedictine monks, neat and dapper with well-oiled short hair, usually dressed in Indian white pyjamas and highly polished black leather slip-ons, residing with his family in a British-built bungalow in Dehradun, a former British military garrison town, should come to address a 'stoned' crowd of 'hippies' at Glastonbury Fayre, speaking between rock bands sandwiched on either side of his appearance.

More significantly, this convergence of Prem Rawat and Glastonbury Fayre in 1971 reveals an important piece in the developing jigsaw that forms the bricolage that came to be known as 'New Age' or, more neutrally, contemporary spirituality. Both Glastonbury and Prem Rawat have gone on to re-emerge in significantly different identities to the one presented in 1971. In June 2019, both will celebrate fiftieth anniversaries of this significant milestone in their respective histories: Prem Rawat, his arrival in the West and the beginnings of his global mission to promote a message of peace; Glastonbury, its beginnings as the premier event for all popular musicians and for thousands of festival goers at the height of British summertime. Few today are aware of the controversies that surrounded the young Prem Rawat during the 1970s or the 'spiritual' origins of the festival and the significance of the meeting that took place in 1971 in forming elements of popular culture, which may still be regarded as eccentric but have in various forms entered the mainstream.

The following contents are not concerned with the festival's undeniable legendary status in the annals of rock music and other popular genres. I am not a musicologist, even though a lover of most forms of popular music, but a scholar of religion and my interest in this case study is in the fusion of Eastern religions, esotericism and indigenous religious revivals, combined with the discovery of new and embodied sacred spaces that led to new forms of spirituality in the latter decades of the twentieth century.

To tell the tale, I shall rely heavily on the narratives of those who attended the event, whether festival goers or the followers of Prem Rawat. I am aware that several of the key players are now dead but some have left written testimonies whether online, in biographies or in the handful of written accounts on the Glastonbury Festival. I am aware that memory plays tricks on us and that even fresh testimony would be highly influenced by heightened emotions and perceptions. However, spiritual or religious feelings are in themselves highly emotive, arising primarily from the experiential dimension of life. The formation of religious 'truths', some of which were life-changing, will remain in the memory as stepping-stone moments in the uniquely human occupation of making sense of our lives. I am not so much concerned with the 'truth' of these recalled narratives, or the possible distortion of facts conveyed by these various sets of informants, but how events and narratives shape lives and formed a new subjectivity in British popular culture. I am aware that in many cases the key informants, including myself, are looking back on events across fifty years. Glastonbury Fayre, Prem Rawat and 1960s counterculture are part of modern cultural mythmaking and, in some cases, part of the construction of spiritual or religious narratives to support newly emerging movements. Danièle Hervieu-Léger argues that religion exists when 'the authority of tradition' has been invoked 'in support of the act of believing' (2000: 76). She declares that 'one would describe any form of believing as religious which sees its commitment to a chain of belief it adopts as all-absorbing' (ibid.: 81). Hervieu-Léger's theory of religion as a chain of memory is useful for my approach to the memories of my informants. These stories carry meaning beyond the surface, as in all myths whether thousands of years past in origin or constructed in more recent times. For the scholar of religion, both ancient and contemporary myths are fascinating insights into human behaviour and social history. For scholars of contemporary religion, these new myths provide insights into how religions develop as distinctly human formations. In addition to testimonies, I shall draw upon media accounts and secondary sources to analyse and place in context such transformations, particularly with a view to challenge or nuance some of the existing theories of counterculture spirituality.

I need to fully disclose my position. I stood on the Pyramid Stage at Glastonbury Fayre with the young Prem Rawat and accompanied him to the event and returned with him to London that night. I recognize some of the testimonies from others as accurate depictions of the occasion but there are some that to my recollection are inaccurate. My memories are also suspect, so where necessary I shall supplement them by gathering evidence from as many eye witness accounts as possible. The advantage of having been there is that I know the key players, where they are now, and that they are willing to speak to me as an old acquaintance, an ally in a particular view of the world, or simply because of my professional status in the latter part of my life. Any interviews that were carried out I have called 'conversations' as my insider's privileged position meant that such discussions were conducted in a mood of reminiscing between friends rather than formal structured anthropological interviews. My life has been formed by the events that unfolded as were theirs and I am aware that this book will be part of the mythologizing process to some as well as demythologizing to others. Of course, there is a downside to my subjectivity. In the study of religions and anthropology, this is known as the insider/outsider or emic/etic dichotomy.[5]

Emic/etic issues

I have challenged the insider/outsider dichotomy throughout my career. I accept that there are drawbacks and strengths to each position (Geaves, 2019). Yet it strikes me as too simplistic. Life is rarely compartmentalized into rigid polarized positions. Self is fluid, so is identity. Very often in the study of religion, or in writing about religious people, it is assumed that once conviction is established it remains immutable bar exceptional circumstances. Even in cases of dramatic conversion, it is unlikely that faith will remain static throughout a life. When we assume fixed positions, it oversimplifies, reduces our humanity and tells a false narrative of religious experience. Even in the course of one day, positions can fluctuate from faith to no faith and back again. In all my investigations into religious phenomena, I am sometimes an insider, sometimes an outsider. I affirm some discoveries about a particular religious tradition and I deny others. At one end of the insider/outsider spectrum, I am an individual and therefore an outsider to all others; at the other extreme I share in a common humanity, so I am an insider to everyone. Personally, I would go even further and affirm my sense of empathy with all other life forms that share the gift of existence. Between these two poles, there are infinite expressions of belonging and not belonging. As a scholar of religion with an interest in lived religion, I am trained in empathy, the ability to walk in the shoes of the 'other', but that does not mean I endorse the 'other' in all circumstances. I rarely reject totally even when I would not endorse or participate in certain human behaviour or worldviews. The 'self' that walked on the stage with Prem Rawat in 1971 is not the 'self' I inhabit today but certain elements remain. I was formed by counterculture membership from the age of 16 and although my views have changed, been reconsidered, reembraced and dismissed, I still consider myself as outside the mainstream. I acknowledge that this distant 'self' helped to form me as I exist today but I am to some degree surprised to see myself as I was then and appear as a figure of curiosity to myself in the captured images of the event.

Even so that 'self' needs to be declared in the interest of my positionality. There will be those, both academic and non-academic, who would have demanded that I declare myself and my interest in the events described and my objectivity in telling the tale. So be it, but let the above provisos warn the suspicious. Anthropologists demand the reflexive from the field researcher, and the contemporary study of religion increasingly demands the same standard within the methodological process. I will not recount the full story of my engagement with Prem Rawat in this introduction as it will inform parts of later chapters. Suffice it to say that I have known him for nearly half a century. This will create challenges that I have not faced with previous books, as I will not only have to deal with my 'insider' status but I will also have to insert myself into the story as a principal informant. I have never played both interviewer and interviewed before. I am part of this story. I remain one of the only contemporary academics in the study of religion who has written articles on Prem Rawat and the various institutional organizational manifestations that he has created and dissolved as his work progressed or transformed and that has in part initiated my interest for this longer analysis of his part in the history of twentieth-century counterculture (2004, 2006a, 2006b, 2007, 2009, 2013). The other academic to write recently is Stephen Kent (2001) who describes how encountering Prem Rawat in 1974 was influential in determining the direction of his career (p. xv). Kent would focus on the shift from political activism to Eastern spirituality in the early 1970s. He acknowledged the role of Prem Rawat in this process. Other scholars of religion have written about this era in the context of creating a new cluster of spiritualities in modern Western society. Chris Partridge has written on the historical formation of 'occulture' (2004, 2006, 2017) and the development of 'high culture' (2018), exploring the use of drugs in various counterculture manifestations. Paul Heelas (1996, 2012) has written extensively on New Age. Steven Sutcliffe (2013) has advocated the positioning of New Age and other contemporary spiritualities to be moved from the margins of the study of religion and be treated with the same theoretical respect as major religious formations. I am indebted to all these scholars and many more for their theorizing of the field, but more significantly I note that all of them have admitted to countercultural belonging at some stages of their life. I am certain that there are many others whose names I have not mentioned. I am not alone in my endeavours to explore phenomena that formed part of my own life story. Religion and spirituality are subjectivities that determine powerful allegiances and feelings, both positive and negative, and it is not surprising that scholars are drawn to explore their own creation of meaning within the academic study of religion.

Survivors of the encounter between Prem Rawat and Glastonbury are decreasing year by year. There are even fewer who can speak of their experiences that helped to form the bricolage that became counterculture spirituality in the early 1970s. I am one of them. Throughout the 1960s I had moved through left-wing political activism, joining anti-war demonstrators and protesting outside the South African and Iranian embassies against apartheid and the Shah's regime. I had travelled to Europe to attend anarchist conferences and marched with the Provo in Holland.[6] In all these activities, I had worked as a freelance reporter for *Freedom*, the oldest anarchist newspaper in Europe.[7] From the mid-1960s, I had begun to experiment with psychedelics and opiates and developed an interest in Indian religions and Sufism. My influences were the beat generation; the poets Lawrence Ferlinghetti, Gregory Corso and Allen Ginsberg; and the novels of Jack Kerouac and William Burroughs. I was reading Jalaluddin Rumi, Alan Watts, Lobsang Rampa, Aleister Crowley, Alan Davies and Jean Genet and listening to the music of Jimi Hendrix, the Doors, Traffic, Cream, Bob Dylan and Frank Zappa, among many others. I attended the free concerts in Hyde Park and spent my weekends at Middle Earth in Covent Garden and the Roundhouse in Camden Town. I lived in Oxford and Soho and listened to jazz and folk in the beat pubs of the West End and Notting Hill Gate. The drugs and involvement in flower power did not bring an end to my political activism. I marched with the anarchists in the spring of 1968 into Grosvenor Square protesting against the Vietnam War, took part in the demonstrations against the *Daily Mirror* in 1968 outraged at the shooting of Rudi Dutschke[8] and supported the French demonstrations on the streets of Paris and the struggles of the anarcho-communist groups in Germany. I read *Private Eye* and the *International Times* along with Marvel Comics and *Oz*.

I believed with many others that the world was about to change dramatically. In late 1968 I left for India, hitchhiking with a girlfriend, hoping to find Enlightenment. In India, I lived as a Hindu sadhu in Varanasi. It was in India that I met with the 11-year-old Prem Rawat, who I would know for many years as Guru Maharaj Ji. I had returned to the UK in 1969 and helped begin the first ashram of Prem Rawat in London. I was at Heathrow when he arrived in 1971. He asked me to be at his side until he left the country and I was witness to the attempts to bring him to Glastonbury Fayre. I knew most of the key players. I have considered how to introduce myself in the book's contents. I have decided not to use the personal pronoun 'I' once the book moves past the Introduction. Using my surname in the third person appears odd except when citing a text. After some deliberation, I have decided to recall my testimony as 'the author'.

The literature

Considerable academic literature exists on the New Age (history, causes, definitions, theories), for example, Lewis and Melton (1992), Kyle (1995), York (1995), Hanegraaff (1996), Heelas (1996), Sutcliffe (2003), Partridge (2004), Kemp and Lewis (2007) and Sutcliffe and Gilhus (2013). These books provide the contextual literature for this work and enable the author to assess existing theories and the importance of both Prem Rawat and Glastonbury Fayre, particularly the encounter between the guru and the festival in the building of a narrative that explains the shifting sands of counterculture spirituality in the 1970s. Marion Bowman has written extensively on Glastonbury (the Tor and the Abbey) as a sacred site but not on the festival/Fayre, but her work helps to explain the significance of the site, both as a Christian sacred space and in British esotericism (2003, 2005, 2006, 2007a, 2007b, 2009a, 2009b, 2011, 2015a, 2015b).

No in-depth academic treatment of Glastonbury Fayre exists but Steven Sutcliffe (2003) provides a comparable approach to the formation of the New Age by focusing on a particular case study (Findhorn) as a place of historical significance in counterculture spiritualities. George McKay (2000, 2015) has written on the Fayre as part of 'festival culture' but does not say much about its spiritual origins, although Christopher Partridge has written a short article in 2006 on the sacralization of festival culture that mentions Glastonbury as an important site in that process, but his focus is the later period of 'rave' culture. I have drawn extensively on the work of musicologists and historians of contemporary culture, especially those writing on rock festivals in the period under discussion. They do not necessarily perceive these events as religious or spiritual, but my contention is that the music of the counterculture performed a religious function for the participants.

There is popular literature on Glastonbury Festival. These works provide insights or very brief windows into the motivations of the founders of Glastonbury Fayre and photographs of the event, for example, John Bailey's (ed.) (2013), *Glastonbury: The Complete Story of the Festival* or Crispin Aubrey and John Shearlaw (eds) (2004), *Glastonbury Festival Tales*. These works are more coffee table books than academic works but George McKay's (2000) *Glastonbury: A Very English Fair* does provide a more scholarly treatment but focuses on all the Glastonbury events from the perspective of festival culture. It does not provide a focus on the spiritual aspects of the 1971 Fayre, although it recognizes its significance within the formation of popular culture. There is also a history of the Free Festival Movement by Sam Knee published in 2017, but there is no comparable book that focuses only on Glastonbury Fayre. Andrew Kerr (2011), one of the co-founders, has written an autobiography that covers his major role in organizing the festival; however, this is more of a primary source, especially useful when interviews cannot be carried out due to the deaths of major players.

Very little serious assessment has taken place of Prem Rawat's role in counterculture spirituality in the 1970s and most of the web material of his visit to Glastonbury is controversially subjective. The popular biography by Andrea Sagan (2007) does not contextualize or examine the guru's contribution to transformations in the counterculture of the time, although it is useful to provide Prem Rawat's life story as narrated through the lens of key followers. Most contributions on Prem Rawat are either written by past or present students with a positive or negative polemical intention. The exceptions would be the exploration of Prem Rawat's place in Indian religious movements historically and

Figure 2 Prem Rawat in Dehradun aged 11 in school uniform. Copyright RKV Delhi.

his organizational attempts to anchor his message in the UK and North America written by the author and a small number of sociologists writing shortly after the period covered by this book, most notably James Downton (1979), which still remains the only monograph written solely on the guru's activities in the United States in the aftermath of his success in the 1970s. Stephen Kent (2001) shows the divisions within the US counterculture caused by the success of the young guru, particularly in the context of the clash between Eastern spirituality and political activism. A number of sociological texts contain chapters on Prem Rawat's early activities but these were mainly written in the 1980s in the context of the anti-cult movement and academic attempts to assess the fierce polemic often led by ex-members.[9] These works are of little relevance to this volume other than providing some insights into the causes of Prem Rawat's success and to reposition his organizational activities as one of a number of new religious movements of significance to counterculture.

There are a number of useful works by followers and ex-followers, especially those who write from the perspective of being former counterculture exponents who discovered the guru's message of peace and were transformed by it. These accounts help position the guru in counterculture narratives and also indicate the variety of spiritualities influencing individuals at the time of their contact with the guru. Key among these are Charles Cameron and Rennie Davies (1973), Sophie Collier (1978), David Lovejoy (2005), Jos Lammers (2007) and Michael Finch (2009). These accounts are intensely positioned subjectivities written on either side of cult and anti-cult debates but their relevance to this volume is not concerned with their creation of truth claims but that they all provide accounts of counterculture spirituality located within personal transformation during the period of interest. Together these works, enhanced by interviews with key survivors of the encounter between Prem Rawat and the counterculture milieu of Glastonbury Fayre, can help to build the narrative of the event and its importance. The key theorizing that arises from the narrative concerns the relationship between Indian spirituality (Easternization), esotericism and the creation of an occulture, which includes within it New Age spirituality. It is argued that the term 'Easternization' essentializes the wide diversity that forms Indian worldviews, especially those referred to as 'Hinduism', and that Eastern religions transmigrating to the West could be highly antagonistic toward late 1960s counterculture and part of its destruction in the early 1970s and therefore remained in existence outside the orbit of an occulture bricolage.

The contents

In Chapter 2, the various theories concerning New Age and Contemporary Spirituality will be identified and assessed drawing upon the existing literature, especially in the light of the bewildering attempts to categorize the phenomena in any meaningful way. In particular, along with Easternization, Christopher Partridge's concept of 'occulture' will be explored in order to consider its usefulness for this study along with Andrew Rawlinson's categories of Eastern Masters and Elizabeth Nelson's identification of the key elements of 1960s and early 1970s counterculture. The relationship between counterculture and Eastern spiritualities is also introduced. The chapter concludes that Steven Sutcliffe, Ingvild Gilhus and Lisapotte Frisk (2013) are the best theorists to understand the New Age within in any attempt to assess Prem Rawat as they lift the concept out of the bewildering confusion of earlier attempts to define New Age and into the mainstream of the study of religion.

Chapter 3 explores the history of Easternization from its roots in European colonial expansion through to the arrival of Indian religious teachers in the decades following the Second World War. The arrival of Prem Rawat in 1971 will be presented in the context of this phenomenon but he is not examined in detail until the following chapter. A number of prominent gurus who came to the West are introduced from the perspective of their various influences on the Easternization of counterculture. It will be argued that there is no apparent single cause for the number of teachers arriving in the UK and the United States during the 1960s or earlier. It will also be asserted that there is no common element that can be found in those who choose to bring their messages to the Western world, although Rawlinson's identification of 'Inner Hinduism' is introduced as a possible common factor. In the context of the considerable range of differences between doctrines and practices in Hinduism, Harvey Cox's (1977) identification of 'immediacy' as a possible common element of attraction to the counterculture is introduced to support Rawlinson.

Rawlinson's analysis of Western teachers who taught Eastern spirituality is brought into play to show that elements that might be shared are the following: a direction from their own teacher, a desire to promote Eastern spirituality in the perceived materialism of the Western world or significant meeting with Western travellers. It is noted that each of the individuals who came to the West as teachers represented very different disciplines or trends within Indian spirituality and that Hinduism, unlike other 'world religions', does not possess a single trunk from where all its sub-traditions emerged. Consequently, it is necessary to nuance the theories surrounding Easternization in the light of academia's tendency to essentialize major religions, especially Hinduism.

Chapter 4 will focus only on Prem Rawat, particularly the circumstances that brought him to the West in 1971. It will locate him within the history of religions in India, especially the sant tradition as explored by Gold (1987) and Schomer and McLeod (1987), introducing the concept of a 'solitary sant' as the best possible 'fit' for Prem Rawat's worldview. The chapter will provide a critical overview of scholarly interpretations, especially those perceived through the lens of mostly sociological studies carried out at the time, when he came to be perceived as the foremost Indian teacher of the counterculture.

Chapter 5 explores the development of the counterculture through from the mid-1960s by introducing counterculture music and festival culture, in particular the development of the Free Festival movement. The chapters provide the background to Glastonbury Fayre in 1971, showing how music and festival culture became part and parcel of counterculture distinctiveness and exhibited strong elements of spirituality derived from the East. Key festivals will be introduced such as the Mantra-In, the Human Be-In and Woodstock in the United States. The development of psychedelic ('soul-searching') rock will be explored as a vehicle for spiritual experience alongside drug usage, especially LSD (acid). George McKay's identification of 'festival culture' shows how these rock music venues emerged as a unique arena for the celebration of 'immediacy' but, of more relevance to the motives for creating the Fayre, demonstrates how commercialization provided the motivation for some countercultural individuals to seek authenticity.

Chapter 6 will assess the significance of Glastonbury as a repository of British spirituality, exploring both the Christian and esoteric emphasis on Glastonbury as a sacred space. Glastonbury Fayre will be identified as a reaction to the commercialization of festival culture. The Fayre was not the first festival in Britain nor is it the largest in terms of numbers or the mainstream success of the bands that played there. It does, however, have iconic status as an emblem of the era. I have allowed this chapter to emerge as a narrative, primarily created from the testimonies of the organizers, especially Andrew Kerr (2011). The focus will be on how contemporary or traditional religious beliefs were framed to create an event at Glastonbury on the summer solstice. The emerging importance of synchronicity or synergy among New Age adherents will be examined in the light of testimonies from the creators of the event.

As in the account of the Fayre, Chapter 7 will narrate the story of Prem Rawat's encounter with Glastonbury drawing on a number of voices including eye-witness accounts. It will include the convergence of key Glastonbury organizers with the teachings of Prem Rawat, most notably Andrew Kerr, but also recognize the major differences that existed in the perceptions of the guru at the time. Finally, there will be assessment of the immediate impact on British counterculture individuals caused by Prem Rawat's attendance at the Fayre. Chapter 8 will explore the impact of Glastonbury Fayre and Prem Rawat's encounter with the counterculture on contemporary spirituality in the 1970s after his visit to the Fayre in 1971. It will show how the festival was a key element in developing various trends in counterculture spirituality that would flourish in the 1970s and beyond. At the same time, it will show how Prem Rawat's success with the counterculture was enhanced by his visit to the Fayre but significantly how there were major discrepancies between his worldview and the developing spirituality of the counterculture, which would sometimes reflect divisions already existing in the counterculture. Easternization is reassessed in terms of its relationship with occulture and it is argued that sometimes Indian gurus were less than happy with countercultural lifestyles and appropriation of Eastern beliefs and determined to eradicate them from their followers.

Chapter 9 will round up all the theorization and events described in the previous chapters, exploring divergences in the context of countercultural expectations and Eastern teachers, especially Prem Rawat. In the process, there will be a reassessment of the 'solitary sant' categorization and its possible synergy with counterculture spiritual aspirations. The conclusion will be that there were more contradictions than similarities and this would in the end combine with circumstances to end Prem Rawat's period as the 'foremost counter-culture guru' of the era. It is hoped that in the process of revealing these more nuanced case study understandings of the diversity of Indian traditions transporting to the West, a more nuanced light is thrown on such concepts as Easternization, occulture, New Age and festival culture. Chapter 10 will provide a short postscript that shows how both the festival and Prem Rawat have transformed in later decades to emerge as they are at the end of the second decade of the twenty-first century and each approaches important fifty-year anniversaries in 2021.

2

Theorizing New Age and contemporary spiritualities

The rapid transformations in British and North American religious forms and spiritualities in the second half of the twentieth century brought about renewed academic interest ranging from sociological studies of secularization to examination of new religious movements (NRMs), especially those attracting the post-war counterculture generation coming to adulthood in the mid-1960s. The fragmentation of NRMs into the more amorphous New Age spiritualities and the latter's subsequent movement into mainstream society, or at least, selected elements of it, would also come under academic scrutiny from the mid-1980s. Although my primary interest was in the arrival of religions from South Asia, introduced by post-war migrations, and dramatically transforming the landscape of British religious life, I ventured into the terrain of NRM research with the publication of an article in *Nova Religio* in 2004 exploring the change in organizational structures that had been created to transmit the message of Prem Rawat in a global scenario. These changes had taken place in the 1980s and were perceived by ex-members as a deliberate strategy to nullify accusations of 'cult' status (Geaves, 2004). The article would raise howls of protests from ex-members who challenged my 'objectivity' and the right of insiders to write on movements where they had an ongoing commitment. I had first presented my analysis of the transformations at a conference in 2003[1] and later published it in the second edition of *Journal of Alternative Spirituality and New Age Studies* in 2006 (Geaves, 2006a). The contact with leading New Age and contemporary spirituality scholars at the conference led to an interesting lunch-time conversation in which Prem Rawat was defined as a 'New Age Guru'.

This did not conform with my understanding, especially as I was aware that audiences from both rural and urban areas of India numbering in hundreds of thousands gathered to listen to Prem Rawat with little or no concept of 'New Age'. It also raised questions of self-definition (emic) as opposed to academic classification (etic). I was certain that Prem Rawat would strenuously deny any links with New Age forms of spirituality or even acknowledge that he was 'spiritual'. In 2007, I tried to demonstrate that Prem Rawat had roots in Indian spirituality which located him in what Karen Schomer calls 'sant tradition', with little surety that he would agree with that definition either, even though the evidence was more supportive of his teachings than that of 'New Age' (Geaves, 2007). Prem Rawat had arrived in the West at the height of counterculture activity, overwhelmingly drawing the mainstay of his support from 'hippies' in both Britain and North America, and this had transformed his position as a 'guru' as understood in Indian terms. He had spoken from the Pyramid Stage at Glastonbury Fayre in the early summer of 1971 and gone on to become the most prominent counterculture guru throughout the 1970s, having a profound impact on the shape and form of the counterculture itself. It is possible that the formation and disbanding of various organizations including the well-known Divine Light Mission (DLM) led to the mistaken nomenclature of 'New Age Guru'. Prem Rawat would deny the category without hesitation, as he accepts neither 'religion' nor 'spirituality' as sufficient categories for his teachings. In view of the early organizational forms created on his arrival in the West and continuing throughout the 1970s, the definition of NRM would seem to have more mileage than 'New Age'. Both terms have been under scrutiny by scholars in the field but it appeared to me that Prem Rawat provided an interesting case study to reassess the relationship between 'New Age' spirituality made up of various bricolages, generally perceived to exhibit mixtures of Western esotericism and Easternization and shaping religious life in Britain and the United States within countercultural milieu from the nineteenth century.

The development of 'New Age' theorization

The earliest definitions of New Age not surprisingly came from insiders who were content to use the label. One of the first of these emic categorizations would appear in 1970, although the author describes the phenomenon without using the term 'New Age', preferring to use 'New Religions'. Jacob Needleman writes,

> It is about holistic medicine, Transcendental Meditation (TM), Yoga and Zen, the liberation of consciousness, the Buddhist enlightenment, Christian mystical tradition, relaxation to embrace divine energy, communication with the dead,

near-death experiences, acupuncture, reflexology, Hinduism, Taoism, Jainism, Animism, Sufism, the noosphere of Teilhard de Chardin, utopian communities, the celebration of world peace and love. (1970b: 30)

In 1976, in the first edition of the *New Age Dictionary* Alan Jack described the New Age in a similar vein as 'a movement of emerging planetary consciousness devoted to making Earth a healthier, happy, and more peaceful place, to live based on a respect for humanity's diverse traditional ways of life in harmony with the environment'. He goes on to list a number of defining features including a holistic community of practitioners of yoga, meditation, natural foods, spiritual development, humanistic psychology, environmental and peace activism and psychic arts and sciences. He also lists some key elements of transformation, for example, a belief in the Aquarian Age as a coming era of peace and spiritual awareness; an added dimension to daily lives where ordinary living is rejuvenated with a sense of the unexpected; a waking up from 'somnambulistic existence' resulting in a love-centred rather than fear-centred approach to life where beliefs that cannot serve the planet are replaced; group idealism replaces selfish or greed-based behaviour. He states that these elements together will 'create a major and unprecedented cultural transformation' (Jack, 1976).

David Tacey in 2003 writing nearly thirty years later is more sceptical in tone. He argues that the New Age is only one element of a 'spirituality revolution'. In his view over the intervening years the New Age has commercialized into something which is 'frequently an exploitation of the new public interest in the spirit, rather than a creative response to it' (2003: 3). Tacey may be referring to either the shift of various elements of 'New Age' spirituality into the mainstream as demonstrated by Paul Heelas and Linda Woodhead in 2004 or the emerging networks of spiritual products functioning as a parallel consumer society for alternative subcultures. Tacey's sceptical tone towards 'New Age' is, however, only one of terminology. His 'spirituality revolution' described as 'a universal spiritual wisdom that could transform our fractured world' (2003: 1) appeared remarkably similar to the 'New Age' described by Jack and Needleman. Tacey argues that there is a democratization of spirituality, in that 'the spiritual life is no longer a specialist concern' that is the domain of religious movements. He argues that the 'revolution' he describes has made spirituality the concern of all, something that requires no group membership. He asserts that it is a grass-roots spontaneous rising of the spirit leading to a new interest in holistic living, well-being and health. Tacey sees the cause of this new spirituality as the realization among people that secularism runs 'on an empty tank' and that we have outgrown the values of modernity where the individual is viewed as a 'sort of efficient machine' (ibid.).

From the above emic descriptions, it is possible to discern the challenge that would arise for scholars of religion once they began to investigate the phenomena. William Frost (1992) correctly points out that the New Age is a 'gathering place of many beliefs and practices'. This is bewilderingly true and not helped by the fact that many practitioners of these manifold practices do not answer to the label of 'New Age'. George Chryssides uses the term 'amorphous' to describe New Age and lists spiritual healing, yoga, meditation, crystal healing, astrology, UFOs, crop circles and Eastern religions (2012: 247). Steven Sutcliffe and Ingvild Gilhus agree, adding tarot, and forms of divination, 'practices of possession, channelling and mediumship; magical ideas about 'multiple bodies' and occult ideas about hidden anatomies ... popular psychotherapies and counselling ideologies ... and a blend of pagan religions and Eastern philosophies' to the mix, stating that it is 'sometimes bewildering', asking the question, 'What are we talking about?' (2013: 3). It would seem that both etic and emic understandings of 'New Age' are in agreement on the diversity of beliefs and practices, yet Chryssides' list, as with others, is in itself liable to cause some problems of categorization. Yoga and meditation are associated with ancient Eastern religions and can be practised within movements with more rigid borders than that usually associated with the 'pick and mix' of New Age spirituality. The appearance of New Age in a collection of essays in a work that explores NRMs can also obfuscate the matter. Although Heelas argues that the term 'New Age' includes some NRMs, citing ISKCON (International Society for Krishna Consciousness), commonly known as 'Hare Krishna', and Osho as examples, it is unlikely that the former would agree, even though individual members may uphold some of the New Age tropes. Osho, on the other hand, was highly influenced by Californian Esalen students and teachers who introduced psycho technologies, techniques for developing human potential, dreamwork, channelling and alternative healing to an Eastern religion.

Needleman's very early study in 1970 also appears to be confused between 'New Age' and NRMs when he posits that the 'New Age' originated in the arrival 'in our country (referring to the USA) of certain unusual men from the East who brought with them practical teachings and forms of organization' (p. xii). Needleman may be referring to a small number of Indian gurus who arrived in North America in the late 1960s and early 1970s and may well include Prem Rawat who had toured the United States in July 1970. Needleman claims that the teachings and organizational forms were not only new to the West but also to the world. Needleman's apparent understanding that the phenomenon originated in the United States is also echoed by Wouter Hanegraaff writing in 2001.

Hanegraaff argues that the 'New Age' is a product of the globalization of American culture where spirituality becomes a consumer product (2001: 16). He focuses on the 'pick and mix' elements of the 'New Age' spirituality as a consumerization of religion but there are problems with the locating of 'New Age' in the United States. It is equally viable to argue that the process was an Easternization of the West that had begun in the late nineteenth century and was part of a re-enchantment process and a form of rationalization thesis as proposed by Max Weber and discussed by Partridge (2004). Chryssides warns against the trap of confusing or conflating NRMs with 'New Age' (2012: 247) and in associating the arrival of Eastern gurus with the phenomenon. Needleman fails to point out that these charismatic figures usually created movements more in line with NRMs and it is not exactly clear how one moved to the other or in what forms such a conflation took place.

Nor are earlier studies any clearer on a contextualized positioning of 'New Age' within wider cultural or religious transformations from the Enlightenment onwards, especially the Victorian period. Needleman does point out that the 'New Age' also includes an element of the occult, defined as 'acquisition of mysterious powers, spiritualism's conversing with the dead, astral projection and mind reading' including vibrations, emanations, auras and cosmic forces (1970b: 33). This is echoed by Lewis and Melton (1992), who argued that the 'New Age's' earlier formation was the 'occult-metaphysical community, represented organizationally by such groups as the Theosophical Society' (p. 1), and Michael York (1995) who suggests that the 'New Age' is a 'blend of Pagan religions, Eastern philosophies and occult-psychic phenomena' (p. 34). The linking to spiritualism, astral projection and emanations would seem to suggest an earlier period of belief in psychic phenomena, especially in the late nineteenth and early twentieth century when such movements as Theosophy and Spiritualism became popular. This would suggest that 'New Age' was not particularly new at all but a continuation of earlier trends. It would seem that the phenomenon of 'New Age' was calling out for academics to provide a more precise definition. The confusion with NRMs, earlier religious forms that belonged to the Victorian and Edwardian periods, the vast panoply of beliefs and practices and the statements of origin in North America were rendering any precision in classification impossible. This apparent confusion would lead Steven Sutcliffe to state that the 'New Age' was not 'a meaningful category as it was impossible to specify what counts as New Age activity and what does not' (cited in Chryssides, 2012: 248).

Sutcliffe and Gilhus would further state that the obfuscation was partly caused by the World Religion's paradigm which leaves religious phenomena outside their terrain as problematic. They state 'modelling "religion" only in terms of strongly institutionalized forms, whether conceptionalized as "world" or "polis" is only one approach to category formation and carries inbuilt normative commitments' (2013: 9–10).

Lewis (1992) had identified the problem of separating the 'New Age' from the 'pre-existing spiritual sub-culture of which it had emerged' but one of the first attempts to clarify the situation was made by Hanegraaff in 2001. His solution was to distinguish between a restricted sense (*senso stricto*) of the 'New Age' and a general sense of the term (*senso lato*). Hanegraaff refers specifically to a form of 'esotericism based upon the 1950s interest in UFOs and apocalyptic expectations' as *senso stricto*. Chryssides describes *senso lato* as a term used to describe a wide range of esoteric activities that include channelling, healing, spiritual growth and neo-paganism (2012: 247) and is arguably too broad and therefore becomes meaningless as an analytical category unless refined. *Senso stricto* is too limited and does not describe adequately later developments especially when 'New Age' practices or beliefs infiltrate mainstream society.

Sutcliffe (2014) expands on *senso stricto* to draw upon emic understandings of a millennialistic transformation on a global scale in which a spiritual awakening would take place following the collapse of the capitalist, militaristic and material exploitation of the world (p. 41). This is sometimes specifically referred to as the Age of Aquarius and the end of the Piscean period. There is a Gnostic Christian element to the latter as it posits that Jesus Christ's age was the Piscean and ended in tragedy but the Aquarian will see a victory for a cosmic consciousness in which the Christos will be manifest through an awakening in all humans. Dominic Corrywright refers to this as the 'post-Christian nature of the New Age' and suggests a number of influences including William Blake, Emanuel Swedenborg, Ralph Emerson, Alice Bailey, Anton Mesmer, Edgar Cayce and Gurdjieff (cited in Chryssides, 2012: 248). The impact of these various figures on the contemporary 'New Age' clusters is beyond the scope of this study, but each of them in some way contributed towards the thinking of early-1960s countercultures.

Pearson (2002) notes that the 'New Age' has entered 'vast areas of life' since its heyday in 1960s counterculture. She states that one of the problems of definition is the lack of demarcated borders that belonged to older religious movements (p. 1). As a consequence it can be found within existing movements, independent of them and also dispersed into mainstream cultures. We can begin to see why

Needleman pleaded for the next generation of research to be based on providing a clearer definition of 'New Age' (1970b: 21), although he does begin to seek a common denominator which he identifies as an absence or even rejection of dualism and materialist reductionism (ibid.: 22).

Later theorizations of 'New Age'

By the late 1970s, the study of NRMs had entered academia and become institutionalized. Beginning in the sociology of religion, it attracted sociologists interested in recruitment, conversion, charisma and institutionalization, defection and processes of belief maintenance (Chryssides and Zeller, 2014: 19). It gradually moved into the study of religion sitting alongside other major religions. *Nova Religio: The Journal of Alternative and Emergent Religions* (1997) and the *International Journal of the Study of New Religions* (2010) appeared as dedicated journals to the phenomena. The former describes itself as keeping scholars informed on not only 'new religions and new movements within established religious traditions' but also 'neo-indigenous, neo-polytheistic and revival movements; ancient wisdom; and New Age groups'.

The decline of institutionalized NRMs, possibly as a result of the 'moral panic model' which described their membership as 'cult' indoctrination (Chryssides and Zeller, 2014: xviii), would lead to the emergence of organizations seeking to offer more informative or 'neutral' knowledge and understanding to concerned bodies such as the media, policy makers, parents and families.[2] In turn, various organizations of ex-members mainly utilizing the internet to generate 'moral panic' provided an opposition. The rise of the New Age seemed more benign and able to fly under the radar of the moral panic controversies and would lead to the establishment of ASANAS (the Association of the Study of Alternative and New Age) and the *Journal of Alternative Spiritualities and New Age Studies*, both founded in 2006. The New Age too was transforming and by the late 1970s the *senso stricto* understanding appeared to be in decline or subsumed into *senso lato*. Chryssides would argue that since the 1970s New Age had become

> an umbrella term for a more 'this worldly', corporeal and even sensual cluster of beliefs and practices promoting an expanded sense of spirituality, practical healing and enhanced insight and knowledge set within a re-enchanted cosmos populated by a variety of deities and powers, but with the 'spiritual growth' of human beings placed firmly at the centre. (cited in Sutcliffe, 2014: 41)

The move away from *senso stricto* would further loosen the borders of New Age religious forms and would lead to a focus on networks rather than discrete movements to understand the phenomena. For example, York would theorize the New Age as a Segmented Polycentric Integrated Network (SPIN), often operating as 'client cults' made up of individuals offering spiritual services on a commercial basis (York, 1995). These apparent commercial transactions would lead to studies which placed the New Age within a paradigm of the globalization of consumer capitalism with Hanegraaff describing it as a 'heavily secularized interpretation of Western esotericism' (cited in Needleman, 1970b: 22). SPIN was first identified by Luther Gerlach in his study of certain social movements in the 1960s. Gerlach describes SPIN as *Segmentary*, that is, formed of many diverse groups, which 'grow and die, divide and fuse, proliferate and contract'; *Polycentric*, demonstrating multiple and often temporary associations, with sometimes competing leaders or centres of influence; and *Networked*, forming a loose, 'reticulate, integrated network with multiple linkages through travellers and overlapping membership' (2001: 289–90). Dominic Corrywright would offer an alternative 'web' network theory (2004) that would be more akin to Gerlach's definition of 'Networked'. In general, those who propose such theories argue that networks are a reaction to secularization in Western societies, a strategy of embattled groups or a more effective way of challenging and changing society and culture than a centralized organization (Gerlach, 2001: 290).

Counterculture

The close attention from scholars on both sides of the Atlantic would result in the recognition of the connection between counterculture and the New Age. Later studies would shift the attention away from late-nineteenth- and early-twentieth-century occult figures mentioned above and seek for later more alternative spirituality inspirations, such as Lobsang Rampa,[3] the *Aquarian Gospel*,[4] the beat poets, for example, Laurence Ferlinghetti (1919–), Gregory Corso (1930–2001), Allen Ginsberg (1926–1997) and Jack Kerouac (1922–1969), particularly the invention of Dharma Bums[5] inspired by the writings of Alan Watts (1915–1973)[6] and D. T. Suzuki (1870–1966).[7] Other writings of influence were the novels of Herman Hesse (1877–1962), particularly *Siddharta* and the *Glass Bead Game*[8] and the influential *The Teachings of Don Juan* by Carlos Castanada written in 1968.[9] A decade later, Pirsig's *Zen and the Art of Motorcycle Maintenance*[10] would be a bestseller but the popularization of New Age and its shift from counterculture to the mainstream would occur in the 1980s with the books written by Shirley MacLaine and the explosion of mind, body, spirit sections in all major bookshops. Other scholars would identify centres such as Esalen,[11] Findhorn[12] and Gandalf's Garden[13] alongside the advent of festivals to promote spiritual inspiration.]

The earlier authors of influence mentioned above along with the beat poets were born in the nineteenth century or in the first half of the twentieth and compel acceptance of an historical development of the 1960s counterculture from its beginnings in Theosophy and other esoteric movements of the late Victorian period. Into this mix would be added the arrival of Indian gurus, surpassing the very small numbers that had arrived in the late nineteenth and early twentieth centuries, but in the main these too would be men born in the earlier period. This would lead Robert Burrows to state that the 'New Age emerged from the counter-culture of the 1960s when US youth turned for inspiration to the sacred traditions of Eastern mysticism and Western occultism, which they regarded as ancient wisdom' (1986: 17). Likewise, Russell Chandler (1988) would assert that 'the counter-culture size and radical disaffection with the cultural mainstream reinforced the sense that something novel and revolutionary was under way'. It could be argued that the 'novel and revolutionary' was more a matter of quantity and mass commodification than a qualitative divergence from earlier Bohemianism and its attraction to the East.

Although the above two authors could be accused of a strong Christian bias against the New Age, it is Chandler who first identifies the role of Prem Rawat whom he describes as a 'guru' of the New Age and the 'centre of the flower power people in the 1970s', a claim that will require some assessment (ibid.). The rapid expansion of 1960s counterculture propelled by the anti-war movement, the civil rights movement and protests against apartheid in South Africa and the Shah's regime in Iran would threaten the foundations of US and Western European society and government and led to a concern for peace, environmental issues, new spiritualities and a raising of consciousness that would transform the Western world. New protest politics would merge in hybrid forms with various new spiritualities, sometimes leading to New Age syncretism and on other occasions create uneasy bedfellows (Kent, 2001). Much has been written on the counterculture of the 1960s and following decades, but Prem Rawat's popularity will be assessed utilizing the identification categories described by Elizabeth Nelson (1989). Nelson does not deal with counterculture spirituality but her identification of counterculture's various parts, namely play, drugs, festivals, communes and revolution, is useful to explain thousands of counterculture individuals of both genders on either side of the Atlantic to Prem Rawat. Also, in this context, Andrew Rawlinson's (1997) analysis of Eastern gurus and counterculture spirituality is also useful. Rawlinson describes Eastern masters, albeit Western teachers in the Eastern tradition, as those who are part of established Eastern traditions (pp. 13–24), independent teachers (pp. 25–9), travellers on the inner path (pp. 29–30), embodiments of truth (pp. 30–3) and practitioners of new spiritual psychologies (pp. 33–5). The categorization will help assess the relationship of Eastern teachers with New Age formations and contextualize Prem Rawat and his activities.

The variety of possible sources of counterculture spirituality would lead to comparative studies of folk or vernacular traditions and their role in forming the bricolage that constitutes contemporary spirituality, especially found in the works of Marion Bowman (2003, 2007a, 2007b, 2015a, 2015b). We have seen above that others, for example, Corrywright and York, would prefer analyses of networks, while some scholars would focus on nuanced histories and significance of particular 'enclaves', for example, Sutcliffe's study of Findhorn (2000, 2003) or Bowman's work on Glastonbury as a site of pilgrimage (2005, 2006, 2009a, 2009b). Partridge would attempt to provide detailed encyclopaedic histories of 'occulture' attempting to trace a lineage of New Age development from the nineteenth- and early-twentieth-century esoteric movements (2004, 2015a). Paul Heelas would argue that there was nothing new about 'New Age' at all but rather it was a continuation of esotericism (1996). Nelson considers the counterculture to be an extension of Bohemianism (1989: 84). Sutcliffe also challenges the construction of a sui generis religious phenomenon that could be defined as a 'viable social or religious "movement" called "New Age"'. Instead, he argues for an expression of contemporary Anglo-American 'popular religion' that demonstrates 'signs of incompleteness, heterogeneity and cultural diffusion' (2003).

Occulture

The lack of agreement among scholars reflects the amorphous nature of New Age spirituality and even the uncertainty to where its borders were positioned. Sociologists and scholars of religion from other disciplines were more used to discrete boundaries secured by doctrine, ritual, sacred texts and sacred spaces. The situation was not helped by the refusal of many adherents to acknowledge the term 'New Age' or by the cultic milieu that preceded the New Age where

[handwritten margin note: Understandably, A term of abuse]

a number of NRMs, especially those of Eastern origin, displayed elements of immediate religious experience or even monistic theosophies but were prepared to define their boundaries. Christopher Partridge attempts to cut through the confusion and define these forms of alternative spiritualities as 'occulture'. He defines the term as 'hidden, rejected, and oppositional beliefs and practices associated with esotericism, theosophy, mysticism, New Age Paganism and a range of other subcultural beliefs and practices' (2004: 68). Partridge's occulture is inclusive enough not only to contain New Age but also to incorporate other contemporary spiritualities such as Paganism or Wicca whose followers may not be comfortable with the latter label. It can cope with the amorphous nature of overlapping borders, transitory networking and also provide an historical overview that can show development from more traditional understandings of the occult as perceived in the nineteenth, early twentieth century or even further back in time. Occulture would permit comparison with the past and the present allowing for a historical overview of bridges and developments. Later in 2015, Partridge would write,

> Within this progressively secular environment, where modernization appeared to be highly corrosive of religion, there is a conspicuous, widespread, and vibrant interest in the paranormal, the pursuit of experiences of transcendence, the acquisition of occult knowledge, and the development of some form of mysticism or inner-life spirituality. (2015a: 10)

Partridge is also one of the few scholars of contemporary religion to have assessed the counterculture's use of drugs, music and festivals in the context of spirituality (2015b, 2017, 2018).

Re-enchantment and Easternization

Partridge's extension of New Age to being one component of occulture permits an analysis of how and why these various complex elements of esotericism, mysticism, pantheism, psychic and the occult, and folk religion entered into counterculture from the mid-1960s, becoming a central plank of popular culture in the 1980s, influencing music, literature and film. Partridge notes that one central element of occulture is the romanticizing of the past whether it is a return to the wisdom of the ancients as embodied in constructions of a mythical East or an innate oneness with nature and the environment found within indigenous peoples. He states, 'Whether drawing on Eastern spirituality or Gnosticism, there is a broad occultural agreement that the key to vibrant, authentic contemporary spirituality is the resurgence of ancient traditions' (2004: 77). He argues that the counterpart and antagonist to these authentic and lost ancient wisdoms is the later institutionalized religions complete with dogma and authoritarian systems of control (ibid.), especially those among them which allied themselves to power. Within this critique of institutionalized religion, there is also a deep suspicion of the modern and the rational. Traditional or orthodox institutional Christianity is often perceived to be the manifestation of all that has gone wrong in the world of religion and alternatives are looked for in the East. Yet as we will see in the next chapter, constructions of Eastern religions in New Age, especially Buddhism and Hinduism, are carefully monitored to ensure that they 'fit' the occultural worldview.

Partridge perceives the process of Easternization as an important element in what he calls the 're-enchantment of the West'. He lists it along with Romanticism, mystical traditions and Western esotericism as particularly significant (2004: 87). Heelas argues that the counterculture declined in the 1970s but 'Eastern imports' especially those offering opportunities of 'austere versions of the search within' were resilient (1996: 54). Heelas suggests that this growth in Eastern movements and emphasis on world rejection should not be perceived in its Eastern forms as 'New Age' but that it becomes so when moved out of their traditional settings and moved to the West (p. 55). Yet, I would argue that a constructed East that diffuses into the New Age is very different from the far more focused doctrines and practices of the Eastern-origin NRMs that entered the West in the 1970s. The occultural filter of Eastern beliefs such as karma, reincarnation or the appropriation of yoga may be at odds with these various imported movements, and in that context, New Age understandings of the world may not sit easily alongside the policed boundaries of some Indian teachers. This will vary from movement to movement and requires case-study consideration.

Finally, it is important to observe that most writers on contemporary spirituality in the West failed to recognize the significance of altered states deriving from drugs and the role of music. Although much has been written on counterculture music and the use of mind-altering substances, the contribution by scholars has rarely come from the discipline of religion. Christopher Partridge is a notable exception. Bridging music and the drug experience, he writes, 'Early psychedelic music, which emerged within the neo-Romantic, hippie cultures of folk rock and blues in the United States (principally California) and also in Britain (principally London), was closely entwined with spirituality' (2017: 295). In his book *High Culture*, he identifies drugs as 'technologies of transcendence' (2018: 13) and acknowledges that the 'identification of altered states as "religious" raises a number of questions for theologians and scholars of religion' (p. 14), perhaps explaining why commentators on 'New Age' or contemporary spiritualities have on the whole avoided these topics. In this book, I acknowledge Partridge's interpretation of counterculture in the late 1960s as essentially spiritual, and that music and drugs formed part of the life-transforming experience that was sought at the time. Among the New Age theorists, the most useful for the conclusions of this book are Sutcliffe (2013), Gilhus (2013) and Frisk (2013). Gilhus's problematizing of the New Age and her categories drawing upon John Z. Smith's (2003) of 'religion there', 'religion here', 'religion anywhere' and 'religion everywhere' complement Sutcliffe's cogent analysis of the politics of classification in the study of religions. Frisk comments,

> In the context of New Age, there are certainly no clear cut borders between what should be considered religious and what should be considered secular. 'Enlightenment' or 'self realization' may, for example, be interpreted by the individual practitioners as either psychological or religious, but most probably the individual is not even thinking in those terms. (2013: 61)

This needs to be evaluated in the context of new paradigms for studying religion put forward by all three scholars. It is in their respective searches to liberate New Age from the marginal to the mainstream, which offers them as the main theorists to assess Prem Rawat in the final conclusions of this book.

Some concluding remarks

In this chapter, I have attempted to demonstrate the complexity of defining New Age and attempts by a number of scholars to begin to take the phenomena seriously and to offer theories and methods that facilitate analysis of its significance in contemporary Western societies. On route, I have introduced the significance of 1960s, counterculture, Easternization as part of a re-enchantment of the West and occulture as a way of expanding on and even challenging New Age as the sole category of religious formation. A number of questions are raised that require further investigation. The historical approach implicit in Partridge's occulture requires more understanding of the actual links between earlier-nineteenth- or early-twentieth-century occultism and middle-twentieth-century counterculture spirituality, especially the fulcrum decade of the 1960s. What was the milieu in which occulture flourished as part of counterculture during the early 1970s? How were these beliefs and practices viewed by Indian teachers establishing movements in the West in the early 1970s? In what ways was the East reinvented and, in particular, was Elizabeth Puttick right in claiming that the teachings of the Indian gurus lacked an 'organic connection with Western spiritual and cultural traditions' (2000: 207)? Finally, it is clear that some scholars are not so sure about the boundaries between NRMs and New Age spirituality and more needs to be said about the way in which they coexist with each other. In the next chapter, Prem Rawat will be situated within the context of Indian gurus who came to prominence in the West, framed in the wider context of Easternization and the transmigration of a variety of Eastern movements from India to Britain, North America and beyond.

3

Easternization: Indian gurus and the West

Scholars like Partridge, Heelas and Tingay are aware that the history of the influence of the Orient on Western spirituality goes back several centuries, and especially after the conquest of India, movement of individuals and organizations back and forth between Britain and the 'jewel in the crown' of the empire were to impact on ideas and art. Yet there is little knowledge to what degree the spiritual seekers of the 1960s counterculture were aware of these previous excursions of Eastern spirituality into the West. Nor are we fully aware what stimulated a variety of Indian teachers to expand into the West in the same period. It appears that far more significance has to be given to the contemporary search for the experiential in the spiritual domain, which Harvey Cox describes as the pursuit of immediacy. He defines immediacy as a close encounter with the holy, a need for inner peace or a longing for a deep experience of the divine (1977: 96). However, this desire to turn away from institutionalized Christianity, perceived as 'tired, authoritarian, patriarchal and sermonizing' (pp. 95–100), to more experiential forms of religion needs to be positioned alongside an anti-rational search for the miraculous and the wondrous, perhaps linked to the Romantic search for the 'Magic Garden', which according to Weber had been lost in industrialized nations of the West. The search for immediacy would also appear in the counterculture's pursuit of hedonism, marked by music, festivals, sexual encounters and drugs.

The early period

Partridge cites the founding of the Theosophical Society in 1875 as a key moment in the West turning eastwards for spiritual inspiration (2004: 90). Both Olav Hammer (2015) and Kevin Tingay (2000) concur. The founders of theosophy drew upon the Indian concepts of karma and reincarnation to understand the evolution of the soul towards perfection, yet their ideas draw upon neo-Platonic mysticism nearly to the same extent as they do upon Hinduism and Buddhism. Certainly, theosophy, along with spiritualism, Freemasonry and the Rosicrucian Order founded in 1915, helped to form nineteenth- and early-twentieth-century fusions of Eastern spirituality and Western occultism, to form an occultural bricolage of the period. Interestingly, it is this milieu that also provided the vehicle for the transmission of Islam into London in the early twentieth century. The first Muslim missionaries to the West arrived from India. Hazrat Inayat Khan (1882–1927) arrived in London in 1910 and moved on to the United States. He founded the Sufi Order of the West in London in 1914. Born in Baroda in 1882, Hazrat Inayat Khan trained as a musician under the instruction of his grandfather. As his musical ability grew, Hazrat Inayat utilized his travels throughout India to meet with the nation's holy men. Raised in an atmosphere of religious acceptance, Khan considered Sufism to be above the outer forms of any one religious tradition. However, his own awakening took place in the famous tomb of the founder of the Chishti *tariqa* in Ajmer and under the instruction of his teacher, Shaykh Sayyid Muhammad Abu Hashim Madani. It is said that a Hindu Brahmin seer first foretold that Hazrat Inayat Khan's life work would be in the West. Khan's eclectic spirituality derived not only from the Sufis he had made contact with during his travels as a musician but also from the ancient wisdom of India, especially the synthesis of Hindu and Islamic mysticism that marked certain periods of the Mughal Empire (Geaves, 2005a). This apparent universalism would attract a number of cultured middle-class seekers, mostly women, drawn from the same circles that were influenced by the theosophy of Madame Blavatsky and Annie Besant and including well-known Bohemian artists such as the dancers Mata Hari[1] and Ruth St Denis.[2] It is unlikely that any of these followers would have considered that they had become Muslims or, indeed, would have formally converted to Islam.

The more Islamically orthodox Ahmadiyya missionaries arrived in London between 1912 and 1914 and were drawn to the same milieu (Geaves, 2017). Both their Woking and London missionaries used the growing interest in esotericism and Eastern spirituality to seek converts, speaking at spiritualist, theosophical and other such gatherings (Germain, 2008: 97). Alex Owen points out that by the 1890s, there was a widespread emergent new spirituality represented by a number of movements seeking esoteric meanings to the world's sacred literature and an 'unmediated experience of the divine' (2004: 4). He indicates that these people were, on the whole, educated and middle-class individuals in search of answers to fundamental questions and no longer convinced by traditional

Christian doctrines (pp. 4–5). Not only were such new thinkers the precursors to New Age thought, in that they believed optimistically that a revolution in spirituality would accompany late Victorian scientific and technological development, but many of them also considered the East to possess a 'higher spirituality', and some looked for enlightened or esoteric saviour figures in India and Tibet (p. 5). Contacts between Eastern missionaries and theosophists and spiritualists were common in both Woking and London. Islam in Britain would begin to appeal to such an audience, with the added familiarity of Abrahamic monotheism, as opposed to Hindu or Buddhist worldviews.

Hindu and Buddhist teachers were arriving in the West approximately two decades earlier. The year of 1893 was pivotal. The World Parliament of Religions took place in Chicago that year and featured key figures representing Buddhism and Hinduism and also representatives from Shinto, Zoroastrianism and a range of speakers from various branches of Islam (Seager, 2009). Two motives that appeared to dominate the Christian organizers of the event were either to seek the possibility of a unity based on the Golden Rule to bring religions together against irreligion or to compare Christianity in a favourable light against the truths of other faiths (Braybrooke, 1992: 13). Two speakers are worthy of mention. The Ceylonese Buddhist monk, a convert from Christianity, Dharmapala (1864–1933) had arrived in Britain before travelling to the United States for the conference. He returned in 1896 and in 1904 Dharmapala had been a follower of Henry Olcott (1832–1907), who had been one of the early founders of the Theosophical Society and had formally converted to Buddhism before travelling to India and Ceylon (Gombrich and Obeysekere, 1988: 71ff.).

The visit of the Hindu sannyasin Vivekananda (1863–1902), disciple of the famed mystic Ramakrishna Paramhansa (1836–1886) and founder of the Ramakrishna Mission in India, was of more significance, especially for Hindu confidence. Vivekananda was a staunch defender of Hinduism, especially the monistic philosophy of Advaita Vedanta. Instead of agreeing with the liberal Christian quest for unity, he posited that the same principles could only be discovered through the ancient truths inherent within Hinduism (Glyn, 1999). He would extensively tour the United States and Europe and became a celebrity in his native land. Vivekananda was certainly the first to proclaim that the balance of West and East would result in a genuine human renaissance based on a fusion of spirituality and material development (www.vivekananda.net/ PROSE/EastWest.html). Also influential was the arrival of the Zen teacher, D. T. Suzuki (1870–1966), in the United States where he remained from 1897 to 1908, and through the activities of his disciple Nyogen Senzaki (1876–1958) various

Zen centres were established between the 1920s and the 1950s. In Britain, the Buddhist Society of Great Britain and Ireland was formed in 1907, receiving visits from Ananda Mettaya (Charles Henry Allen Bennett) with three other Burmese monks in 1908 (Partridge, 2004: 91). Buddhism had been known in Britain for several decades especially through the epic poem describing the life of the Buddha, *The Light of Asia*, written by Sir Edwin Arnold but it was Ananda Mettaya who provided the first experiential dimension and attracted converts. Previously, Bennett had been a member of the Hermetic Order of the Golden Dawn and a mentor to Aleister Crowley. As with Olcott who was intensely interested in spiritualism, these early Western Buddhists arrived at Eastern spirituality through their interest in Western esotericism ('Ananda Mettaya').

These predecessors to the Indian teachers who arrived in the late 1960s and early 1970s were, according to Partridge, 'far more authentic sources of Eastern wisdom in the West' (2004: 91). Yet they pose a predicament. Partridge's argument that Easternization is part of a wider occulture is supported by the life journeys of several of the earlier key players of the era. Olcott had been instrumental in reviving Buddhism in Ceylon but had also been a key member of the Theosophical Society and had explored spiritualism prior to his contact with Madame Blavatsky. Bennett was a practitioner of the occult. Erik Davis warns against the temptation to collapse 'the popular emergence of Western Buddhism and non-ethnic Hinduism in the 1960s into the occult *per se*' (2015: 636). Davis prefers to identify a 'spiritual counterculture' containing Eastern religions in addition to an overlapping but 'more specifically characterised occult currents' (ibid.). He makes the point that the East has been an influence on Western occultism since theosophy and early Crowley. However, he distinguishes the doctrines and practices of Eastern religions and Western occultism when he states that 'Tibetan Buddhism, Taoism, yoga, and even Zen, have their own forms of "magic"' (ibid.).

Herein is an important distinction. Partridge's claim of 'far more authentic sources of Eastern wisdom in the West' needs to be understood in the context of popular 'folk' mythologies and the hagiographical tales contained within the term 'magic' described by Davis. These elements of religion described as 'apotropaic', which is the realm of religion that seeks magical means or supernatural beings to control malign forces or prevent disaster or achieve well-being and prosperity, are widespread in the East (Spiro, 1970: 31–65). The first teachers from the East arriving in the late nineteenth or early twentieth centuries, however, tended to promote a 'Nibbanic' version of Eastern religions, that is, one where the focus was on the means of liberation from this world by close observance of doctrines as enshrined in sacred texts or the teachings of founders (ibid.). To some degree, this emphasis was an apologetic discourse, elaborated and emphasized to offset colonial and Christian criticisms of the East as backward and superstitious. This dynamic tension between apotropaic folk religions and Nibbanic quests for human fulfilment through liberation or salvation paths is important in order to understand how Easternization takes place and to resolve the differences between Partridge and Davis. It can also help to understand the development of Eastern NRMs and their relationship to New Age religions. Sutcliffe makes the critical point that New Age demonstrates continuity with the popular beliefs and practices 'expressed within and across a range of different world religions' and rather than being regarded as deviant should be explored in the context of Durkheim's elementary forms of religion manifesting in a Western context (Sutcliffe, 2013: 17–18). The Eastern teachers, from both Hindu and Buddhist origins, were dismissive of such practices as 'superstition'. Sutcliffe points to the issue of how prevailing concepts in the study of religion continue to influence how we construct our data; in this instance, he argues, along with the author (2005b) and Fitzgerald (1990), that the World Religion's paradigm has created this conceptual problem in studying South Asian religions (Sutcliffe, 2013: 17).

In this context, Davis's mention of theosophy is important. Although Partridge points out that Madame Blavatsky appropriated core Indian concepts and repositioned them within key occult understandings of the soul's development, there is a far more significant element in Blavatsky's appropriation. Among her core theosophical doctrines was the significance of the 'Masters' or 'Mahatmas' in human spiritual development. In theosophical discourse, 'Masters' are beings that are able to communicate the esoteric or arcane knowledge of the East that belonged to ancient adepts and possessors of wisdom and who have developed beyond the level of normal beings (Hammer, 2015: 251). Blavatsky initially claimed that she met such a Master in Hyde Park in 1851 (ibid.), and she soon developed a cosmology of hierarchically ordered Masters living far beyond human evolution and who guide humanity from remote fastnesses in Tibet (pp. 255–6). Blavatsky claimed that she succeeded in entering Tibet and was trained by the Masters in Tibet from 1868 to 1870 and that she was chosen to restore the wisdom of the Ancients (Tingay, 2000: 39). In addition, the later theosophists developed the idea of the advent of a World Teacher and that spiritual change was imminent. The movement chose to fulfil this ambition by promoting Jiddu Krishnamurti (1895–1986), a young Indian boy, as the chosen vehicle of Maitreya, an advanced member of the spiritual hierarchy of Masters (p. 45). Blavatsky is able to combine elements of esotericism to wonderful Eastern narratives that would appear to be derived in transcendental modes of religion,[3] rather than Durkheim's elementary forms, which exist in vast multiplicity alongside modes of liberation and conduct in Indian religions. Theosophy was thus able to compete with Christian doctrine and gain converts from the intelligentsia in the West. Eastern pragmatic or apotropaic practices rarely appear in New Age narratives of the East even though, as Sutcliffe (2013) argues, practitioners have developed many Western correspondences with such Eastern practices.[4]

The search for spiritually elevated masters in the East would pervade George Gurdjieff's (d.1949) *Meetings with Remarkable Men* published in Russian in 1927 and translated into English in 1963.[5] Gurdjieff provided a narrative of a group of individuals whom he named the 'seekers of truth'. In some way, each one is instrumental in finding spiritual texts and/or masters in various Eastern lands. As with Blavatsky, Gurdjieff posits that individuals belonging to ancient civilizations were at higher levels of spiritual consciousness than those of today, presuming that modern times were in some way fallen from advanced spiritual knowledge in spite of material development. In Yogananda Paramahansa's book *Autobiography of a Yogi*, first published in 1946, the theme of spiritual men and women with advanced knowledge and superpowers residing in the East was continued. Yogananda's autobiography describes his search for his guru, Yukteswar Giri, through to his journey from India to America in 1920 and the establishment of his Self-Realization Fellowship in the West. Yogananda not only ascribes a number of miraculous or psychic powers to his guru and his predecessor, the nineteenth-century yogi Lahiri Mahasaya, he also claimed that the latter was a direct disciple of Mahavatar Babaji, an incarnation of Shiva, who continues to reside for centuries in a remote Himalayan region of India, seen in person by only a small number of disciples and a few chosen others. Typical of Yogananda's miraculous encounters is the meeting with Giri Bala, the female yogi who never eats (Weil, 2000). Lobsang Rampa's *The Third Eye*, published in 1964, also describes a highly romanticized semi-fictional account of life in Tibet's monasteries replete with lamas who can astral travel, have mastered telepathy, practise invisibility, levitate and meet with yetis and who are contrasted with Western development in technology to place them as superior in human self-development.

Transmission to counterculture

All these texts and their respective authors would be influential in counterculture circles in the late 1960s. Gurdjieff is cited as influential in transforming New

Age adherents from reading about to actually practising transformational techniques (Heelas, 1996: 47). *Autobiography of a Yogi* was one of the few books available to Western seekers in the 1960s that described in detail an Indian path to self-realization. George Harrison received his first copy from Ravi Shankar in 1966 and, according to Shankar, 'that was where his interest in Vedic culture and Indian-ness began' (O'Mahony, 2008). Gary Wright (2014), the American musician who played keyboards on Harrison's influential album *All Things Must Pass* released in 1970, mentions that the ex-Beatle had given him a copy of the book a few days before they both travelled to India in 1972. Steve Jobs, the co-founder of Apple, read it as a teenager and reread it annually (Isaacson, 2001: 527). The book was given out as a gift to those who attended his funeral (Farber, 2013).

All these works present the East as a fabled land, an Eldorado, inhabited by wondrous beings who possess not only ancient wisdom but who can live for centuries, communicate by telepathy, be in two places simultaneously, survive without eating, walk on water, travel astrally but, more significantly, watch over and intervene in the spiritual evolution of the human race. Even though *Autobiography of a Yogi* describes the practices and disciplines required of a yogic practitioner, it does so through the lens of 'wondrous tales from an exotic land' (Weil, 2000). Aravamudan Srinivas (2005) is less flattering of its contents describing the book as a 'miracle-infested territory' whose 'single most memorable feature ... is a repetitive insistence on collating the miraculous and the quotidian. ... The autobiography is an eclectic directory of sorts that might be dubbed a hitchhiker's guide to the paranormal galaxy' (pp. 60–1, 246).

This sense of a secret knowledge held in the East by advanced beings (human or divine) would continue through to individuals in the counterculture of the 1960s and lead to the idea of travel in search of enlightenment and the enlightened. However, the reality of Indian religious life is a long way from the exotic representations described above. Aravamudan's description of *Autobiography of a Yogi* as a 'guide to the paranormal' suggests that such depictions of Indian spirituality can easily locate themselves within Partridge's occulture, merging with Western occult traditions to create a bricolage of the wondrous that together become part of the New Age worldscape. For those travellers to the East, who came into contact with and committed themselves to age-old paths of religious life found within Buddhism or Hinduism, the journey would demand rigorous daily discipline that would require organization and structure with a possible condemnation of an interest in the wondrous and the paranormal. From these contacts would arise the plethora of Eastern-origin NRMs and their often contested relationship with the more ephemeral search for the psychic and the occult. This relationship would be complex and sometimes fraught with tensions as these new movements in the West sought to police borders and protect truth claims.

Indian gurus in the West

Philip Goldburg considers that three gurus changed the face of spirituality in the West (2011). He adds Maharishi Mahesh Yogi (1918–2008)[6] to the already mentioned Swami Vivekananda and Yogananda. Although Yogananda was known to the 1960s counterculture, Vivekananda was far more well known in India and may have been an original inspiration for Indian gurus deciding to engage in reverse mission to the West. There is no doubt that Maharishi Mahesh Yogi enabled meditation to become known in popular culture and raised the public awareness of gurus in the West. The *Hindustan Times* (8 February 2008) would declare that the Maharishi left a legacy that popularized meditation, which he made available to everyone and is considered responsible for bringing meditation into the mainstream in the West. Goldburg states that 'Maharishi's face became the global symbol of guruhood' (2011). Maharishi's fame would arise from his discovery by the Beatles in 1967[7] but he had been travelling throughout the world for a decade earlier teaching Transcendental Meditation (TM),[8] including regular visits to the United States, first attracting small numbers of middle-class seekers and then gathering a student audience, allowing him to cross over into the counterculture. Michael York argues that the Maharishi was the most effective spokesman for the argument that a critical mass of people becoming enlightened through the practice of meditation would trigger the New Age's millennial expectations of an age of peace (2006: 16).

Harvard University's Pluralism project offers an online article called 'The Rush of Gurus' and agrees with Goldburg that the term 'Guru' had become a household word in the United States from the late 1960s. It is debateable to what degree the arrival of gurus during this period could be described as a 'rush' but there were certainly a number of intrepid spiritual travellers sharing in common the desire to expand their teachings globally. The same article also mentions Maharishi Mahesh Yogi as a pioneer but adds Swami A. C. Bhaktivedanta Prabhupada who arrived penniless in New York in 1965, quickly founding the International Society for Krishna Consciousness (ISKCON). Allen Ginsberg met the swami in New York (Muster, 1997: 25) and helped him to extend his visa, thus ensuring his counterculture credentials (Goswami and Dasi, 2011: 76–7). Ginsberg would often chant the Hare Krishna mantra when performing and made the mantra part of his way of life (Brooks, 1992: 78–9). He endorsed the mantra as a way of producing a state of ecstasy when addressing counterculture audiences (Szatmary 1996: 149). Ginsberg considered Prabhupada to be an authentic swami who would introduce Hindu chanting to America. Other countercultural figures like Timothy Leary, Gary Snyder and Alan Watts would also endorse Prabhupada and hoped that the chanting of the Hare Krishna mantra would become part of the hippie movement.[9] Prabhupada would take part in the Mantra-Rock Dance concert where Ginsberg would introduce him to the Haight-Ashbury counterculture (Brooks, 1992: 78–9). Swami Satchidananda would speak at Woodstock in 1969 and went on to teach yoga at his Yogaville ashram in rural Virginia, the headquarters of Integral Yoga International. In the same year, Swami Rama visited the United States and initiated the Himalayan Institute in Honesdale, Pennsylvania, to bring East and West together through holistic health and yoga practices; Swami Muktananda launched the Siddha Yoga Dham Movement in 1970 and by 1976 claimed eighty meditation centres and five ashrams; and in June 1971 Prem Rawat flew into London visiting France and Germany before going on to the United States. Before his departure from London, Divine Light Mission was established as a vehicle to promote his message (The Rush of Gurus). To this list can be added Sri Chinmoy (1931–2007) who arrived in New York as early as 1964 apparently in response to an inner call 'to be of service to people in the West searching for spiritual fulfilment' (Chinmoy, 2000: 48) after living for many years in the ashram of Sri Aurobindo in Pondicherry (Dua, 2005: 18, 22) and Yogi Bhajan, also known as Harbhajan Singh Khalsa (1929–2004), who founded the Triple H (Healthy, Happy, Holy) movement in 1969, introducing a mixture of Kundalini Yoga and the teachings of Guru Nanak, the founder of Sikhism, to West Coast counterculture (Cowley et al., 1975: 65).

Also not mentioned on the Harvard website is Meher Baba (1894–1969). Although born into a Zoroastrian family, Meher Baba claimed to be an avatar.[10] After a period of time in his youth, in which he claimed to have been taught by five masters, Meher Baba set out to teach and gather his own disciples in 1922 at the age of 27 (Haynes, 1993: 38–9). From 1925, he took a lifetime vow of silence and would communicate by hand gestures or an alphabet board (p. 2). Meher Baba began to visit the West from 1931 and suffered a serious road accident in the United States during a visit in 1952 in which his ability to move was seriously impaired (p. 60). In 1962, he invited his Western followers to an East-West gathering in India (Awakener Magazine, 1963: 1) and began to preach against the use of psychedelic drugs to aid spiritual experience. He would continue this warning until his death in 1969 (Baba, 1966; Brecher et al., 1972). His tomb in Meherabad remains a site of international pilgrimage (Haynes, 1993: 62).

Although Meher Baba maintains an institutional presence through the Avatar Meher Baba Charitable Trust, established by him in 1959, it is some of his teachings that are more significant for the growing counterculture spirituality of the late 1960s, especially his doctrines of the 'Perfect Master'.[11] Baba claimed that there are fifty-six incarnate God-realized souls on earth at any one time and that of these souls there are always five who constitute the 'five Perfect Masters' of their era (Kalchuri, 1986: 944). When one of the five Perfect Masters dies, Baba stated that another God-realized soul among the fifty-six immediately replaced him or her (Adriel, 1947: 49). The Avatar, according to Baba, is a special Perfect Master, the first soul to achieve God realization. This soul, the original Perfect Master, or the 'Ancient One', never ceases to incarnate and helps other evolved souls to attain their aims. Baba's doctrine of the 'Perfect Master' has similarities to the teachings of Yogananda and the theosophists and would feed the ideas developing in the countercultural milieu concerning miraculous beings with special powers able to influence the spiritual destiny of the human race. Meher Baba is also relevant as he was one of the first Indian teachers to establish a relationship with popular culture in the West, attracting the rock band, The Who, and influencing their rock opera, *Tommy*.

Western seekers in India

There are also a number of gurus and organizations in India whose ashrams became centres of attraction for Western seekers and who would subsequently establish movements in Britain and the United States or alternatively create or inspire pockets of spirituality that would add to the developing bricolage that Partridge calls occulture. Swami Sivananda's (1887–1963) ashram in Rishikesh would place the ancient Hindu pilgrimage city as a foremost destination for counterculture spiritual seekers from the early 1960s, even attracting a small number of the beat generation in the 1950s. Sivananda had turned a number of deserted cowsheds on the banks of the Ganga into an ashram in the late 1930s. He taught a synthesis of the major schools of yoga and created the Divine Life Society in 1936. Throughout the 1940s, Sivananda expanded his activities, undertaking tours of India and Sri Lanka, organizing the All-World

Religions Federation on 28 December 1945 and established the All-World Sadhus Federation on 19 February 1947. The Yoga-Vedanta Forest Academy was established in 1948 to provide systematic spiritual training to the residents and visiting seekers. In 1953, the World Parliament of Religions was convened at the ashram in Rishikesh (http://www.dlshq.org/saints/siva.htm).

In 1968, Mirra Alfasa (1878–1973), known as 'The Mother', founded Auroville, in addition to the Sri Aurobindo Ashram established in 1926, in Pondicherry. Sri Aurobindo had handed over his activities to his close collaborator, Mirra Alfasa, on his retirement from the world in 1926. Auroville was established as a universal city populated by spiritual seekers. As stated in the Mother's inaugural speech, 'Auroville wants to be a universal town where men and women of all countries are able to live in peace and progressive harmony, above all creeds, all politics and all nationalities. The purpose of Auroville is to realize human unity' (Lotfallah, 1993). The four-point charter setting out the Mother's vision of integral living clearly shows its close affinity to the goals of the New Age movement: (1) Auroville belongs to nobody in particular. Auroville belongs to humanity as a whole. But to live in Auroville, one must be the willing servitor of the Divine Consciousness; (2) Auroville will be the place of an unending education, of constant progress and a youth that never ages; (3) Auroville wants to be the bridge between the past and the future. Taking advantage of all discoveries from without and from within, Auroville will boldly spring towards future realizations; and (4) Auroville will be a site of material and spiritual researches for a living embodiment of an actual human unity (the Auroville Charter). Today, the city has around 2,852 residents (2,155 adults, 697 children) from fifty-six countries (Census – Auroville population).

Meher Baba, Auroville and the Sivananda ashram provided teachings that would permeate through the counterculture made possible by individuals who would visit their centres in India or have contact with their writings. None of them would establish major centres in the West. The next two movements introduced would establish major centres in India attracting Western adherents and go on to create important loci in Britain and the United States.

Radhasoamis

The Radhasoamis are one of the earliest movements to attract Westerners in significant numbers. These contacts occurred early enough in the twentieth century to provide a link to both theosophy and Western occultism. Radhasoami began in the 1860s in Agra with the teachings of Swami Shiv Dayal Singh (d.1878) and developed into over twenty offshoots depending on a lineage of gurus claiming to be successors of the founder (Juergensmeyer, 1991: 3–4). The teachings are said to be a mix of Sikh and the Nath Yogis, with influences from Kabir and Hindu Vaishnavite bhakti traditions (p. 3). The essence of Radhasoami teachings lies in the experience brought about by initiation into sacred sounds and access to an inner sound current (*shabd*) and the saving grace of a spiritual master. In combination, these two elements have the capacity to transform the self and offer access to inner spiritual realms (ibid.).

A small number of Radhasoami movements were to achieve transglobal status. In 1887, Rai Saligram, a close follower of Shiv Dayal Singh, retired from government service to attempt to establish order into the fragmentation of the movement that had accompanied the death of his master. In Punjab, Jaimal Singh retired from military service in 1889 and established the Beas branch of the movement. This development led to the creation of two spiritual colonies, Dayalbagh in Agra and Beas in the Punjab. Even as early as the late nineteenth century, a small number of Westerners had been attracted to Rai Saligram, the first was possibly a German theosophist travelling to India along with an American woman who sent her son to India to find out more about visions she was receiving in her yoga practice (p. 52).

However, it was the Beas branch that became particularly successful in attracting foreigners. Sawan Singh had succeeded Jaimal Singh and created a small city on the banks of the Beas river in Punjab. They claim to have initiated 125,000 people during Sawan Singh's forty-three-year leadership (p. 49). From the 1930s onwards, both Dayalbagh and Beas centres record increasing numbers of Westerners coming to stay. In 1948, a successor of Sawan Singh, Kripal Singh, established a new organization in Delhi, named the Ruhani Satsang, and began the practice of touring abroad (p. 52). Foreign initiates increased rapidly throughout the 1960s and 1970s and the movement claimed over thirteen thousand foreign followers, comprising 10 per cent of its total (ibid.). In 1951, Charan Singh took over the leadership in Beas and began to promote the movement as a universal religion, demonstrating in its literature that the sacred sound accessed through the Radhasoami initiation can be traced in Taoism, Gnostic philosophy and the Logos theology of the New Testament (ibid.). The promotion of the message was aided by the use of English as the movement's chosen vehicle for promotion (p. 53).

Juergensmeyer analyses Radhasoami success with Western seekers. He points out that in 1911 the movement established the concept of 'proxy initiation'. An American dentist and his wife requested initiation from the United States and an Indian immigrant living in the United States was granted the authority to initiate on the guru's behalf. This permitted the movement to spread among followers in the West without travel to India (p. 54). Today, there are claimed to be over twenty thousand active members outside India, allowing Radhasoami in India to warrant the prestige attached to reverse mission and to confirm that the message transcends its Indian roots (p. 54).

The first Western followers who stayed in Radhasoami centres in India during the first half of the twentieth century were from the same background as those who joined theosophy, including theosophists who became Radhasoamis. Their numbers were in the hundreds. In the 1960s and 1970s, the Radhasoami masters made several world tours and centres were started in most European nations.[12] In India, the proximity of Beas to the border with Pakistan made it a convenient spiritual stopover for counterculture individuals on the overland trail to India popular from the mid-1960s onwards.

In Juergensmeyer's view, individuals attracted to theosophy or the Vedanta Society groups established after Vivekananda visited Chicago in 1893, found in Radhasoami a more authentic Hinduism. He notes that theosophy blended Western occultism with Indian ideas but was essentially a Western movement and that the Vedanta Society groups in the United States adopted Christian styles of worship and addressed Western philosophic issues (p. 205). In the later period of the 1960s, Radhasoamis would offer meditation practices based on technique and knowledge rather than piety and dogma, and meeting the demand for Hindu yoga popularized in the period. Radhasoami's ability to package their teachings as 'universal truth' would have had a particular appeal for Western seekers. By the 1980s, the popularity of the movement among Westerners declined but would remain strong among Indian migrants to the West, especially those of Punjabi origin (p. 207). The decline appeared to be due to the aging profile of the Western membership and its inability to attract counterculture youth during the 1960s and 1970s. The inability to move from esoteric interest in the early decades of the twentieth century to the different expectations of the late 1960s marked other movements established in the first half of the twentieth century. The issue seems to have been lifestyle, particularly drugs and promiscuity (Geaves, 2000: 175–6). This may suggest that there was less continuity than claimed in occultural or esotericist explanations of the counterculture in the second half of the twentieth century.

Bhagwan Rajneesh (1931–1990)

Bhagwan Shree Rajneesh, also known as Osho, the founder of the Rajneesh movement, also attracted considerable attention from counterculture individuals in the West. His first Western disciples were 'hippies' travelling around India who came to stay in his ashram in Pune. By the early 1970s, he was one of the most influential gurus from India who would impact on the direction of counterculture spirituality and their synthesis of East and West. While movements such as the Radhasoamis and ISKCON presented themselves to Western adherents as elements of authentic Hinduism, representing both transcendental and dharmic configurations, supported by Indian sacred texts, Rajneesh would consciously seek a fusion between new psychotherapies arising from the Human Potential Movement (HPM), described as 'psychospiritual wing of the counterculture' (Puttick, 2000:204), and Eastern-based meditations (p. 208). Combining the two formed a new psychospirituality (ibid.) and permitted a high degree of experimentation within the Rajneesh movement which included Tantric-influenced sex therapies and opened the door for Western practitioners to become major figures in the movement. The meeting of psychotherapy and meditation first took place in 1972 when Paul and Patricia Lowe, the founders of a human growth organization in London named Quaesitor, visited Pune (pp. 207–8). The Lowes were initiated into Osho's sennyasins, an inner circle that would give the movement its popular label of 'Orange People', and persuaded other key HPM therapists to join.

The HPM therapists would develop Osho's praxis into a programme of body-based encounter-style cathartic exercises developed to deal with emotional repression, progressing through encounter groups to Buddhist meditations, finally resulting in Vipassana practice (p. 208). By the mid-1970s, the movement had become possibly the fastest-growing NRM among Western countercultures (ibid.), arguably overtaking the declining Divine Light Mission, but Rajneesh would be the last guru to attract a mass following outside of India. By the arrival of the next decade (1980s), the 'glut of gurus' was over. Rajneesh would establish a community in the small town of Antelope, Oregon, renamed Rajneeshpuram, which would collapse in 1985 after the guru's arrest. However, his impact on New Age and Easternization is important. Whereas the Radhasoamis bridge the earlier-nineteenth-century occultism located in theosophy's fusion to a more authentic Hindu participation by Western seekers, the Rajneesh movement allows those who sought enlightenment in the East to acknowledge the significance of a Western contribution to the process derived from indigenous counterculture spirituality. The circle was complete.

Puttick points out that the challenge Indian gurus faced was that they had 'no organic connection with Western spiritual and cultural traditions' (2000: 204) or, in Partridge's terms, were not able to create the fusion necessary for occultural synthesis. The experimentation permitted within the Rajneesh movement, however, would encourage the 'pick and mix' synthesis that would become a feature of the later New Age movement, whereas others, such as ISKCON and Prem Rawat, would be more exclusive.

Western gurus

A number of Western seekers in the East would become gurus in their own right and make a major contribution to counterculture spirituality. Foremost among these was Richard Alpert, a professor of psychology at Harvard University, who found his guru, Neem Karoli Baba, in the Himalayas and went on to change his own name to Ram Dass. His book *Be here Now*, published in 1971, was almost compulsory reading among counterculture spiritual seekers in the 1970s.

Joyce Green was a Jewish housewife in Brooklyn who became Ma Jaya Sati Bhagavati. She had been influenced by the teachings of Jesus, Swami Nityananda and Neem Karoli Baba and taught at the Kashi Ashram in Florida. Rudranada, the guru of Swami Chetanananda of the Nityananda Institute, was also an American and studied with the Shankaracharya of Puri, Swami Nityananda and Muktananda, before becoming a teacher himself. These well-known American gurus would originally be students of an Indian spiritual guide(s) but develop their understanding to the degree that they would become teachers themselves and assist in the process of indigenizing Eastern traditions. Rawlinson provides a thorough exploration of these Western gurus in Eastern traditions and attempts to provide a typology. Although his analysis is unsophisticated to describe a very complex variety of individuals and not intended to describe the Indian masters who came to the West, it is a useful tool for categorization that can help to avoid the error of placing them together as a single group, therefore failing to recognize the breadth and depth of Hindu and Buddhist traditions.

Positioning Indian gurus within the Hindu worldview

Rawlinson comments that Hinduism consists of many overlapping subtraditions which are not consistent with a main tradition with subbranches, which arguably is the case with the Abrahamic religions and Buddhism. He states that there is not an original Hindu tradition 'but rather several trunks which have twined around each other, each with many branches' (1997: 13). In this respect, he agrees with Fitzgerald (1990) and Geaves (2005b), who argue that any attempt to perceive Hinduism as a 'single trunk' religion leads to essentialism and, furthermore, Rawlinson is not satisfied with utilizing separate subtraditions such as Shaivism, Vaishnavism or Vedanta because of the tendency of Hinduism to proliferate within and across subtraditions (1997: 14). If this is so, it is reasonable to ask whether categorizing Hindu gurus is useful at all, but in the context of this book, Rawlinson's (1997) reference to 'inner Hinduism' provides a useful tool to frame Prem Rawat's success in the West.

Rawlinson argues that many of the above subtraditions can be subsumed within paths to enlightenment or understandings of our true nature and suggests that all the gurus who came to the West belonged to 'inner Hinduism', where spiritual attainment exists as the ultimate test of authority regardless of the subtradition (p. 15). So although we find representatives of Vedanta (Sivananda), Shaivism (Mahesh Yogi), Vaishnavism (Prabupada), yoga schools (Shri Chinmoy), Tantra (Rajneesh) and Sant Mat (Radhasoamis), among the Indian teachers who came to the West, including a number of swamis belonging to or claiming lineages to the great founder of Advaita Vedanta, Shankarcharya, each claims to possess a level of personal realization and therefore does not have to seek authentication from a tradition, although some such as Prabhupada do. It is also true that they do not necessarily refer to their teachers for authority and remain independent of them when it comes to teaching or establishing movements in the West (ibid.). Rawlinson states categorically, 'Realization is authority' (ibid.). Rawlinson goes on to subcategorize 'inner Hinduism' as universal Hinduism, which accepts all paths, including traditions outside Hinduism; representatives of particular Hindu subtradition; originally authorized by their guru to teach; or, finally set up as independent teachers (pp. 15–18). These categories too overlap with each other. Another category that is not mentioned by Rawlinson belongs to those who transcend the category of 'inner Hinduism', especially after arriving in the West. Rawlinson (1997) particularly refers to Western Hindu teachers as 'someone who's teachings is traceable to the Hindu tradition (in any of its variant forms)' but who does not necessarily 'teach what Indian Hindus teach' (p. 15). In the next chapter, these categories will be used to attempt a positioning of Prem Rawat and to ascertain how he was different from the other Indian teachers and, in later chapters, demonstrate why he was able to attract so many adherents of the counterculture.

Concluding remarks

The 'Rush of Gurus' described in Harvard University's Pluralism Project was relatively short-lived. Beginning in the late 1960s, it was effectively finished by the mid-1970s, although the movements that they founded or inspired in the West remain with us to the present time even if going through several transformations and demonstrating the adaptability of religious forms. This chapter has introduced the main figures and argues that they did not necessarily form part of Chris Partridge's understanding of occulture, although individuals who were inspired by them may have retained a variety of Western esoteric beliefs. Arising out of the countless sects that form today's Hinduism, these individuals and movements represented a number of the broad range of schools and traditions that have historically developed in India. As such, they reflected a spectrum of beliefs that veered from inclusivism to strict exclusivism, and some may have changed their views as a result of Western contact. Depending on where they stand on this spectrum of exclusivism and inclusivism, or insistence in maintaining strict sectarian borders, would impact massively on their attitude towards the vast collation of beliefs that constitute Western occultism that had filtered into counterculture or their respective inclinations towards their followers adopting and utilizing elements extracted from the occulture mix alongside their respective teachings.

Those that would present meditation and yoga as a science, such as Maharishi Yogi, were not much concerned with other beliefs and practices maintained by TM practitioners but such eclectic mixes would have been more difficult for the exclusivist theism of the ISKCON movement, especially for those who would commit fully through living in temples or ashrams. Rajneesh, on the other hand, developed his teachings to include Western occulture, especially holistic healing practices and sexual psychotherapies, and therefore positively encouraged East/West fusions. Prem Rawat would appear to change and remove all the trappings of Hindu teachings during the 1980s but faced a massive challenge deconstructing both Hindu and New Age tropes in the 1970s.

Theosophy had declined by the second half of the century and both Tingay and Hammer comment on its demise. Tingay states that the Theosophical Society is a 'faded shadow' of its former self, now 'submerged by the brightly packaged products of the New Age' (2000: 48) and Hammer argues that 'membership dwindled, and although all the main bodies of Theosophists exist today, they lead rather a subdued existence' (2015: 258). The author was not aware of theosophical teachings playing a major role in late 1960s spiritual quests;

however, the search for the miraculous and an evolutionary approach to spiritual soul travelling was often on display. It also needs to be pointed out that most counterculture individuals in the late 1960s and early 1970s did not visit India. They stayed at home. Paul Heelas notes that not many joined the movements begun by the relatively few Indian gurus and describes self-spirituality in the 1960s as 'inchoate' (1996: 50). Describing his experience, he writes,

> Speaking from personal experience, only a couple of friends became involved in well-organized spirituality. The greater majority, including myself, used our own resources to make contact with what we took to exist beyond the material world. We did not have a very good idea of what we were looking for. But off we went: perhaps to a favoured farm, located in the Welsh borders, where we would talk of mysteries, take hallucinogens, watch sunsets, use the I-Ching or tarot, listen to the Incredible String Band, read Carlos Castaneda's The Teachings of Don Juan (1968) or Herman Hesse's *Siddhartha*. (p. 51)

To these 'stay at home seekers', occultural bricolages seem to have been the norm, but many would come into contact with the Indian gurus arriving in the West where they may have found opposition to self-created spirituality.

There would appear to be little in common between the various teachers who established themselves in the West or in their motivation to arrive when they did. Although it was common knowledge and a matter of pride in India that Vivekananda had spoken at the conference in Chicago in 1893, there is no direct evidence to suggest that anyone came to the West as a direct inspiration from his actions. Although several of the gurus are connected by their emphasis on yoga of various types, a common motif would be the emphasis on the experiential or immediacy in their message as suggested by Rawlinson. Most would speak of God or self-realization as opposed to an emphasis on faith. Some would be discovered by Western travellers in India and others were directed to come to the West by their teachers. Several mention being called to bring Indian or Eastern spirituality to offset the materialism of the West and in this respect they do echo Vivekananda's rallying cry that the East excels in spiritual knowledge as opposed to the West's material dominance. The 'pull' factor of the growth in counterculture spirituality and its gaze on the East for authenticity and immediacy may have been more a factor than the 'push' factor of Indian teachers looking West for global expansion. Most would market their teachings as universal truth, expected or required to be taught to a global audience that transcended Hinduism in order for the world to secure peace, happiness or enlightenment.

The key elements in the debate over the relationship between Easternization and occulture depend to a large extent on the exclusivism of the individual movement's truth claims. I have compared ISKCON with TM, for example, suggesting that the total package of beliefs surrounding devotion to Krishna as the sole means of salvation would not be conducive to maintaining Western occult beliefs and practices whereas the market-orientated approach of TM was not so much concerned to eradicate previous belief systems. Those who accepted initiation from Prem Rawat were formally requested to leave the teachings of any other guru (Lovejoy, 2005: 52; Kerr, 2011: 266) while Rajneesh's inner circle consciously sought for fusions. For those who joined movements, there was likely to be daily regimes of practice and possible world-renouncing lifestyles to maintain.[13] For these adherents, Easternization was likely to be a total lifestyle change, including cessation of drug taking, possible change of dress codes, diet and sexual behaviour. The wider diffused occulture, described by Heelas, could be perceived as ignorance of the truth discovered in a movement and those who lived in the diffused occulture were likely to be seen as a marketplace for the movement's teachings. On the other hand, the majority who imbibed a range of sources from East and West could be described as being part of occulture where Easternization was diffused and superficial.

The development of salvation myths

Although theosophy had declined, it had contributed a form of messianism, an expectation of a world saviour arising from the East, to the counterculture set of beliefs. The teachings of Meher Baba and the Radhasoamis had introduced the concept of living human avatars or perfect masters to theosophy's eternal masters residing in the remote fastnesses of Tibet. ISKCON had brought with it intense devotional love to Krishna, and a religious immediacy based upon sensory experience sublimated to the divine. Each of these movements in its own way fed into expectations of transformation that prevailed in the counterculture milieu of the late 1960s. As such, they were 'New Age' only to the degree that they fed into millennial transformation on a global scale in which a spiritual awakening would take place following the collapse of the capitalist, militaristic and material exploitation of the world (Sutcliffe, 2014: 41). This collapse of the system was associated with messianic beliefs that drew upon Christian expectations of 'return' and Eastern ideas of the advent of a world messiah or messiahs. With the possible exception of Rajneesh, they were not 'New Age' in the general sense (*senso lato*) but could be described as contributory to *senso stricto*. It was into this bewildering milieu that the 13-year-old Prem Rawat arrived in London on 17 June 1971. The following chapter will focus on Prem Rawat, his biography, teachings and impact on the Western counterculture utilizing Rawlinson's 'inner Hinduism' and introducing Gold's (1987) category of 'solitary Sant' to understand how Prem Rawat might be understood in the context of the history of Indian religions.

4

Prem Rawat and contextualizing Indian religions in the West

It was in this context of Indian gurus arriving in the West and being accepted by counterculture youth that the young Prem Rawat arrived in London on 17 June 1971. As with other Indian teachers who came out of India, it was not his first contact with British and American seekers. The first individual to come across Prem Rawat and his family was Brian Kitt, an Englishman who had travelled overland to India in 1968 and became a sadhu, taking initiation from several gurus. He had come across the teachings of Prem Rawat after meeting an Indian student who had suggested that he should visit the ashram of Divine Light Mission (DLM) in New Delhi. Brian Kitt was renamed Saphalanand Ji, after joining the saffron-robed sannyasi order of male and female renunciates founded by Prem Rawat's father Shri Hans Ji Maharaj (d.1966). In June 1969, Saphalanand Ji requested permission to leave the ashram to seek out more Western followers. He met four travelling hippies who lived on the roof of old Delhi railway station. The meeting took place in the unlikely location of a night club in New Delhi frequented by travellers who went to listen to the music of counterculture icons such as Bob Dylan and Jimi Hendrix. The author was one of the four. Three would stay in the ashram in New Delhi and later as guests in the family home in Dehradun while the author travelled to Varanasi where he became a Shaivite sadhu. He would later return and stay in Prem Rawat's Premnagar ashram located in Haridwar. In late summer of 1969, all five travelled back to London, fully committed to communicating Prem Rawat's message to whoever would listen. Before leaving India, two more British travellers had been invited to stay at Prem Rawat's family home in Dehradun. On the way back through Afghanistan, a meeting took place with Joan Apter, an American, on her way to India to discover 'truth'. She would seek out Prem Rawat and become the first North American follower, organizing his tour to the United States in July 1971.

In September 1969, an Indian mahatma, Charnanand, was sent to London with permission to initiate along with Saphalanand, an example of 'proxy initiation' as described by Juergensmeyer and which allowed for initiation to take place outside India (1991: 76). A small basement apartment was rented in Fairholme Road, Fulham, and the four first Westerners, including the author, began to support the two mahatmas and communicate to those whom we met in various counterculture locations in London. Word went out through the 'jungle drums' of counterculture communication, and individuals in various states of dereliction and stages of truth-seeking began to arrive at the door. Fairholme Road was located in an area of small cheap rented accommodation within a stone's throw of various counterculture centres including Gandalf's Garden, Kensington Market, King's Road and Notting Hill Gate. It was close to several of London's large parks, especially Holland Park, where hippies would gather to jam and smoke hashish or partake in LSD. Every night, the room in Fairholme Road would be packed, as dozens crammed into the small space, sitting on the rush mats in front of Charnanand who would speak or sit listening to whoever he had requested to address the audience. The room carried no Indian deities and was bare of decoration, but there were small photographs of Prem Rawat and his father by the mahatma's bed. Indian incense would burn incessantly, partly to remove the smell of feet as shoes were removed in the ashram. Charnanand would also travel regularly to speak by invitation at Hindu temples and Sikh gurdwaras that were beginning to open up in London as the post-war South Asian migrant's presence from India began to increase in numbers. Interactions between these two sets of consumers of Indian religiosity were minimal. The author would sometimes be invited to speak when Charnanand attended Indian festive events. Aji Bai's Hindu temple in Golders Green, North London, created in the front room of her suburban house, was the only venue where counterculture spirituality and Hindu migrants would sometimes overlap. There, on occasions, you would find ISKCON devotees, members of the strongly Hindu-influenced rock band Quintessence and the new followers of Prem Rawat gathered together with Indian migrants, joining in with puja (worship) to the Hindu deities, but these mixed gatherings were not the norm. Charnanand would stay with an Indian family in London on his arrival in 1969 but left after experiencing their unease when long-haired hippies began to visit him there (Charnanand, 1996: 4).

It was not expected that Prem Rawat would visit the West so soon. His mother had informed Western followers in India that he would come after completing his schooling and attending university (p. 5). In November 1970, a large event was held in Ram Lila grounds, Delhi, to commemorate the birthday of Sri Hans Ji Maharaj. The event had been coined the 'Peace Bomb Festival'. Two sets of new British followers decided to travel overland and purchased second-hand vehicles, one an old ambulance, to attend the event and stay with Prem Rawat at Premnagar Ashram in Haridwar. Psychedelic lightshows were taken at the request of Prem Rawat's eldest brother to form part of an exhibition to be shown at the event. The two mahatmas also departed. During this time, larger premises were rented in Golders Green to replace the woefully inadequate basement flat in Fulham. This was to be a turning point in the history of the fledgling movement. The contact of around a dozen Western counterculture individuals with Prem Rawat in India was life-transforming. David Lovejoy would describe the experience as a 'life-altering time for all of us, with consequences extending three decades or more into the future' (2005: 77). All would return from India committed to dedicate their lives in service to their teacher through the promotion of his teachings. David Lovejoy would go to Australia; others would travel to Sri Lanka, Japan, Lebanon and France. Some would go to Goa to reach out to the hippie travellers who congregated on the beaches. The new ashram, a three-bedroom house in North London, provided the means to further develop the growing activities. The mahatmas would return along with a third Indian missionary, Ashokanand, who would begin to demonstrate formidable organizational abilities, developing the infrastructures of the fledgling DLM throughout the early 1970s. Finances were raised by donations, charity shops and later whole food and natural clothing businesses but money was in short supply, partly due to the countercultural attitudes towards it.

In April 1971, there were around one hundred initiated followers in Britain who consciously identified themselves as students of Prem Rawat, known as premies (derived from prem, meaning love). In the United States, the numbers were much smaller, only a handful who had met the guru in India as there was no one there to provide proxy initiation. The progress was slow. Charnanand once again left for India to attend the celebration of Vaisakhi, the Hindu spring festival. Shortly after his return, an unexpected telephone call came from Bombay where Prem Rawat was speaking during his school holidays. The caller announced that Prem Rawat was coming to London in June and could the London followers be ready to host him. It was from this not very prepossessing origin that DLM would come into existence as one of the most influential and controversial new religious movements (NRMs) of the 1970s.[1] It was only with the arrival of Prem Rawat and his subsequent appearance at the first Glastonbury festival that the teachings really caught on and spread like a forest fire through the milieu of the disenchanted counterculture of Britain and the United States in the early 1970s. DLM was also established in the United States and by 1972 had its international office in Denver, Colorado, where it was renamed Divine United Organization (DUO). By 1973, the movement in the United States was able to attract around twenty thousand mainly counterculture youth to the Houston Astrodome to hear Prem Rawat speak.

Academic studies of Prem Rawat

Although Chandler (1988) and others were to identify Prem Rawat as the 'centre of the flower power people in the 1970s', little serious academic treatment of Prem Rawat had taken place at the time. Most scholarly attention came from sociological analyses of religion, especially focusing on the arrival of NRMs attracting counterculture youth. A number of scholars referred to Weberian classifications of religious authority and described Prem Rawat as a charismatic leader (Dupertuis, 1986; Geaves, 2004b) with J. Gordon Melton (2003) attributing the rapid rise of the guru's message within the counterculture milieu to his personal charisma and Thomas Pilarzyk (1978) claiming that the distribution of authority in DLM was based on the charismatic 'appeal' of Prem Rawat, which he described as being somewhat ambiguous as many followers were not certain about his position in the organizational scheme of the movement, or the claim that he was the only true spiritual master. By the 1980s, a period outside the scope of this work, Meredith McGuire (1981) noted a transition from charismatic to rational management but attributed this process to Prem Rawat's desire to consolidate power and authority to himself within the United States (p. 175). Paul Schnabel (1982) would, however, continue to describe Prem Rawat as a pure example of a charismatic leader. Schnabel would appear to agree with Van der Lans and Fran Derks (1986) who considered that Prem Rawat stimulated an uncritical attitude, which gave them an opportunity to project their fantasies of divinity onto his person. According to Schnabel, attributing divinity to a guru is a common element within Eastern religions, but when removed from its cultural context, and confused with the Western understanding of God as a father, 'what is lost is the difference between the guru's person and that which the guru symbolizes – resulting in what he describes as limitless personality worship' (p. 142). There is considerable evidence, however, in the discourses of Prem Rawat that suggests he makes considerable reference to his humanity and denies divinity, at least, in any Western understanding of the term.

Figure 3 Hans ji Maharaj at Premnagar Ashram, late 1950s. Copyright RKV Delhi.

Yet none of the above provided an analysis of Prem Rawat's charisma or explored where the authority for such charismatic leadership originated, although Schnabel's point that Indian understandings of divinity were mixed with Christian understandings of God by Western counterculture followers is important and will be explored in Chapter 9. Lucy Dupertuis (1986), a one-time follower who had assisted James Downton in one of the first detailed studies of DLM, described Prem Rawat's authority as a master emerging from three interrelated phenomena: that is traditional or theological definitions of a satguru in Indian religions, the first-hand experiences of followers and accounts and discussions of the master among devotees in which tales of his extraordinariness were circulated. David Bromley (2007) also argued that charismatic leaders of many NRMs were held in awe by their early followers who ascribed extraordinary powers to them that set them apart from other human beings (p. 156). Stephen Hunt (2003) would completely disagree with these attempts to define Prem Rawat in terms of sociological charismatic theory and stated that the guru's major focus was on stillness, peace and contentment within the individual, established through his 'Knowledge', which was not discursive but consisted of techniques that were revealed in order to obtain these inner qualities.[2] Hunt maintains that this inner transformation was not derived from personal charisma but from Prem Rawat's teachings and the benefits accrued to individuals applying them (ibid.). The author (2006b) has also written that Prem Rawat made and continues to make significant efforts to assert his humanity and dismantle the hagiography that had developed around him and refocus attention on his message. In these interventions, it is argued that Prem Rawat, rather than considering himself a charismatic leader, has de-emphasized the sealing of the master–disciple relationship and focused instead on correct practice and staying in touch through participation or listening (ibid.). This view of development in the West is also stated by Melton (2003):

> In the early 1980s, Prem Rawat moved to disband the DLM and he personally renounced the trappings of Indian culture and religion, disbanding the mission, he founded Elan Vital, an organization to support his future role as teacher [...] Prem Rawat had made every attempt to abandon the traditional Indian religious trappings in which the techniques originated and to make his presentation acceptable to all the various cultural settings in which followers live. He sees his teachings as independent of culture, religion, beliefs, or lifestyles, and regularly addresses audiences in places as culturally diverse as India, Japan, Taiwan, the Ivory Coast, Slovenia, Mauritius and Venezuela, as well as North America, Europe and the South Pacific. (pp. 23–28)

Melton's attribution of an independent teaching to Prem Rawat coincides with Rawlinson's (1997) subcategories of 'Inner Hinduism', which he divides into teachers operating within a known tradition, including those who are part of a guru lineage; independent teachers who either set up on their own basing their authority solely on their inner experience; or those who teach without appeal to any tradition or previous teacher(s) (pp. 18–25). Rawlinson also refers to teachers who consider themselves to be authorized by membership of a spiritual hierarchy, those who claim to live in 'accordance with a transcendental source whether personal or impersonal' (p. 28). Individual teachers can possess one or more of these attributes and that is certainly true of Prem Rawat as will be demonstrated.

This academic debate with regard to Prem Rawat's charisma and authority would become highly charged after the academic study of NRMs and popular perceptions felt the impact of anti-cult discourses late in the decade of the 1970s and when throughout the 1990s a small but vociferous number of ex-followers[3] drew upon the emerging anti-cult milieu sometimes led by media crusades feeding upon and fuelling public outrage.[4] Although sociologists of religion would consider the movement to be benign, even beneficial, these disenchanted followers would draw upon 'brainwashing' theory, controversial mass suicides

Figure 4 Charnanand in Switzerland, 1972. Copyright RKV Delhi.

and acts of violence taking place elsewhere in the late 1970s and 1980s. These were allied to the guru's personal lifestyle which was never that of an ascetic in order to depict Prem Rawat as something more sinister, captured under the vilification of a 'cult leader' label.

Academics were more cautious and Downton (1979) who had studied Prem Rawat's followers for five years in the 1970s declared that 'these young people had a spiritual experience which deeply affected them and changed the course of their lives. It was an experience which moved many to tears of joy, for they had found the answer they had been seeking' (p. 156). He went on to state that by 1976, the majority of Prem Rawat's students viewed the guru as 'their spiritual teacher, guide and inspiration'. He explained that the typical view among students was that 'the only thing he (Rawat) wants is to see people living happily and harmoniously together' (p. 198). Downton concluded that the students had changed in a positive way, 'more peaceful, loving, confident and appreciative of life' (p. 210).

Sant iconoclasm

Typical of sociological analyses, no one would consider Prem Rawat's place in the complex and variegated history of religions in his place of origin, partly because of the marginalization of NRMs in the West which failed to assess them within the mainstream of the study of religions that tended to focus on the major world religions as discrete entities. Generally speaking, as argued earlier, the gurus from India and their organizations were perceived as a common phenomenon and grouped together as Hindu-origin sectarian or cult leaders. Followers were often pathologized. Gradually, scholars of religion would begin to rectify the large gap in the literature with a new methodological approach and begin to explore origins of the newly arrived movements, which could often be centuries old in Asia, for example, Knott's treatment of ISKCON (1986) or Chryssides' study of the religious origins of the Unification Church (1991).

The author would contribute to this fresh approach with a number of articles published between 2003 and 2007. These were written three decades after the arrival of Prem Rawat in London and his subsequent success as a counterculture guru in the early 1970s. My reasons for writing them were that I had noted not only the lacuna in both the academic treatment of NRMs and the scholarly consideration of Prem Rawat but also a number of factual errors concerning his origins that had resulted from over-reliance on anti-cult information on the World Wide Web. The early studies that existed tended to be written by sociologists and focused on the organizational structures in the West that grew around Prem Rawat. Thus, my first two interventions put forward the argument that it is necessary to take into account the worldview of the insider in order to appreciate the coherence or 'rationality' of actions by religious/spiritual teachers and their adherents in any analysis of religious organization. I examined the transformations that had occurred in the organizational forms utilized by Prem Rawat and argued that these developments owed more to his perception of his role as a teacher and his wish to universalize his message to reach out to all human beings irrespective of religion. I would suggest that this transformation was historically located in the teachings of individual sant iconoclasts, a centuries-old Indian phenomenon that exhibited strong anti-establishment elements that could be seen to parallel or approximate those of the Western counterculture that had embraced him. These articles argued that these influences were greater than any external or internal pressures brought to bear upon the organizational forms themselves, although these may have existed as secondary factors responsive to sociological analysis (Geaves 2004a, 2006a, 2006b).

Further articles would penetrate deeper into Prem Rawat's origins (2007, 2009, 2013). I had noted in my visits to India in 1969 and 1971 that a certain animosity existed towards Prem Rawat among the Brahmin-caste gurus who controlled ashrams in the Haridwar region and also in the Arya Samaj, a prominent Hindu reformist movement.[5] This was, in part, due to Prem Rawat's age of 8 when he

Figure 5 Western followers in Premnagar, 1970. Copyright RKV Delhi.

began to teach and the fact that his father, Shri Hans Ji Maharaj, had been a householder with four children. It could also be attributed to Shri Hans Ji Maharaj's Kabir-like critical stance on most, if not all, Hindu traditions.[6] In 1971, there would be anger generated towards the number of Americans staying in the ashram in Haridwar as war had broken out after India's intervention to secure Bangladesh's independence from Pakistan and rumours were rife, including claims that Prem Rawat was an agent of the CIA even though only just turned 13. Even journalists of respected newspapers put forward wild theories that the guru's age was fabricated and he was really around 40 years old.

It is unlikely that many of the counterculture followers flocking to the guru in the early 1970s knew much about his origins in India or where Prem Rawat could be contextually positioned in the vast diversity of Indian religious life as they were too involved in creating their own narratives concerning his divinity and credentials as a world messiah, yet they were certain that the rumour circuit contained considerable factual errors and this assisted them to construct their narratives of a world that historically would not accept reality or truth as revealed by a living master.

DLM had rapidly developed into a vigorous NRM with its own distinctive appearance combining the typical characteristics of a contemporary North Indian sant panth (organization) in which nirguna bhakti (love and devotion towards the formless God) was combined with intense reverence for the living satguru and the millennial expectations of the Western counterculture. Many of the characteristics of the Indian movement founded by Prem Rawat's father who had died in 1966 were imported wholesale into the Western environment. Ashrams were established with a lifetime commitment of celibacy expected from those who joined. Members were expected to forswear drugs and alcohol and to adopt a strict vegetarian diet. Outside the ashrams, members were advised to marry and live according to monogamous family units. The teachings were primarily given by saffron-robed mahatmas who came from India and toured the West. Rawlinson affirms that 'Guru Maharaj Ji's teachings were precise – and demanding'. He notes that in addition to these strictures, meditation took place twice a day, early morning and last thing at night, for a minimum of an hour each session (1997: 597). He also points out that 'the foundation of spiritual life was not just a certain lifestyle nor even a particular meditative practice but Guru Maharaj Ji himself' whose grace enabled 'initiates to advance on the inner path' (ibid.). The wider worldview was essentially Hindu in origin and accepted transmigration of souls, karma, human avatars and was imbedded in an interpretation of the *Upanishads*, the *Bhagavad Gita* and other Indian sacred texts. The reference to grace as essential to salvation showed the movement's origins in the *bhakti* (devotional) traditions within Hinduism but very different from the ISKCON focus on Krishna as an *ishvara* (personal form of God).

A discerning listener would have recognized the radical voice of the North Indian *nirguna sants*, especially Nanak (1469–1539) and Kabir (fifteenth century), in the message of universalism, equality and the focus on inwardness rather than the outer ritual forms of temple Hinduism or devotion to a deity. It was this apparent renewal of the *sant* idiom that led the few scholars of religion who wrote on the guru to mistake DLM for an offshoot of the Radhasoami movement. Olsen (1995), for example, asserts that DLM was a Radhasoami-inspired movement that had the 'greatest public American presence'. Dupertuis goes even further and claims that 'the gurus of DLM traced their spiritual lineage from Sant Mat and Radhasoami traditions' (1986: 114). She asserts that 'DLM was founded in India by Shri Hans Ji Maharaj who, despite the usual successional disputes, assumed leadership of his particular Radhasoami lineage upon his guru's death' (ibid.). Melton (1996: 890) further compounds the theory by identifying Shri Hans Ji Maharaj's guru as 'Dada Guru' who he claims is of the Sant Mat tradition and who initiated Prem Rawat's father into *surat shabd yoga* (the yoga of the sound current). 'Dada Guru' is a common title in Hindu *paramparas* (sectarian lineages) and refers to the founding guru who is usually taken as no further back than two generations from the present incumbent, even in longer lineages. *The Encyclopaedic Handbook of Cults in America* identifies the Dada Guru in this case as Swarupanand Ji, 'a guru of the Sant Mat tradition' who had initiated Shri Hans Ji Maharaj (Melton, 1999: 217). The paper further compounds the belief in a Sant Mat heritage by claiming that Swarupanand Ji was Sawan Singh, 'a prominent Sant Mat Guru' of one of the many Radhasoami lineages (ibid.) and continues to claim that Prem Rawat's teachings are derived from Sant Mat and describes them as a variation of Sikhism with Hindu influences (ibid.).

A possible conflation with Sant Mat may arise from the common language to verbalize experience that goes back to the medieval sants of North India, including the founder gurus of Sikhism and used by contemporary Sant Mat movements such as the various Radhasoami offshoots. Maharaj Charan Singh, a former master of the Beas branch, claims that the Radhasoami movement is united by its method of 'God-realization', identified as (1) the *simran* or remembrance of the Lord's Holy Names; (2) the *dhyan* or contemplation of the immortal form of the master; and (3) the *bhajan* or listening to the *anhad shabd* that is constantly reverberating within (cited from Sawan Singh (1965), *Spiritual Gems* in Juergensmeyer (1987: 331–2). These common elements identified by the guru reveal the Radhasoami link back to the sants of North India. In 2003, I had demonstrated that the metaphors used to describe the inner experience of immanence within the sant tradition are so alike as to provide a common language. The experience of the divine was veiled in various images of light, sound, nectar and finally the Word or Name of God. Rawlinson refers to such tropes within Indian religions as identifying a category he calls 'travellers on the inner path' identified by the belief that 'the soul is trapped in the physical world (and the physical body) but can go back to its source by following the inner path to God, using light and sound, guided by a master who has already traversed the path' (1997: 29). Juergensmeyer identifies that several contemporary Sant Mat teachers have linked the references to 'Word' to the logos theology at the beginning of St John's Gospel to demonstrate the universality of the teaching and thus transcend Hinduism (1991: 52–3). This common symbolic language could be found in both Sant Mat movements and marked DLM discourse until the early 1980s. Sant Mat can be described as a complex of interlinked gurus who attempt to revive the sant tradition of Northern India in the present time. Vaudeville adds to this understanding of the common attributes of the many sects (*sampradayas*) that can be defined as sant by asserting,

Whether they be born as Saiva, Vaisnava or Muslim, all the Sant poets stress the necessity of devotion to and practice of the divine Name (nama), devotion to the divine guru (satguru) and the great importance of 'the company of the Sants' (satsang). The Name, the divine guru and the satsang are the three pillars of the Sant sadhana. (1987: 31)

Shri Hans Ji Maharaj's book, *Hans Yog Prakash*, written sometime in the late 1930s, also reveals his inclination towards the North Indian *bhaktas* of the sant tradition and his conviction that his teachings and theirs were a continuation of an ancient revelation going back at least as far as the Upanishadic sages of ancient India.

Although the followers of Prem Rawat in India would draw extensively on the sant idiom, the idea of a Radhasoami connection in Prem Rawat's lineage seems to have arisen as a result of an error that confused Swarupanand Ji with Anand Swarup (d.1937)[7] and the mistaken belief that the two traditions share the same four techniques of practice.[8] Prem Rawat's actual historical location can be found in the lineage of Advait Mat, a north Indian cluster of movements which perceive themselves as originating from Totapuri, the teacher of Ramakrishna Paramhansa[9] with claimed ancient links back to Shankaracharya (788–820)[10] through a succession of Dasnami sadhus.[11] Prem Rawat has acknowledged this lineage as his own on his now redundant website as follows: Shri Totapuri ji Maharaj (1780-1866), Shri Anandpuri ji Maharaj (1782-1872), Param Hans Dayal Shri Advaitanand ji (1840-1919), Shri Swarupanand ji Maharaj (1884-1936) and Yogiraj Param Hans Satgurudev Shri Hans ji Maharaj (1900-1966).[12] Yet the link to Shankaracharya lineages is not evident in the teachings. The official lineages from the founder of Advaita Vedanta are extremely orthodox and would have frowned on many elements within the Advait Mat lineage, including the initiation of women, lower castes, Westerners and even the creation of female orders of renunciates.

Shri Hans Ji Maharaj was a prominent disciple of Shri Swarupanand Ji[13] and the lineage from Totapuri to Swarupanand Ji is documented in a biography written by a close follower of Swarupanandji in 1998. Although there are a number of offshoot organizations that dispute the succession at each stage as one master dies and another succeeds, it is not disputed that there is a master/disciple link between each new claimant back to Totapuri. However, the link to Totapuri is difficult to establish.[14]

Caution has to be taken in making too much of Prem Rawat's lineage in ascertaining how far he considers himself to be confined by his predecessors. His own emphasis has always been on the centrality of experiential knowledge and the role of the master that leads to such knowledge and inspirational guidance. He draws upon life experiences and examples from a range of sources to illustrate this central message. This echoes the teachings of the masters who came before him, although they drew upon scriptural references more readily as is the style in India. None of his predecessors proclaimed that the teachings belonged to a particular *sampradaya* or even a particular branch of Hinduism. In fact, all proclaimed that the teachings were independent of any religious tradition.[15] In Prem Rawat's case, this has resulted in the dissociation of the techniques from any Indian location and the loss of the sant idiom in his discourse as he has promoted the teachings worldwide in recent decades. In this respect, he bears resemblance to Rawlinson's independent teacher who arises from within a known tradition, including being part of a guru lineage, but who set up on their own basing their authority solely on their inner experience and teach without appeal to any tradition or previous teacher(s).

Arguably, Prem Rawat's charisma owes itself to a combination of factors that enabled individuals to perceive something far more dynamic than an established Indian *sampradaya* lineage could provide. His age, his ability to speak spontaneously drawing upon real-life experiences, anecdotes and his

Figure 6 Indian mahatmas in the West, circa 1972–3. Copyright RKV Delhi.

own experience, rather than scriptural interpretation, and the intense devotion of his following based upon their own inner experiences combined with an already developing hagiography led to the conviction of an individual master, uncluttered by tradition. In India, this had resulted in an intense *gurubhakti* (Guru devotion) which led many in India to regard Prem Rawat as an avatar of Krishna or Ram.

Although the author has stated that each master in Prem Rawat's lineage appeared to have total autonomy, free from tradition (Geaves, 2009), the events that led to the succession of Shri Hans Ji Maharaj and those pertaining to Prem Rawat are important in the way that the guru understood his authority as a teacher and were arguably even more pertinent at the time Prem Rawat came to the West as a child than in more recent decades. His father had been dead for only three years when the first Western followers met the child guru in India. The enthusiasm that they displayed for the guru to come to the West was reciprocated and has to be understood in the context of expectations which, if not exactly messianic, certainly contained a strong soteriological element, in which the young guru would bring out to the world a knowledge of the inner presence of the divine that had been hidden in India for millennia.

Shri Hans Ji Maharaj, according to the accounts of his followers, had, like Swarupanand Ji before him, been one of his master's inner circle with a special enthusiasm for promoting the teachings. He had been given permission to teach the techniques that led to the inner experience but it is unlikely that he would have been accepted as having equal status by the travelling *sannyasi* order that had been developed by Swarupanand Ji. Shri Hans Ji Maharaj was married, and in spite of the ethos of equality that was inherent in his guru's teachings, the long conditioning of Hindu culture and the traditional view of the superiority of the renunciate over the householder would have prevailed with many of the monks. The narrative of his followers states that Shri Hans Ji Maharaj was away when his master died in Nangli, a small village in Uttar Pradesh on the Grand Trunk Road (Tunden, 1970: 3). Various senior *sannyasis* gathered to discuss the succession and they were to choose from among themselves Vairaganand Ji to continue the lineage (ibid.). It is highly unlikely that they would have considered anyone who was not a monk especially in view of the fact that the previous masters had all been Indian renunciates and yogis.

Shri Hans Ji Maharaj contested this succession on his arrival at the ashram but the monks denied his claim. It is said Swarupanand Ji had stated, 'I am in

Hans' heart and Hans is in my heart' and had once lifted Shri Hans Ji Maharaj's hand and declared that the disciples should follow him after his death (p. 2). Whatever the circumstances, Shri Hans Ji Maharaj was fully convinced that he had inherited his master's mantle and departed the ashram with a very small group who had committed themselves to him and eventually began his own work to promote the teachings throughout India. Penniless, Shri Hans Ji Maharaj began to travel from place to place, slowly collecting a following that recognized him as their master. He first began to teach in Punjab basing himself in Lahore. At Partition in 1947, he moved to Delhi and began to promote the teachings among the workers at the Delhi Cloth Mill.

On Shri Hans Ji Maharaj's death in 1966, it is said that he appointed his youngest son, Prem Pal Singh Rawat, as his successor. Although there were other claimants, the family and senior followers of his father endorsed the young 8-year-old's claim to be the master.[16] It is important to note that the succession of Prem Rawat was never considered to be a hereditary one. The new master was believed by his father's students to possess his own charisma, and hagiographic narratives abound of his childhood exploits, especially in regard to his early attempts to speak out in public gatherings organized for his father. The 8-year-old Prem Rawat took to the task of promoting the message with the same enthusiasm which his father and Swarupanand Ji had displayed and achieved notable growth when his age is considered and that his own succession has not been without problems. Within a few years, he succeeded in transforming a little-known North Indian movement into a global phenomenon that today reaches out to most of the nations of the world.

The succession from Swarupanand Ji to Shri Hans Ji Maharaj brought about a significant transformation in that the guruship moved from a renunciate *sannyasi* to a householder but essentially the structure of DLM remained similar in form to the kind of organization that existed in Swarupanand's lifetime. The focus of authority was the charismatic leadership of the living satguru and authenticity was invested in the personal experience achieved by the individual follower as a result of the inward journey made possible by the practice of the techniques. Although a householder, married with four sons, Shri Hans Ji Maharaj maintained a large *sannyasi* order of both monks and nuns as his own guru had done. These formed the backbone of his efforts to communicate his message throughout India. The young Prem Rawat inherited all this from his father but increasingly began to dismantle the Indian forms of organization beginning shortly after his own marriage to an American in 1974.

Charisma and institutionalization

Prem Rawat's location in Indian spirituality shows his belonging to a continuous chain of masters who can be identified by their resistance to institutionalization and religion building. All of the masters identified in Prem Rawat's lineage have demonstrated iconoclastic and antinomian tendencies, and each has walked away from the material and religious infrastructures inherited at the death of the previous master in order to begin again with a new or renewed vision. I have called this phenomenon elsewhere '*traditionless* tradition' maintained to uphold the integrity of the 'experiential iconoclasm' worldview of each master (2009). Prem Rawat would appear to reveal this position even more than his predecessors, breaking with tradition and not offering any external authority to support his actions, whether by reference to sacred text or previous masters. A pragmatic sense of the 'eternal' in the 'now' perhaps conveys something of his position but it is neither a world-renouncing nor world-denying perspective; rather, the focus is on the preciousness of life and the miraculous presence of divinity within. This would appear to undermine Rawlinson's claim of a teaching that sees the 'soul trapped' with its corresponding dualistic view of the body and the world.

All of the above would seem to indicate an attempt to maintain a charismatic moment against the processes of institution in Weberian terms. Charisma is difficult to precisely define other than in terms of personal qualities associated with leadership which are attractive to others. From a student's perspective, Prem Rawat can be defined as charismatic with many personal accounts indicating the intense affective bonds based on gratitude and appreciation with which those who acknowledge him as their master hold him in regard. However, from his perspective, charisma is played down with a focus on the message and the transformative powers of the message contained within his teachings given far more emphasis. Utilizing the post-Weberian sociological analysis developed by Thomas O'Dea, any understanding of Prem Rawat's motivations would have to take into account the challenge to maintain the purity of his teachings from any sign of institutionalization. O'Dea argued that the founder-innovator is only concerned with communicating the message and maintaining the spontaneity of the transcendental experience (1961: 30–9). Although O'Dea perceived these conflicts and tensions chronologically as a way of exploring the development of charismatic authority to institutional authority, an analysis of this modern sant phenomenon still at the first stage of development provides an example of how a contemporary sant master, the first to globalize his teachings fully, grapples with and seeks innovative solutions to the problems of institutionalization.

Two scholars of the sant phenomenon in Northern India provide us with stages in the development of sant lineages from the original charismatic moment embedded in the teaching of a 'solitary sant' resistant to religion building through to the emergence of fully developed religious institutions after death. Building on these analyses of the sant tradition by Daniel Gold (1987) and Charlotte Vaudeville (1987), it can be argued that Prem Rawat be perceived as a 'solitary sant' whose authority derives from his teachings and is not part of any overarching formal organization, and that he does not have to subscribe to any particular worldview originating in any of the established religions. Gold argues that such figures have little inclination to establish a panth or sectarian institution (1987: 85). As such, Prem Rawat can be placed within the sant phenomenon as a starting point of understanding but any further research must demonstrate how far he has transcended that label to forge for himself a unique category that is to be understood on its own terms. I have argued in another paper that although there may be pragmatic concerns, such as financial stability, the attitudes of the wider society and the opposition of former practitioners, focusing on these as the prime factors of change and adaptation misses the opportunity for far more significant study of the relationship between charisma and institutionalization and overemphasizes the impact of reaction to external forces as the dominant motivation in understanding new religions. In particular, Prem Rawat's activities promise fascinating insights into the fine balance of maintaining the integrity of teaching and experience over the apparently inevitable processes of organizational and sectarian development. Prem Rawat has chosen a route of perpetual transformation in which organizational forms are created and utilized and then destroyed, thus providing flexibility to deal with rapidly changing social attitudes, to provide pragmatic solutions to internal problems and, above all, to keep his students focused on the core message that he wishes to transmit.

Religion and spirituality

Over the years, Prem Rawat has demonstrated his antipathy to categorization in a number of discourses in which he has claimed that his teachings have nothing to do with either religion or spirituality. A closer examination reveals that Prem Rawat is defining both these categories within very narrow parameters. The former is somewhat easier to deal with than the latter. There are a number of reasons why Prem Rawat would not want to acknowledge his teachings under the umbrella of religion. Prem Rawat's affinities with the medieval *nirguna bhaktas* of Northern India, although he would not define himself as such, preclude the possibility of categorization as religion. Prem Rawat shares with these exceptional figures in world spirituality an iconoclasm bordering on the antinomian that exalts inner experience of the sacred over and above the ceremonial, ritual, social and doctrinal dimensions of religion. Prem Rawat has been defined as a sant (Geaves, 2006b; Melton, 2003: 890) following the classic definition of such figures provided by Charlotte Vaudeville:

> A holy man of a rather special type, who cannot be accommodated in the traditional categories of Indian holy men – and he may just as well be a woman. The Sant is not a renunciate. ... He is neither a *yogi* nor a *siddha*, practices no *asanas*, boasts of no secret *bhij mantras* and has no claim to magical powers. The true Sant wears no special dress or insignia, having eschewed the social consideration and material benefits which in India attach to the profession of asceticism. ... The Sant ideal of sanctity is a lay ideal, open to all; it is an ideal that transcends both sectarian and caste barriers. (1987: 34)

It is certainly true that well-known sants, for example, Nanak and Kabir, were ambivalent towards the religions as practised in their time. Nanak, the founding guru of Sikhism, emphasized the sant's freedom from subservience to religious doctrinal or ideological worldviews very strongly:

> There are many dogmas, there are many systems,
>
> There are many scriptural revelations,
>
> Many modes to fetter the mind:
>
> But the *Sant* seeks for release through Truth. (Singh et al., 1973: 74–5)

Prem Rawat goes further than the sants in that his universalism frees him from the need to express his vision within the cosmological frameworks of any existent religious tradition. He remains non-speculative, refusing to engage with culture- or religion-specific doctrines concerning an afterlife, the nature of divinity or even its existence. His discourses reveal a pragmatism and even a strong scepticism towards the unproven such as doctrines concerning heaven and hell, reincarnation and ontological categories of good and evil. He tends to see religions as concerned primarily with the next life rather than this one. However, Prem Rawat's linguistic origins lie in India where 'religion' has no comparable term. The nearest approximation would be 'dharma', a concept

Figure 7 Prem Rawat and father on stage in India, circa 1963. Copyright RKV Delhi.

summoning up a whole complex of behaviour associated with a divinely given way of life. It is quite clear that Prem Rawat's teachings bear no resemblance to Indian dharmic systems and do not provide a code or a way of life that regulates behaviour. Indeed, it is doubtful that Prem Rawat would see himself within any category of religious specialist and would certainly refuse the label of 'holy man' given by Vaudeville (1987) in her definition of a sant.

There would be many in the West who would describe the above positioning as 'spiritual' as opposed to religious. However, it is eschewed by Prem Rawat whose discourse seems to suggest that he sees this contemporary and fashionable label so prevalent in New Age discourse as a discredited and imprecise label, appropriated by a consumerist, 'pick and mix' culture of 'spiritual' seeking and given esoteric significance, neither of which echo with his pragmatic iconoclasm or his requirement to commit to one focused discipline. On the other hand, if Paul Heelas's definition of spirituality as 'subjective-life forms of the sacred, which emphasize inner sources of significance and authority and the cultivation of unique subjective-lives' is taken as the benchmark, then certainly as far as the West is concerned those who become inspired by Prem Rawat's message to the point of initiation into the four techniques known as Knowledge can be placed as part of the move away from institutionalized forms of religion that emphasize conformity with external principles (Heelas and Woodhead, 2004). Stephen Hunt commented that the Western followers of Prem Rawat do not see themselves as members of a religion but rather as adherents of a system of teachings focused on the goal of enjoying life to the full (Hunt, 2003: 117) which would appear to confirm contemporary endorsement of spirituality over religion. However, the sociologically identified shift from religion to spirituality in the West would not appear to be applicable to Prem Rawat's success in the East where emic understandings would insist that the search for 'subjective life of the sacred' has been an ongoing human project for millennia.

Conclusion

This chapter has assessed both the sociological literature and the handful of studies by scholars of religion that were written after the dramatic success of Prem Rawat in the West after his arrival from India in 1971. It is deemed important to establish the antecedents of Prem Rawat and his particular understanding of the human dilemma within the history of Indian religious traditions as it is necessary to demonstrate that each of the Indian gurus who arrived in the West originated in vastly different historical, doctrinal and ritual dimensions of Indian religious life. As we have seen in the previous chapter, there are some common threads which can be identified. Several arrived as a fulfilment of a desire or prophetic statement from their own teachers; others were discovered by Western counterculture spiritual seekers, and it could be argued that each was influenced by Vivekananda's reverse mission to reposition India's place in world history by establishing the practices of yoga in Western nations. The latter motivation could be explicit or implicit.

The paucity of material on Prem Rawat's background has been supplemented through drawing upon the author's research undertaken in the first decade of the twenty-first century. I have tried to dispel some of the misunderstandings that connect DLM to Radhasoamis and a contemporary resurgence of Sant Mat. It is clear that the historical lineage is not proven to be connected to the Radhasoamis, although it develops historically in the same period and in the same region of Northern India and has some similarities regarding organization and symbolic language at various stages of its development. It is also questionable to label the lineage as Advait Mat as opposed to Sant Mat as the term 'Advait Mat' seems to have been initiated by the various institutionalized developments after the death of Swarupanand Ji. It does not figure in the language of the masters themselves, including Shri Hans Ji Maharaj and Prem Rawat. Swarupanand Ji had promoted the teachings of his guru on a large scale in rural and urban areas of Punjab, and this had brought about both organizational changes and a transformation of the symbolic language used to express the teachings. It is this change which appears to bring the tradition closer to Sant Mat and has probably created the confusion of a Radhasoami connection. The response of the masses who received the techniques from Swarupanand Ji was to declare their master an avatar of Krishna. This is not a usual feature of the *nirguna bhakti* of northern *sant* tradition and probably arises from the Hindu devotion to Krishna in the region combined with the remnants of Advaita discursive language that focuses on the *Bhagavad Gita*. It should be noted that identification with Krishna does not necessarily mean that the gurus understood themselves to be divine, but rather they regarded the human incarnations of Vishnu, that is Krishna and Ram, as masters who had been mythologized into deities. However, the masses in India may well have not had such an understanding and Western followers interpreted such narratives along with the scriptural references to St John's Gospel to view Prem Rawat as a world saviour – even an incarnation. These were then linked to millennial hopes arising from New Age expectations.

I have positioned Prem Rawat in a line of masters who have little in common with each other, other than their focus on the need for human beings to find a master who is able to transform human existence through correct knowledge of the immanent divine and their promotion of the need for experience rather than ritual or other dimensions of religion. I have argued that the lineage is more akin to that of single charismatic masters such as Kabir or Nanak who had little interest in founding institutions and can be understood as sant teachers. Prem Rawat has dropped any association to Hinduism and created a global presence that has little reference back to India or Indian traditions. It would thus appear that the kind of spiritual fulfilment taught by his predecessors was able to cross the boundaries of traditional Hindu *darshanas* and *sampradayas* and assist in the creation of new manifestations of charisma. In the hands of Prem Rawat, it has gone even further and been removed from all cultural moorings.

If Prem Rawat is to be defined within the realm of religion, it would require a definition of religion which espouses experience and rejects the necessity of any other outward activity or the maintenance of any particular cosmology. The main driving force for such a revolutionary transformation has been immediacy. In Chapter 9, there will be an assessment of how this focus on immediacy rooted in sant theosophy chimed with countercultural seekers but before doing this the following chapters will explore the advent of music festivals as part of the

Figure 8 Prem Rawat aged 8 announces his succession as satguru. Copyright RKV Delhi.

1960s counterculture and the special place of Glastonbury Fayre in that milieu, in order to understand the significance of the child guru headlining on the Pyramid Stage.

5

Festivals and music: Counterculture's religiosity?

Introduction

A superficial analysis of counterculture music venues in the second half of the 1960s might easily miss the relationship between music and the transformative mood of counterculture spirituality and it appears to have been overlooked by most scholars of contemporary religion. This may be due to academe's tendency to marginalize new spiritualities as explored by Sutcliffe who talks critically of a 'league table of religious entities' in which the smorgasbord of New Age phenomena is placed very low (2013: 22). Even those who take the New Age seriously rarely list consciousness exploration or 'raising' through transformative substance use or the bacchanalian elements of festival culture, possibly due to the normative constructions of a religious/secular divide that prevails in sociology and the study of religion. In this context, Sutcliffe speaks of steering 'New Age studies away from constructing marginalia and exotica' (p. 17), and perhaps it is considered that drug use, rock music and festivals belong in these categories. On the other hand, these categories of counterculture life can show how contemporary spiritualities belong to both the 'local' and the 'popular' as stated convincingly by Sutcliffe and fulfil his wish that New Age studies should move towards the 'recovery of a hitherto camouflaged data set located as much "within" as outside traditional formations, and which also straddles the religious secular divide' (pp. 17–18).

George McKay (2015) has examined festival culture from its early roots to its present manifestations as part of British summertime cultural mainstream experience and highlights the role of music in counterculture; however, Partridge remains one of the few scholars to fully explore this relationship between music and occulture (2004, 2015b, 2018) and has investigated what he calls 'High Culture' providing an in-depth analysis of the role of drugs in various countercultures (2018). It is necessary to provide a detailed description of music, drug use and the development of a festival culture in order to place the events that occurred in Glastonbury in 1971 and in the context of Prem Rawat's visit to the Fayre. Essential to the archaeology of these elements of late-1960s and early-1970s counterculture is the emphasis on their role as indicators of spirituality for many participants, even for an increasing minority, who found the heart of their religious experiences articulated in the teachings of an Eastern guru demanding allegiance. This chapter will posit that the song writers, the poets and the musicians of the counterculture were far more influential as spokespersons for the growing movement than the Indian gurus but, even so, were important in articulating the teachings of writers and Eastern philosophers into popular forms. Although Partridge's article written in 2006 is primarily concerned with the spirituality of the later rave movement, it explores its origins in the earlier countercultural forms with the latter's creation of 'sites of countercultural ideology and alternative spirituality' (p. 41), embodied in the free festival and the performance of psychedelic music as a unique vehicle to carry the message of those 'who wanted retreat from a society they perceived to be inhibited, violent and repressive. The free festival represented a microcosm of a new utopian community on the edges of an old, decadent, and staid society' (p. 42). Partridge particularly points towards the powerful spiritual dimensions of the festivals held at Stonehenge and Glastonbury as symbols of the authentic free festival (p. 43).

Psychedelic (soul-revealing) music

By 1967, known as the 'Summer of Love', American West Coast psychedelic[1] music had arrived in Britain, and the bands sang of the lifestyles, relationships, drugs, psychedelic experiences and spirituality of the counterculture. The term 'Summer of Love' began with the formation of the Council for the Summer of Love during the spring of 1967 responding to the convergence of young people on the Haight-Ashbury district in San Francisco. The council was composed of The Family Dog, The Straight Theatre, The Diggers, The San Francisco Oracle and approximately twenty-five other people, who sought to solve some of the problems anticipated from the influx of people expected in the area during the summer of 1967 (Chet Helms).

An examination of 1960s and 1970s rock music reveals a number of songs inspired by the literature that was influencing counterculture spirituality, especially the increasing impact of Eastern religions. The novel *Siddhartha* was immensely influential. In 1969, Nick Drake wrote the song 'River Man' and Ralph McTell recorded 'The Ferryman' for his 1971 album *You Well-Meaning Brought Me Here*. In 1972, the rock band Yes wrote 'Close to the Edge' on their album of the same name; Pete Townshend of the Who would also name a song 'The Ferryman' written for a modern production of *Siddhartha* in 1976. Even as late as the 1990s, the novel was influencing contemporary alternative bands; for example, the Slovenian alternative rock band formed in 1995 was named Siddharta after the novel and the self-styled independent rock band originating in San Francisco, Ten Mile Tide, wrote a song entitled 'Siddhartha' which provided a musical version of the novel (Partridge, 2015b).

The associations with Eastern spirituality would go further than songwriting. West Coast psychedelic bands would name themselves with obscure references to mystical or occult literature or left-wing revolutionaries, even sharing the stage with Indian gurus, beat poets, and donating money to create the sacred spaces for transmigration of Indian religious movements. Jim Morrison of the Doors would perceive himself as a saviour figure for the counterculture.

The Grateful Dead's first album, *The Grateful Dead*, was released in 1967 and the skull and roses design on the cover became emblematic of the band and is attributed to a black and white drawing by Edmund Joseph Sullivan in the 1913 edition of the *Rubaiyat of Omar Khayyam* (The Grateful Dead – Skull and Roses). The band had performed their first show in San Jose, California, on 4 December 1965, at one of Ken Kesey's Acid Tests (Stanton, 2003: 102) and at the beginning of 1967 they performed at the Mantra-Rock Dance in the Avalon Ballroom organized by the San Francisco Hare Krishna temple. The Grateful Dead, along with the Hare Krishna founder Bhaktivedanta Swami, the poet Allen Ginsberg, bands Moby Grape and Big Brother and the Holding Company with Janis Joplin, all donated proceeds to the ISKCON Krishna temple (Bromley and Shinn, 1989: 106).

The Doors were also formed in 1965 in Los Angeles and derived their name from singer Jim Morrison's suggestion from the title of Aldous Huxley's book *The Doors of Perception*, which itself was a reference to a quote made by William Blake, 'If the doors of perception were cleansed, everything would appear to man as it is, infinite' (http://www.doorshistory.com/doors1965.html). Morrison perceived himself as a counterculture bard, almost a messianic figure. Ray Manzarek, the co-founder of The Doors, describes Morrison's transformation after long sessions of LSD and reading Huxley's *Doors of Perception*. He claimed that Jim Morrison wanted to be the door by which others could experience the unknown and ultimately change a person's/society's way of thinking by becoming open to all things possible. He goes on to describe the singer in messianic terms stating that Morrison wanted to change the world's narrow perceptions and dedicated his life as a sacrifice to be the one to do so. His words, resonant of Christ's life, describe Morrison as the one who will pass through the door with the fear of death gone and alongside an awakening of something greater than life (http://www.doorshistory.com).

Also formed in 1965, Country Joe and the Fish would represent a different strand of the counterculture, one imbedded in American socialist politics. They would record two albums in 1967, *Electric Music for the Mind and Body* and later in the year *I-Feel-Like-I'm-Fixin'-to-Die*. The lyrical content of both albums demonstrated their commitment to political protest, recreational drug use and free love. The founders Joe MacDonald and Barry Melton had their roots in the left-wing underground and the band's name was a reference to Josef Stalin and to Mao Zedong's description of revolutionaries as 'the fish who swim in the sea of the people' (Eder, Bruce). Both had begun their musical careers in the folk scene and were strongly influenced by Woodie Guthrie. McDonald had been a publisher of the underground magazine *Et Tu Brute*, which later became *Rag Baby*, containing poetry, drawings and political messages of the Underground (James, Gary). By early 1965, McDonald had become involved in the folk scene in Berkeley and the Free Speech Movement that was organizing demonstrations in the University of California, Berkeley, which opposed the war in Vietnam. The title track of the second album, *I-Feel-Like-I'm-Fixin'-to-Die* is considered one of the most recognized and celebrated protest songs of the era (Perone, 2001: 40).

The explosion of psychedelic albums would lead Eric Davis to identify album art as an important contribution to the counterculture's development of its own cultural forms, pointing out the Incredible String Band's *The 5000 Spirits or the Layers of the Onion* and Jimi Hendrix Experience's *Axis: Bold as Love* as 'stand-out' examples from 1967 (2015: 640). Davis also mention in passing the representation of Crowley on the album cover of the Beatles' *Sgt Pepper's Hearts Club Band*, also released in 1967 and incidentally showing a number of counterculture literary 'heroes' including Jung, Aldous Huxley and William Burroughs (p. 644).

Arguably, the Beatles' fame commercialized the counterculture and introduced 'pop occulture' more than any other musical contribution of the time. Partridge adds the Indian gurus Sri Yukteswara, Sri Lahiri Mahasaya and Sri Paramahansa Yogananda to the list of figures on the cover of *Sgt Pepper's Hearts Club Band*.

The author remembers gazing at the iconic cover of the album, trying to identify the figures on the sleeve while listening to the music, a common practice at the time of its release (2004: 148). Partridge's identification of Easternization in the Beatles music was played out in the media, with high-profile shots of them covered in flowers and in the company of Maharishi Yogi. Partridge identifies *Revolver* released in 1966 as the beginning of the Beatles' flirtation with Eastern music, spirituality and counterculture. He cites George Harrison's 'Within You, Without You', with its Upanishadic themes and drone sitar, and John Lennon's 'Tomorrow Never Knows' as the product of Lennon's encounter with LSD and the ideas of Richard Alpert and Timothy Leary expressed in their interpretation of the *Tibetan Book of the Dead* through the lens of psychedelic experience (Leary et al., 2008) and Lennon's first use of LSD (Partridge, 2004:148). Partridge cites the book by Ian MacDonald (1995) as stating that 'while Harrison was devoting himself to Indian music ... Lennon had become interested in exploring his mental "inner space" with LSD' (ibid.).

This analysis misses Lennon's interest in counterculture politics that was to become increasingly evident after his involvement with Yoko Ono, the anti-war 'bed-ins' and the politically explicit 'Revolution' or 'Come Together', written when he was protesting against Ronald Reagan's campaign to become governor of California in 1969 (p. 149). While Harrison was becoming increasingly interested in Indian spirituality, Lennon moved towards the political and avant-garde. These two musicians of the counterculture were to understand peace in radically different ways and as with the Grateful Dead and Country Joe represented two influential strands of the late-1960s counterculture. These differences were not always reconciled and in this context Prem Rawat was to play a major role. The counterculture was not a homogeneous entity and comprised many competing strands reflected in the music. Through Bob Dylan, the 1960s music of the counterculture would introduce Greenwich Village, the beat poets and the earlier working-class protests as embodied in the songs of Woodie Guthrie. The soon to become legendary guitarists originating in the English blues scene, such as Jimmy Page, Jeff Beck, Eric Clapton and John Mayall, would introduce black rhythm and blues to British audiences. Blues stars such as Sonny Boy Williamson were touring small clubs in Britain and sent listeners back into the world of black musicians playing prior to the civil rights movement and still affected by the aftermath of slavery. Folk musicians, especially the guitarists David Graham and Bert Jansch, sang the songs of the British beat generation. Others folk musicians would introduce protest music as a means of communicating the peace movement and the civil rights movement.

The occult is not missing from the music of the counterculture. Erik Davis mentions the New York underground folk-rock group The Fugs leading an exorcism of Pentagon demons (2015: 642) and a 'rock endorsement' of Aleister Crowley by Jimmy Page, the lead guitarist of Led Zeppelin (p. 644). Partridge also mentions the folk scene's lyrical involvement with 'folkloric myth and magic' as instrumental in bringing a 'dark and visceral world to their listeners' that would lead to acid folk and folk rock that 'sloughed off from traditional folk' (2015b: 511). Davis concludes that 'the fact that myriad young fans across the globe were exposed to a scandalous Edwardian ceremonial magician through the medium of chart-topping rock and roll is as good a characterisation as any for the dynamics of pop occulture in the 1970s, when the seeds of the counter-culture spread far and wide, high and low' (2015: 644).

A darker side of the counterculture is also manifest in the music of Paul Butterfield and the Paul Butterfield Blues Band. Butterfield had a strong interest in authentic American Blues music (Wolkin et al., 2000: 40). Their second album *East-West* recorded in mid-1965 would influence the West Coast psychedelic musicians. Although containing conventional blues numbers, some rhythm and blues, and jazz, the album contained a thirteen-minute instrumental called 'East-West'. The track introduced Indian classical raga-influenced music with jazz fusion and blues-rock, with extended electric guitar solos. The track has been described as laying 'the roots of psychedelic acid rock' and featuring 'much of acid-rock's eventual DNA' ('Erlwine, Michael'). Pre-empting the long jamming done by the psychedelic bands when performing live, the band would sometimes play live versions of the song lasting nearly an hour, and their performances at the San Francisco Fillmore Auditorium 'were a huge influence on the city's jam bands' (Houghton, 2010: 195).

Bloomfield's influence on the West Coast musicians would help produce a different blend of music leading to acid rock with a harder, louder or heavier electric blues-based sound leading to the East Coast rock as epitomized by Lou Reed and Velvet Underground. These bands brought this darker side to the fore, heavily influenced by the use of opiates and exhibiting gender-challenging sexuality. In 1967, they released *Velvet Underground and Nico* and *White Light, White Heat* in 1968, the latter's celebrating heroin use in New York, both albums influenced by Andy Warhol.

The West coast bands would become legendary for their combination of psychedelic music and embodiment of countercultural lifestyles and values but would be particularly established for their respective performances at significant countercultural events in the late 1960s, especially the foundational

Trips Festival, the Human Be-In and the Mantra In. The Grateful Dead, Jefferson Airplane, Big Brother and the Holding Company and Quicksilver Messenger Service would become counterculture icons and arguably far more significant as spokespersons than the gurus from the East.

The creation of psychedelic spaces in transatlantic cities – United States

The origins of the psychedelic festivals lie in the earlier Beatnik era, where Bohemian tastes in music extended to folk and jazz. These earlier but smaller celebrations of counterculture would morph into the festival culture of the late-1960s 'flower-power'. The Newport Jazz Festival began in 1954 and was attended by thirteen thousand, which rose to twenty thousand the following year ('Newport Jazz Festival'). From its inception, the festival was seen as problematic by the middle-class residents of Newport, a small town on Rhode Island. In 1955, the Belcourt location for the festival was disallowed by local residents on the grounds of potential disturbance. Jazz was not popular within the local community and many of the musicians and their fans were African American. The festival would bring crowds of students to Newport who slept outdoors with or without tents. Middle-class Newport was shocked (Anderson, 2007). Yet the event flourished and grew increasingly eclectic. The presence of major rock stars would attract the new counterculture audiences of the late 1960s. The decision to introduce rock acts to the Newport Jazz Festival was controversial and led to loss of crowd control as hundreds broke down fences to attend (Brennan, 2006). *Rolling Stone* magazine would report,

> Everything went off. The rain. The crowds. Firecrackers. And, above all, establishment paranoia. The fence went again. To prevent more damage to the fence, the gates were opened and bands of wild hippies, LSD on their breath, swarmed through, pushing the bleacher audience forward, vaulting over the VIP box seats, shoving into the press section, slamming the customers into the stage … Sly played on, digging it. (9 August 1969: 10)

George Wein, the organizer of Newport in 1969, introduced rock bands as he had noted the famed Monterey Jazz Festival had already introduced rock acts (Brennan, 2006). Monterey festival had begun in 1958 and like Newport brought many of the great black stars of jazz and blues to its 20-acre site at the Monterey County Fairground. The site would include international food, merchandise outlets and other festivities. It was not until 1967 that the festival introduced Janis Joplin with Big Brother and the Holding Company to its jazz line-up, playing alongside Richie Havens and B. B. King. The coverage by *Rolling Stone* of the Monterey Jazz Festivals of 1968 and 1969 would present jazz festivals as sites of tension between 'old and young, square and hip, traditionalism and the avant garde, and finally, jazz and rock' (ibid.). In the space of a few years, the existing jazz festivals could not provide the milieu for the rapidly growing counterculture fuelled by psychedelic substance use and its own brand of music, nor did they contain the later manifestations of Eastern spirituality mixing in with the revelry. They would be replaced by the rock festival as the site of counterculture celebration. Yet as we shall see, the rock festival would become too commercialized for the diehards of the counterculture after Woodstock. However, this was not the case for the early West Coast events that were perceived as authentically underground occasions.

Even as early as January 1966, the aptly named Trips Festival attracted a crowd of ten thousand to the Longshoreman's Hall in San Francisco. On the second night of the three-day event, Grateful Dead and Big Brother and the Holding Company played to a crowd of six thousand many of whom had taken LSD in spite of the festival being advertised as 'the Acid experience without the Acid' (http://www.postertrip.com). In addition to the bands, the event attempted to recreate the intensity of the psychedelic experience.

According to Phil Lesh, bass guitarist of the Grateful Dead, the event also featured participants from the Open Theatre; Dancers' Workshops; and the Congress of Wonders, an improvisatory acid comedy troupe. Michael McClure read; Bruce Conner showed films; and 'countless unsung freaks added their costumes, movements, and general good vibes to the mix' (2006: 73–5). The first night was billed as 'America Needs Indians' and in addition to psychedelic art celebrated indigenous American Indian culture with representatives from various tribes, perhaps possibly the first event to demonstrate the counterculture's continuing interest in indigenous people and their way of life. The event was very much the brainchild of members of the Pranksters, or Merry Pranksters, who had lived and travelled with Ken Kesey since 1964 and participated in the famous road trip in the psychedelic painted bus named 'Further or Further'. The Pranksters had handed out free LSD as they travelled. The Trips Festival was perceived as a continuation of the road trip and the Acid Tests, a series of parties held by Ken Kesey mainly in the San Francisco Bay Area during the mid-1960s, centred entirely on the use of and advocacy of LSD (https://www.univie.ac.at/Anglistik/easyrider). Tom Wolfe claims that the event created a new night-club and dance-hall genre and within two weeks, Bill Graham, one of the organizers, had secured the Filmore Auditorium as a venue, where they repeated the format of the Trips Festival every weekend. Wolfe goes on to say,

> For the acid heads themselves, the Trips Festival was like the first national convention of an underground movement that had existed on a hush-hush cell-by-cell basis. The heads were amazed at how big their own ranks had become – and euphoric over the fact that they could come out in the open, high as baboons, and the sky, and the law, wouldn't fall down on them. The press went along with the notion that this had been an LSD experience without LSD. Nobody in the hip world of San Francisco had any such delusion, and the Haight-Ashbury era began that weekend. (1968: 258–63)

The Trips Festival was followed by the 6 October 1966 Love Pageant Rally, held in San Francisco to protest the banning of LSD. Held in Golden Gate Park, near the Haight-Ashbury district, the organizers Allen Cohen and artist Michael Bowen, the creators of the *San Francisco Oracle*, were looking to devise a form of protest that was more in line with 'hippie culture'. Cohen would state, 'Without confrontation, we wanted to create a celebration of innocence. We were not guilty of using illegal substances. We were celebrating transcendental consciousness. The beauty of the universe. The beauty of being.' Posters for the event declared, 'Bring photos of personal saints and gurus and heroes of the underground … Bring children … Flowers … Flutes … Drums … Feathers … Bands … Beads … Banners, flags, incense, chimes, gongs, cymbals, symbols, costumes, joy.' The music was provided by the Grateful Dead and Janis Joplin, who played for free. Ken Kesey and the Merry Pranksters attended in the legendary bus. Thousands showed up for the event, read a 'prophecy of a declaration of independence', and many placed a tab of LSD on their tongues and swallowed in unison (Perry, 1988). The protest was possibly the first time mass consumption of LSD was used as political protest and the language of promotion reveals how festival culture was developing as a site of a new spirituality.

Two more events of significance would take place a year later within two weeks of each other. The first was the Human Be-In that took place in Golden Gate Park, San Francisco, on 14 January 1967 where more than twenty thousand people turned up. According to the account by Neville Powell, Richard Alpert, who later became known as Baba Ram Das, had met up with Allen Cohen and Michael Bowen at the Love Pageant Rally where Cohen asked Alpert what he thought of the day. Alpert replied, 'It's a hell of a gathering. It's just being. Humans being. Being together.' 'Yeah,' said Bowen. 'It's a Human Be-In.' It was decided to organize something called the Human Be-In to bring tens of thousands of people together. The event was announced on the cover of the fifth issue of the *San Francisco Oracle* and as with the Love Pageant Rally, the occasion was in protest against the California law banning LSD that had been passed on 6 October 1966. The speakers included Timothy Leary, who in his first San Francisco appearance, dressed all in white with a flower over each ear, announced his famous phrase, 'Turn on, tune in, drop out' (Hartlaub and Whiting, 2017). Richard Alpert, Allen Ginsberg, who chanted Indian mantras, Lawrence Ferlinghetti, Gary Snyder, Jerry Rubin and Alan Watts all spoke. The principal bands who appeared were Jefferson Airplane, The Grateful Dead, Big Brother and the Holding Company, Quicksilver Messenger Service and Blue Cheer, who had all established themselves with strong counterculture credentials. The chemist Owsley Stanley provided massive amounts of his 'White Lightning' LSD, specially produced for the event, as well as seventy-five 20-pound turkeys, for free distribution by the Diggers (Grogan, 1990: 274).

A key element of the Be-In was the attempt to reconcile the two main factions of the San Francisco counterculture, that is, the Berkeley political radicals who were increasingly concerned about the escalation of the Vietnam War and becoming more militant towards the government and the Haight-Ashbury 'hippies' who favoured consciousness-raising through the help of psychedelic drugs and spiritual guides and preferred peaceful protest and joyful celebration. Alan Cohen would call the event a meeting of minds, and the *Berkeley Barb* (6 January 1967), an important underground newspaper, would report that 'the two radical scenes are for the first time beginning to look at each other more closely. What both see is that both are under a big impersonal stick called The Establishment. So they're going to stand up together in what both hope to be a new and strong harmony.' The same issue of the *Barb* would elaborate on the differences and the success of the event to resolve them.

> Berkeley political activists are going to join San Francisco's hippies in a love feast that will, hopefully, wipe out the last remnants of mutual skepticism and suspicion ... In homes on both sides of the Bay while this was being shaped from a dream to a reality, the basic problem was whether to play the word game. The San Franciscans didn't want to play that game any more; it doesn't work, they said, and the non-verbal modes of expression tell it where it's at. The Berkeleyans wanted to play that game because that's where the rest of society plays; that's the only way, they said, to get through to most people. The hip wondered aloud whether the politicos would make the Gathering a haranguing rally. The politicos wondered aloud whether the hip would all happily turn on and any social message would be lost. They solved it. (*The Berkeley Barb*)

The Human Be-In was followed two weeks later by the Mantra Rock Dance held at the Avalon Ballroom in San Francisco. It was organized by ISKCON to promote their spiritual leader Swami A. C. Bhaktivedanta Prabhupada who had recently arrived in the United States in July 1966. The event was also held to raise funds for a West Coast Krishna temple. A number of prominent Californian counterculture bands would play free and major counterculture figures spoke including Allen Ginsberg, who led the singing of the Hare Krishna mantra onstage with Prabhupada, Timothy Leary and Owsley Stanley (Chryssides and Wilkins, 2006: 213).

Swami Prabhupada had been greeted at San Francisco airport by around one hundred 'hippies' chanting and carrying flowers (Goswami and Dasi, 2011: 125). The movement's spokesperson had published an article in the *San Francisco Oracle* announcing the guru's arrival in the city and in a competitive mood, declared, 'Swamiji's chanting and dancing is more effective than Hatha or Raja Yoga or listening to Ali Akbar Khan on acid or going to a mixed media rock dance' (Cohen, 1991: 91, 96). The interest in the guru generated a second article in the *San Francisco Chronicle* in which Prabhupada was asked, 'Do you accept hippies in your temple?' (Siegel, 2004: 11) Although the guru answered that everyone was welcome, the question would implicitly demand a positioning by the guru on counterculture lifestyle, particularly promiscuity and drug use. The three thousand attendees were asked not to take drugs into the event, yet many were smoking marijuana and LSD; however, the atmosphere was peaceful, with the attendees invited to participate in *prasad* (sacred food) consisting of orange slices on entry. The hall combined images of Krishna and projections of the Hare Krishna mantra with strobe lightshows. Prabhupada's biographer, Satsvarupa Dasa Goswami describes the audience,

> Almost everyone who came wore bright or unusual costumes: tribal robes, Mexican ponchos, Indian *kurtas*, 'God's-eyes', feathers, and beads. Some hippies brought their own flutes, lutes, gourds, drums, rattles, horns, and guitars. The Hell's Angels, dirty-haired, wearing jeans, boots, and denim jackets and accompanied by their women, made their entrance, carrying chains, smoking cigarettes, and displaying their regalia of German helmets, emblazoned emblems, and so on – everything but their motorcycles, which they had parked outside. (1981: 12)

Ginsberg welcomed Prabhupada onto the stage and spoke of his own experiences chanting the Hare Krishna mantra and recommended the early-morning chanting at the local Radha-Krishna temple 'for those coming down from LSD who want to stabilize their consciousness upon reentry', calling the temple's activity an 'important community service'. When the swami himself arrived at 10 pm, the crowd of hippies rose to their feet to greet him respectfully with applause and cheers (Goswami, 2011: 154). Gurudas, one of the organizers, describes Prabhupada's arrival, 'Then Swami Bhaktivedanta entered. He looked like a Vedic sage, exalted and otherworldly. As he advanced towards the stage, the crowd parted and made way for him, like the surfer riding a wave. He glided onto the stage, sat down and began playing the kartals' (Siegel, 2004: 8–10). After Prabhupada's speech, Ginsberg chanted 'Hare Krishna' to the accompaniment of sitar, tambura and drums, requesting the audience to 'sink into the sound vibration, and think of peace' (ibid.). Prabhupada joined in leading the audience in dancing and singing, and the Grateful Dead, Big Brother and the Holding Company and Moby Grape accompanied the mantra with their musical instruments (Tuedio and Spector, 2010: 32). The chanting would continue for almost two hours and concluded with the swami's Sanskrit blessings with the audience bowed down on the floor. After Prabhupada left, Janis Joplin took the stage, backed by Big Brother and the Holding Company.

The Mantra-Rock Dance helped raise around $2,000 for the temple and resulted in a large number of visitors at the temple's early morning services. Prabhupada would become an iconic figure to Haight-Ashbury counterculture, even though most would not accept Krishna consciousness or acknowledge the restrictions he required to their lifestyles (Brooks, 1992: 79–80). The Hare Krishna mantra and dancing would, however, become a part of the counterculture and for some an alternative to drug consumption (Ellwood, 1989: 106–7). Prabhupada and his followers would become a common sight in Haight-Ashbury, chanting and dancing and offering *prasad* in the streets of the area (Brooks, 1992: 79–80).

The events above could be described as precursors to the rock festival. The relative failure to integrate the new music with jazz and folk would lead to a number of rock festivals in Northern California in the summer of 1967. The first would be the KFRC Fantasy Fair and Magic Mountain Music Festival held on Mount Tamalpais. Around thirty-six thousand attended the two-day concert on 10 and 11 June, and KFRC is considered to have been America's first rock festival (Hopkins, 1970: 31; Lang, 2009: 58; Santelli, 1980: 16) and the first of a series of such events in the San Francisco area that came to be known as the Summer of Love (Shannon, 2009: 310). Most of the bands played the Fillmore and Avalon ballrooms and were part of the psychedelic rock scene. To reach the amphitheatre half way up the mountain transportation was provided by the 'Trans-Love Bus Lines' and a giant Buddha balloon greeted attendees when they arrived. The festival incorporated 'art-fair' stalls which sold posters, crafts and provided refreshments from booths scattered in the woods. A large geodesic dome of pipes and fittings covered with white plastic contained a light and sound show ('Fantasy Fair'). George McKay describes the Fantasy Fair as the 'first major mediaeval style event' (McKay, 2000: 90) and it is mentioned that it was influenced by the popular Renaissance Pleasure Fair ('Steve Hoffman Music Forums'). The Renaissance Pleasure Faire of Southern California (RPFS) was the first modern Renaissance faire[2] to occur in America. It opened in the spring of 1963 and has been an annual event since then (Thomas et al., 1987). The combination of faire and music festival would become the prototype for large-scale multi-act outdoor rock festivals (Hopkins 1970: 31).

The Californian rock festivals of 1967 would generate a unique identity for the counterculture rock festival and by 1969 promoters across the United States were staging dozens of spin-offs. The East Coast would host its first rock festival in Miami, with a smaller festival in May attracting a crowd of twenty-five thousand. The larger Miami Pop Festival held at the end of December in 1969 attracted over one hundred thousand. It was produced by the same organizers that had created the KFRC Fantasy Fair and Magic Mountain Music Festival. As with earlier festivals in 1968, the event crossed over several music genres and combined bands from both sides of the Atlantic.

1969 would open with the Palm Springs Festival in April and the Big Rock Pow-Wow held in May on a Seminole Indian reservation in Florida, with Grateful Dead headlining and Timothy Leary speaking from the stage. The Northern California Folk-Rock Festival would be repeated in May. In June, the Newport 1969 Pop Festival occurred on the same weekend, the first event of its kind to attract over two hundred thousand. According to Bill Mankin, these early rock festivals were important sociocultural milestones:

> It would not be an exaggeration to say that, over a few short years, rock festivals played a unique, significant – and under appreciated – role in fuelling the countercultural shift that swept not only America but many other countries [during the 1960s]. It seems fitting ... that one of the most enduring labels for the entire generation of that era was derived from a rock festival: the 'Woodstock Generation'. (Mankin, 2012)

Woodstock Festival, held over three days from 15 to 17 August on the 600-acre dairy farm 50 miles from the town, was not the last of such events in 1969 as it was followed by festivals in Vancouver, Texas, New Orleans, Toronto, Palm Beach, Miami and the Altamont Free Concert, but it was certainly the most seminal, with estimates of four hundred thousand in attendance, although only 186,000 tickets were sold. It is estimated that over half million people blocked the roads creating over 8 miles of traffic. The festival came to define a generation with a number of musicians performing songs expressing their opposition to the Vietnam War, enthusiastically shared by the vast majority of the audience. The term 'Woodstock Nation' would be used as a general term to describe the youth counterculture of the 1960s (https://www.history.com/this-day-in-history). Conceived as 'Three Days of Peace and Music', the organizers decided to declare the festival free for everyone in order to control the crowds (http://news.bbc.co.uk/onthisday). Sri Swami Satchidananda opened the festival with the following words:

My Beloved Brothers and Sisters:

I am overwhelmed with joy to see the entire youth of America gathered here in the name of the fine art of music. In fact, through the music, we can work wonders. Music is a celestial sound and it is the sound that controls the whole universe, not atomic vibrations. Sound energy, sound power, is much, much greater than any other power in this world. And, one thing I would very much wish you all to remember is that with sound, we can make – and at the same time, break. Even in the war-field, to make the tender heart an animal, sound is used. Without that war band, that terrific sound, man will not become animal to kill his own brethren. So, that proves that you can break with sound, and if we care, we can make also. (https://www.woodstock.com/lineup/)

The Swami's words would provide the confirmation that Eastern cultures perceived music as sacred, part of the cosmic vibrations of the universe, able to change human consciousness. The event would combine Eastern religious understandings of immanence with immediacy, expressed in Dionysian celebration to form the cocktail of spirituality that was developing in the countercultural spaces. The main organizer, Max Yasgur would declare on the last day, 'You have proven something to the world … that half a million kids can get together for fun and music and have nothing but fun and music.' A film of the concert was released the following year and Woodstock would become synonymous with flower power, the hippie culture and the anti-Vietnam War protests that would continue through into the 1970s (http://news.bbc.co.uk/onthisday).

The British scene

Britain's counterculture would develop with an explosion of interest in authentic American blues within Britain's post-war youth cultures and had led to the creation of the British Blues scene culminating in a number of individuals and bands who would become household names by the middle of the 1960s, including The Rolling Stones, The Animals, Eric Clapton, Fleetwood Mac and Led Zeppelin. London's Soho, the home of the city's red light district, hosted several clubs and venues where blues and jazz musicians would perform. The district would also be the weekend choice for the mod scene in the mid-1960s, where soul bands such as Georgie Fame and Gino Washington would play in Wardour Street. The virtuoso folk guitarists Bert Jansch, Davy Graham and John Renbourn developed a unique style known as Baroque Folk. They remained close to the acoustic blues scene (Sweers, 2005: 184–9) and played in the Lamb and Flag in Cambridge Circus and other public house venues in the Soho area with Donovan appearing from time to time as a guest star.[3] In the nearby Roundhouse Public House, blues guitarist and harpist Cyril Davies would play with Alexis Korner, often called the father of British blues. British jazz musicians, such as Stan Tracy and Chris Barbour, played nearby. As early as 1957, Davies and Korner had formed the Blues Incorporated and were introducing London's youth cultures to high-powered electric blues that was the prototype music for the bands of the later 1960s (Bogdanov et al., 2003: 700). Black musicians of the calibre of Big Bill Broonzy, Muddy Waters and Sonny Boy Williamson were touring Britain's cities playing at small venues. By the mid-1960s, the Marquee Club and The Hundred Club in Soho were hosting top British blues outfits, such as John Mayall and the Bluesbreakers, Blues Incorporated, the Yardbirds (Eric Clapton, Jeff Beck and Jimmy Page), The Pretty Things and the Kinks. Aficionados of the genre and youth culture adherents seeking excitement danced in the steamy hot, underlit clubs listening to musicians who would become household names by the late 1960s. At varying times, Keith Richards, Mick Jagger, Charlie Watts and Brian Jones (Rolling Stones); Jack Bruce and Ginger Baker (Cream); and the British blues stars, Graham Bond, Zoot Money and Long John Baldry would guest with the bands (pp. 1315–16). Blues- and soul-influenced bands began to emerge from other major British cities including The Animals from Newcastle, The Moody Blues and Spencer Davis Group from Birmingham and Them from Belfast (p. 700). Famously, the Liverpool sound developed near the docks of the city and The Beatles were to emerge as the frontrunners of the British popular music scene. Mod bands, such as Small Faces, The Who, Creation and The Action were also musically centred on rhythm and blues and emerged to fill the space for American musicians not available in the small clubs of London's suburbs where the mod subculture was mainly located (pp. 1321–2). The British counterculture would retain strong roots with the earlier manifestations of Bohemia labelled

'Beatnik' but recruited heavily from popular youth cultures drawn to the new Blues played in the clubs of London and Northern cities.

As the 'hippie' subculture began to dominate over other youth cultures in the later 1960s, all of these bands and musicians would begin to develop a style of British psychedelic rock that would explode simultaneously with the United States in 1967 and dominate the rest of the 1960s. Perhaps the most important contribution of British blues was the transmigration of American blues back to America, where, in the wake of the success of bands like the Rolling Stones and Fleetwood Mac, white audiences began to look again at black blues musicians like Muddy Waters, Howlin' Wolf and John Lee Hooker (Kaufman and MacPherson, 2005: 154). Arguably, it was the creative energy emerging out of the British Blues scene that attracted one of the greatest stars of the era to Britain. Jimi Hendrix arrived in London in late 1966 and formed the Jimi Hendrix Experience. In Britain, he was an immediate sensation and the album *Are You Experienced* appeared in 1967 very close in release to The Beatles's *Sergeant Pepper*. The album featured a diversity of musical styles, including blues and rhythm and blues, and also included the experimental science fiction piece, 'Third Stone from the Sun' along with the soundscapes of the title track, and the guitar feedback improvisation of 'I don't Live Today'. The album would proclaim Hendrix as a major proponent of psychedelic rock (Stubbs, 2003: 29, 31–2, 36–7).

Britain's psychedelic musicians would also draw heavily upon Celtic and medieval folk heritage and even music hall to create a whimsical mood in their songwriting. While both British and American bands drew heavily upon the inspiration of Indian and Eastern music, experiment and jazz-type improvisation and drug-inspired imagery, arguably British psychedelic pop was more playful and sunnier in mood, although just as 'freaked-out and forceful' ('British Psychodelia'). However, later in the decade and in the early 1970s, British musicians were combining with American counterparts to form superbands or in the case of Fleetwood Mac rooting themselves in California.

The creation of psychedelic spaces in transatlantic cities – Britain

In the 1950s, both the United States and the UK hosted a number of jazz festivals that would provide platforms for rock and roll artists but Newport in the United States and Beaulieu in the UK were locations of particular significance. In 1956, the grounds of the stately home of the Montagu family became the location of an annual jazz festival and one of Britain's first experiments in festival culture, which included camping overnight, eccentric dress codes, wild music and behaviour (McKay, 2004). It should also be noted that the same period saw the rise of peace marches in Britain where tens of thousands would protest against nuclear weapons. Camping and music were features of the demonstrations. Increasingly, the youth on the march to Aldermaston[4] wanted to sing and play guitars, creating the rise of the folk protest song. In 1960, *Songs against the Bomb* was released featuring a number of protest songs sung on the Aldermaston March, including numbers by Peggy Seeger and Ewan McColl. In 1964, the Cambridge Folk Festival began life with Peggy Seeger, The Watersons and Paul Simon. The festival attracted 1,400 people and the mayor of Cambridge complained to the organizers that they were 'bringing all these hippies into Cambridge!' By 1968, the attendance had risen to five thousand ('History of the Cambridge Folk Festival').

McKay also identifies the early roots of British festival culture as being the jazz festivals at Beaulieu (1956–61) and National Jazz Federation events at Richmond from 1961, declaring that 'they blazed the trail for the hippie festivals of the later 1960s and beyond' (2000: 1). In particular, the Richmond events would showcase the new music emerging from youth culture, and in 1964 the festival changed its name to 'The National Jazz and Blues Festival' to catch up with the changes in musical tastes in the early 1960s. As in the United States, gradually the jazz element of the festival declined. The NJF would move to Windsor where in 1967 it would host the Summer of Love Festival with Donovan, Eric Clapton and Nice. From then on, the festival would feature a mix of progressive rock, folk and blues and draw crowds of around thirty thousand. In 1971, the festival found a permanent home at Reading and became 'The National Jazz, Blues and Rock Festival' ('Timeline: History of the Reading Festival'). The writer of the Reading Festival archive comments that already 'the Festival was past its glory years and was on a long slow, downhill path, not only musically, but in its festival spirit, which had always been pretty friendly and laid back in the 60s and early 70s … its just that the experience was a different one, more booze, less dope' ('The Archive: The Eleventh National Jazz and Blues').

In June 1969, The Bath Festival of Blues was held at the Bath Pavilion Recreational Ground featuring Fleetwood Mac, John Mayall's Bluesbreakers, Ten Years After, Led Zeppelin, The Nice, Chicken Shack, Blodwyn Pig and Principal Edwards Magic Theatre (Watt, 2007: 46–7). The festival would sell thirty thousand tickets and lead the promoters to organize the much larger Bath Festival of Blues and Progressive Music on 29 June 1970. Estimated attendance was 150,000 and for the first time, the top bands of the United States would be heard live by a British audience, although Jefferson Airplane had played at the Isle of Wight festival in 1968. Santana, Led Zeppelin, Country Joe McDonald, The Byrds, Dr. John, Frank Zappa & The Mothers of Invention, Canned Heat, Steppenwolf, Johnny Winter, John Mayall with Peter Green, Pink Floyd, Pentangle and Fairport Convention played, mixing psychedelic West Coast sound with the British Blues bands. It should be noted that an 'alternative festival' was staged in an adjoining field in spite of the megastars playing in the main event, where the Pink Fairies, Yes, Genesis and Hawkwind played on the back of a flatbed truck (Abrahams, 2004: 28). This was a precursor to the many free festivals of the 1970s including Glastonbury and shows that already the counterculture in Britain was seeking to retain its authenticity over rising commercialization. The festival is also noteworthy for the attendance of Michael Eavis who was inspired to hold later that year at Pilton, the prototype event of what would become the Glastonbury festival.

Other notable festivals were the two events held on the Isle of Wight in 1968 and 1970. The first event held on 31 August 1968 was a relatively small affair with around ten thousand attending, held on Ford Farm and featured a number of British counterculture bands but most significantly was headlined by Jefferson Airplane (Hinton, 1995: 21). In 1969, the festival grew exponentially and headlined with Bob Dylan. It took place only eleven days after Woodstock and an estimated 150,000–200,000 attended ('Isle of Wight Guru'). The following year, if the estimates are true, the event attracted the largest crowd to ever attend a rock festival with over six hundred thousand attending to experience over fifty acts including Jimi Hendrix, The Doors, The Who, Donovan, Jethro Tull and Leonard Cohen. The BBC archive would remember the festival in the following words:

> They packed onto the Isle of Wight ferry from the mainland for up to five days (although some stayed considerably longer) of live rock, communal living, free love and mind-bending substances. Besides all the peace, love and latrines, there was the music – non-stop performances from some of the greatest pop musicians of any era. ('Isle of Wight Festival History')

The huge crowds would lead to Parliament adding a section to the Isle of Wight County Council Act 1971, c.lxxi, ss.5–6, preventing overnight open-air gatherings of more than five thousand people on the island without a special licence from the council.

In addition to the rock concerts mentioned above, the Hyde Park Free Concerts held between 1968 and 1971 were seminal. The London parks were increasingly sites of counterculture activity. The *International Times* would publish an article entitled 'Play in the Parks – You Must! You Can!' in 1967 after spontaneous dancing took place when the Exploding Galaxy dance troupe led by David Medalla persuaded a small crowd of London's youth gathered in Regent's Park to join them. The park authorities attempted to break up the happening only for a larger crowd to participate ('The Hyde Park Free Concerts'). Speaker's Corner in Hyde Park was also used for a series of Legalise Pot Rallies from 1968, also known as 'Smoke-Ins' (ibid.). The first free concert took place on 29 June 1968 with Pink Floyd, Tyrannosaurus Rex, Roy Harper and Jethro Tull. John Peel would write in a religious tone, 'Written on the wings of the weekend past which carried with it more love and more hope than I believed possible. Underneath the Saturday skies the blessed drifted and around them music hung in the air and touched the trees' (ibid.).

Throughout the summer of 1968, the concerts happened at monthly intervals with the top counterculture bands performing free. Over the summer, Traffic, Nice, the Pretty Things, Family, Fleetwood Mac, Fairport Convention, Ten Years After, The Move, The Strawbs and Roy Harper played to growing audiences. In June 1969, Blind Faith, Donovan, Richie Havens, Third Ear Band and Edgar Broughton continued the tradition, followed in July by the Stones in the Park concert played as a memorial concert for the recently deceased Brian Jones. Around two hundred thousand would attend the concert (ibid.). The summer would close with Soft Machine and Quintessence. The concerts would continue in 1970.

A precursor to all these events in 1968 and 1969 was the 14 Hour Technicolor Dream, a concert held in the Great Hall of Alexandra Palace (Ally Pally), London, on 29 April 1967 as a fundraising concert for the counterculture paper *International Times* (Manning, 2006: 37). Described as a multiartist event, featuring poets, artists and musicians, the concert was headlined by Pink Floyd (Chapman, 2010: 159). There were two main stages inside the hall, with a smaller central stage designed for poets, performance artists, jugglers and dancers including The Tribe of the Sacred Mushroom, David Medalla and The Exploding Galaxy Dance Troupe. Light shows and strobes lit up every inch of available space from a giant light tower at the centre of the hall. Underground films were screened on white sheets taped to scaffolding and the central attraction was helter-skelter. Pink Floyd appeared just as the sun was beginning to rise at around five o'clock in the morning (ibid.).

The free concerts in Hyde Park would incorporate the music venues at the Roundhouse in Camden Town, Middle Earth in Covent Garden or UFO in

Tottenham Court Road into a London counterculture milieu that would rival Haight-Ashbury in San Francisco. The same bands would play at the clubs, sometimes throughout the weekend. The diehards of the alternative scene would leave the concerts and head for the clubs. Harry Shapiro writes,

> For the *Berkeley Barb* and the *Oracle* read *International Times* and *Oz*; the Roundhouse, UFO and Middle Earth for the Fillmore and the Avalon Ballroom, Ally Pally for the Be-In, Pink Floyd, Soft Machine and Cream for the Dead, Airplane and Quicksilver. Cream and Hendrix straddled both continents. (1988: 146)

Conclusion

The flowering of London as a centre to match San Francisco was perhaps of more significance to the internationalization of psychedelic counterculture. Soho in Central London provided locations for folk, jazz, blues and rock venues as well as public houses friendly to bohemian clientele. The second half of the 1960s saw the creation of the UFO club in Tottenham Court Road and Middle Earth in Covent Garden, later to move to the larger venue of The Roundhouse in Camden Town. London's parks also provided the space for free concerts. These clubs would generate home-grown psychedelic bands that would become well known and regarded as authentic among counterculture audiences. Foremost among them were Pink Floyd and Soft Machine who were house bands at UFO and T-Rex or Tyrannosaurus Rex who played at Middle Earth along with the Pink Fairies. Arthur Brown and Traffic played at the Roundhouse; Jethro Tull regularly performed in small halls in Notting Hill Gate. Pink Floyd would push the frontiers of psychedelic music to the limit, combining with dazzling light shows to create hallucinogenic imitations that would both recreate LSD experiences and enhance the effects of the audience already partaking of the substance. By the mid- to late 1960s, the bands of the counterculture were playing the rock festivals on both sides of the Atlantic.

Although drugs had been linked to both enhancing the creativity of musicians and the enjoyment of the experience of music, psychedelic rock was the first time that a musical form had been named after an experience induced by consciousness-altering substances. In the various subcultures that contributed to mid-1960s counterculture, the beatniks had used various substances including marijuana, and the jazz and folk scenes of earlier decades had been locations for group participation in them on a much smaller scale. The British mods in the mid-1960s had consumed amphetamines to enhance dancing and clubbing experiences, and the jazz clubs of Soho were often associated with opiate availability, but it was the mass availability of LSD (acid) that pushed the experience of users to create a psychedelic milieu that would transform music, art, fashion and religion. The clubs in London, such as UFO, Middle Earth and the Roundhouse, hosted psychedelic bands, developed light shows and catered to the new counterculture. The bands were 'ours'; they sang of counterculture concerns and lifestyles, and the musicians were themselves counterculture members. The events increasingly became a total experience of immersion in a psychedelic experience, a 'happening'. Davis agrees and writes,

> The key catalyst for the emergence of a mass counter-culture was the widespread availability and use of LSD and other charismatic psychoactive substances. For many LSD's extraordinary noetic and emotional affects seemed direct evidence that the individual's alteration or expansion of consciousness, coupled with corresponding shifts in the self and its values, could precipitate a new social and cultural order. (2015: 635)

Chris Partridge would analyse this new social and cultural order under the umbrella term of 'High Culture' (2018). The late-1960s counterculture would quickly develop sites for the expression of 'High Culture' which would provide relatively safe locations for music, dance, relationships, politicizing, developing new spiritualities and participating in group expansion and alteration of consciousness through the use of psychedelics. As the music developed amidst musicians who functioned as the 'high priests' of the movement, the more the sound attempted to recreate the hallucinogenic properties of the substances used. Other art forms would follow suit. Partridge agrees with Michael Clarke that the festivals were often much more than simply music events. Music being 'only one of a variety of activities which, apart from participation in running the site, and preparing and distributing food, may include arts and crafts of various sorts, music and forms of theatre, folk dancing, fireworks and various manifestations of commitment to ecological awareness and to the occult' (1982: 85).

Clarke, Davis and Partridge's identification of a developing subculture at odds with the mainstream would lead to George McKay (2000) using the term 'festival culture' in the preface to his book *Glastonbury: A Very English Fair*. By 'festival culture', he is referring to popular music festivals in Britain and he immediately associates this occurrence with alternative or counterculture development (p. ix). He lists a number of elements that have contributed towards such festivals including gypsy horse fairs, American rock festivals, country fairs and 'rebirthed pagan rituals and jazz events in the 1950s' (ibid.). McKay describes these gatherings of counterculture individuals as 'tribal' and offers a description of the main features as 'a young or youthful audience, open-air performance, popular music, the development of a lifestyle, camping, local opposition, police distrust, and even the odd rural riot' (ibid.). McKay locates festival culture within a political domain but admits that this is problematic as such politics 'admits pleasure, whether of pop and rock music, of temporary (tented) community, of landscape and nature under open skies, of promiscuity, of narcotic' (p. x).

Partridge also uses 'festival culture' to describe music events in which elements of Easternization combined with paganism and neo-Romanticism (2004: 156). He draws upon Kevin Hetherington's and Michael Clarke's (1982) descriptions of free festivals to provide an analysis of the development of festival culture from the late 1960s into the decades that followed (ibid.). He cites Hetherington (1999) as endorsing the escapist elements of such events, stating that 'the most lively escape geographically and physically to the "Never Never Land" of a free festival where they become citizens, indeed rulers, in a new reality' (2004: 156).

Arguably the occult element became more pronounced in the later decades of festival culture as neopaganism and ecology became more significant to counterculture. A point made by Partridge who argues that, somewhat controversially, the free festival movement that emerged from the early 1970s and developed into the rave culture of the 1980s, although owing something to the countercultures and alternative spiritualities of the 1950s and 1960s, was distinct from the 'fashionable hippie culture of the 1960s' and much more 'countercultural and spiritually eclectic' (2006: 1). As this book is concerned with the period described by Partridge as 'fashionable' and including the developments that led up to Glastonbury Fayre in June 1971, described by Partridge as formative in the creation of the free festival movement typical of later rave culture (p. 44), it is essential to understand the same processes of commercialization that marked the rave movement and the same quest for authenticity was part of an ongoing tension in the counterculture that would extend over several decades during and after the 1960s.

One of the major shifts in values can be identified as a celebration of 'immediacy'. A generation wanted its pleasure now and refuted their parents' deferred gratification as a mode of existence. This would have a major impact on the forms of religion that would become popular. Baba Ram Dass (Richard Alpert) encapsulates the new spiritual mood in the title of his book *Be Here Now*. The psychedelic experience 'rushed' the mind to the present moment and challenged mainstream religious focus on social order and the afterlife. God was to be experienced rather than believed in and the LSD experience gave weight to the possibility of cosmic or primal energies rather than the 'old man in the sky' worldviews. Psychedelic experiences pointed towards a unity that linked the universe and supremacy of love as a unitive force, but they said little about codes of mainstream morality. Increasingly Eastern mysticism seemed to be more attuned to the psychedelic experience than mainstream Christianities or vice versa. Harvey Cox's *Turning East* identifies immediacy and 'profound, life-changing religious experience' identified in Eastern religious traditions as a solution to young people's search for 'warmth, affection and close ties of feeling' (cited in Partridge, 2004: 87). Partridge links this quest for immediacy to music, declaring,

> Popular music's important relationship with emotion – its ability to create affective spaces within which identity construction and meaning-making occur – has been explored to great effect since the early 1960s. This confluence of popular music and spirituality has been conspicuous within a number of influential subcultures. (2015b: 509)

Questions about the meaning of life in the 1950s or early 1960s were likely to be met by the response 'It is the way things are'. William Burroughs, one of the key spokesmen for the counterculture, would declare that rock music was one of the key elements that enabled a generation to break out from the 'way things are' and 'reassert a universe of magic' over a 'dead soulless universe'. Many of my informants would speak of a moment when colour first came to the black and white world of the 1950s. This moment occurred when I first heard the Beatles in a South London council house when 'Love me do' was played on Juke Box Jury. The television was black and white. From that moment, like many of my generation, I would choose experience without dogma, both religious and cultural. It is essential to identify music as a key component of counterculture in the period and a powerful element of a developing spirituality. It is the prominence of music and mind-altering substances that mark the late-1960s development of counterculture as different from previous Bohemian periods and bring the counterculture from a fringe activity to mass consumption.

In order to assess Partridge's description of the 1960s counterculture as 'fashionable', it is useful to define the labels used to self-describe the various manifestations of these forms of popular culture. The term 'hippie' was popularly used to describe those who embraced 1960s counterculture as a bridge to earlier bohemian lifestyles.[5] 'Hipster' had been used by beatnik subcultures in the 1950s and the term 'hip' was used to describe someone who ascribed to a bohemian lifestyle (Shiedlower, 2004). It had probably existed in African American urban culture for decades previously. It first appeared in a 1904 novel by George Vere Hobart (1867–1926), *Jim Hickey: A Story of the One-Night Stands*, where an African American character uses the slang phrase, 'Are you hip?' (Hobart, 1904) By the 1940s, the terms *hip*, *hep* and *hepcat* were popular in Harlem jazz slang (Gibson, 1986). According to Malcolm X's 1964 autobiography, the word *hippie* in 1940s Harlem had been used to describe a specific type of white man who 'acted more Negro than Negroes' (Booth, 2004: 212). Andrew Loog Oldham refers to 'all the Chicago hippies' in 1965, seemingly in reference to black blues or R&B musicians, in his rear sleeve notes to the 1965 LP *The Rolling Stones, Now!* In Greenwich Village in the early 1960s, counterculture youth were named *hips* because they were considered 'cool', as opposed to being 'square' (Gibson, 1986). If the term was originally acceptable to young Americans seeking alternative living and who flocked to San Francisco in the mid-sixties, and who participated in events such as the Human Be-In, or attended the Filmore to see their favourite bands, it was not quite so acceptable once commercialization of the music had led to four hundred thousand attending the Isle of Wight Festival in 1969.[6] The psychedelic bands were 'ours' rather than 'theirs' but their mainstream success challenged such belonging and sometimes the counterculture credentials of the musicians. Ian MacDonald would write, 'Though Lennon had yet to launch himself into his fullscale LSD period, he evidently felt sufficiently versed in the "counterculture" associated with the drug to poke fun at those who took it without changing their outlook.' The lyric of *Day Tripper*, he later explained, was an attack on 'weekend hippies' – those who 'donned floral shirts and headbands to listen to "acid rock" between 9-to-5 office-jobs' (MacDonald, 2008: 167–8). The phenomenon of 'weekend hippies' was well known in British counterculture circles and diehards committed to the lifestyle preferred to be known as 'heads' or 'freaks'.[7] 'Heads' was commonly used to describe someone who consumed large amounts of a drug, for example, 'pot head' or 'acid head'. Head shops catered to hippies, selling clothes, comics, beads, candles, jewellery and drug paraphernalia ('Skip Stone'). Partridge's identification of 'fashionable' would apply to the later use of the term 'hippie' but diehard 'freaks' or 'heads', although referred to as 'hippies' by the media, remained outside the mainstream and were deemed socially unacceptable by both working-class and middle-class bourgeoisie.

Clearly, music was crucial to counterculture identity and conjoined with a number of other elements to create what Davis called 'pop occulture'. Davis describes a milieu that would develop wherever significant numbers would gather together, especially prominent in the Haight-Ashbury districts of San Francisco and the Notting Hill Gate area of London. Yet Davis writes that 'within a few short years after its emergence in the middle of the 1960s, the counter-culture had transformed social forms, creative production, personal lifestyles, and religious experience across the globe' (2015: 635). Davis's view of the spread of counterculture into globally mainstream societies is certainly overplayed. In Northern America and Britain, it is certainly true. Arguably, it is the mainstream success of the bands that would be most influential in globalizing psychedelia. It is also true that fashion and media followed suit. Davis mentions comic books, the popularization of meditation and alternative therapies and a more permissive attitude towards sexuality and sexual experimentation, art and literature and a new openness to hedonism as transferrals to mainstream culture (pp. 635–7). He would argue that the counterculture would bring a number of elements into 'centre stage' creating a zeitgeist which would include alternative religious practices, and he goes on to state that the change 'transformed the engines of popular culture' through to the present day where we continue to live in its 'long shadow' (p. 636).

Yet commercialization would bring its own challenges to the late-1960s counterculture individuals. There would be many who would posit the idea that the spread of their ideas, practices and cultural milieu into mainstream acceptance was evidence of a permanent transformation rooted in the idea of the Age of Aquarius or other millennial-type hopes and aspirations. Both the 'New Left' with its struggle against the 'System' and the more utopian romantics seeking spiritual change could agree on this. On the other hand, counterculture demanded authenticity as one of its identity markers. Commercialization would challenge authenticity and those who wished to preserve a counterculture identity within the midst of acceptance by a sometimes despised majority widely described as 'straight' would seek new alternatives.

Festival culture would provide the 1960s counterculture with a gathering place, a location where the revolution could be celebrated and where the numbers attending could bring a sense that the world was being changed. This along with the focused geographical locations of habitat such as Haight-Ashbury, Greenwich Village or Notting Hill Gate and Soho in London provided experiments in living where immediacy, spontaneity and community were practised in safety of numbers away from 'straight society'. The festivals did not need any of the elements of Easternization or occulture to provide a religious experience. Behind the bacchanalian loss of social mores was a rejection of the values of 1950s society, a rejection of materialism as a way of life and a celebration of freedom. The bands, along with the beat poets and the high priests of psychedelia, such as Leary, Kesey and Alpert, with their apparently unlimited supplies of unadulterated LSD handed out freely to raise or change the consciousness of the participants, provided a sacramental element. Any elements from Eastern religions such as the appearance of Indian gurus or Ravi Shankar on Sitar would only direct a few to embrace Indian spirituality with real commitment. The presence of these figures representing ancient ways of life was generally used to reinforce the counterculture's 'high culture' rather than lead to serious commitment in any of the Hindu or Buddhist paths on offer.

The significance of music within the counterculture was recognized by Timothy Leary who declared that in his view, 'there are three groups who are bringing about the great revolution of the new age ... They are the DOPE DEALERS, the ROCK MUSICIANS, and the UNDERGROUND ARTISTS AND WRITERS' (Armstrong, 1981: 56). Mc Kay also notes that 'what festivals also do though is evidence the sheer power and desire of music within the counterculture' (McKay, 'The social and (counter)cultural 1960s'). The music would propel the counterculture into the mainstream, impacting upon youth culture across the Western world. In spite of the sense that the counterculture was expanding, the actual numbers that would 'turn on, tune in, and drop out' were relatively small but the success of the festivals and the popularity of the music would reach out far and wide. The radio DJ Dave Hermann expressed the power of the music succinctly in the following words:

> If the music hadn't happened, nothing would be happening ... The mode of the music changed; it changed in the 1950s, and the walls of the city are shaking. And there would be no women's lib; there would be no Panthers, no Lords, no civil rights movement – no nothing – if we were still listening to Patti Page records. KPMX in San Francisco was 'the first FM stereo station that played psychedelic rock' in 1967, and during the summer of love the top five albums sold in America included the Beatles, Rolling Stones, the Doors, Jefferson Airplane – even if the counter-culture was in fact numerically small (only between two or three per cent of US students considered themselves 'activists' at the height of the 1960s, while 'considerably less than 0.1 per cent of the total American population' were part of the hippie counterculture), its soundtrack was appealing, fashionable, and very popular. (cited in Sarlin, 1973: 198)

Hermann may be exaggerating to claim that major political protests would not have had an impact without the music, but he is right to point out that the music of the hippie counterculture was shared with the political activists and that increasingly black music of the civil rights movement would find its way into festival culture.

The Human Be-In would bring together the activists from Berkeley along with the Haight-Ashbury hippies to form an apparently seamless peace movement that would be expressed in the underground press. There would be tensions. Ken Kesey had laid this out in very stark terms when he expressed his view of a Berkeley anti-war protest in 1965, defiantly claiming, 'You're not gonna stop this war with this rally, by marching ... look at the war and turn your backs and say ... Fuck it' (cited in Farber, 1992: 9). The experiences offered by LSD and to a lesser extent marijuana were seen in religious terms, an insight into the infinity of the cosmos and cosmic energy underlying everything, and as with many religions, where the experiential realm of divinity is paramount, proselytizing the transformation inherent in such experiences is of prime importance. Leary, Alpert, Ginsberg and Kesey were certain that LSD and other psychedelic experiences could transform the world and users would pass on their experiences to others, offering the drug to anyone with enough sense of curiosity to experiment. Both hippies and activists would sample the psychedelic experience and as stated by McKay, 'in the views of some, acid was the tool for social revolution, for some it was the path to personal enlightenment' ('McKay, The Social and Cultural 1960s').

It should be remembered that both the British and the US counterculture had earlier roots in the Campaign for Nuclear Disarmament (CND) protests against nuclear weapons and the anti-Vietnam War demonstrations. On both sides of the Atlantic these were participated in by the earlier beat generation. In London, this political demand for change would find itself fully expressed in the March 1968 anti-Vietnam demonstration outside the American embassy in Grosvenor Square where an estimated ten thousand protestors were involved in a particularly violent reaction when police charged the crowd on horseback ('1968: Anti-Vietnam demo turns violent'). A larger but more peaceful protest took place at the same site in October 1968 with twenty-five thousand participants (ibid.). Exactly a year before, an editorial in the underground outlet, the *International Times* had recognized the synergy between the two elements of counterculture stating, 'We have reached a stage at which it is now possible to talk about a "we" despite the multi-direction and anti-uniformity of our movement' (Hewison, 1986: 125).

It would be easy to dismiss Terry Anderson's description of the Monterey Pop Festival in June 1967 as a manifestation of the trivial when he describes the carnival atmosphere in the following words:

Festival-goers came in peasant dresses, in bell bottoms, leather vests, in colours: mellow yellow, panama red, moby grape, deacon blue, acapulco gold. [LSD chemist Augustus] Owsley [Stanley III] supplied a new batch of LSD called

Monterey Purple, dubbed Purple Haze, and the bands merged the San Francisco sounds with American pop, rock, blues, soul, folk-rock, and the British Invasion. (1995: 174).

Historically, however, the counterculture was for the first time on the march. Arguably, previous manifestations of rebellion away from mainstream norms had been a retreat, a removal from society into bohemian morality and culture, but for the first time, counterculture would believe with millennial fervour that it was about to create a revolution that would change the world. The same article in the *International Times* would continue, '[It is] post/anti political – this is not a movement of protest but one of celebration … the weapons are love and creativity –wild new clothes, fashions, strange new sounds' (Hewison, 1986: 125).

Neville Powis 2003 claims that 'the Human Be-In focused the key ideas of the 1960s counterculture: personal empowerment, cultural and political decentralization, communal living, ecological awareness, higher consciousness (with the aid of psychedelic drugs)' and demonstrated that the counterculture was more than a war protest movement. He argues that the counterculture questioned the authorities of the day in regard to civil rights, women's rights and consumer rights. It shaped its own alternative media, including underground newspapers and radio stations. It also revealed new directions in music, art and technology.

By dedicating the first day of the Human Be-In to North American native culture, the organizers would introduce a key element of later twentieth-century counterculture, the celebration and imitation of indigenous people, their spirituality and ability to live in harmony with nature. This ecological thrust would combine elements of social revolution and personal enlightenment. The Mantra Rock-In would celebrate Eastern religions as a key element in the search for personal enlightenment, perceived as more in tune with the immediacy of counterculture than traditional forms of institutionalized Christianity. The following chapter will explore how the organizers of Glastonbury Fayre would explore these elements of festival culture as both a vehicle for social revolution and personal enlightenment by drawing upon sacred geometry and earth mysteries within a context of scepticism towards the commercialization of festival culture and the renewal of the quest for authenticity within counterculture.

6

The significance of Glastonbury

The question might be asked why Glastonbury Fayre in June 1971 was such a significant milestone in festival culture. The previous chapters have shown both the frequency and increasing attendance at counterculture festivals on both sides of the Atlantic. With rock festivals occurring on at least a monthly basis throughout the summer months between 1967 and 1971, why was Glastonbury Fayre regarded as 'the legendary one' in Britain? Numerically, it was relatively small with an attendance estimated at twelve thousand or less. Nor could it be argued to have had the major frontline bands of the time. Although the Grateful Dead were rumoured to appear, the actual line-up included the Pink Fairies, Hawkwind, Edgar Broughton Band, Fairport Convention, David Bowie, Melanie, Joan Baez, Traffic, Quintessence, Brinsley Schwartz, Family and Arthur Brown. All the bands that played were, however, stalwarts of the counterculture and well known on hippie circuits, but they were not the megastars of the era (McKay, 2000: 96). It could be argued that Glastonbury Fayre in 1971 is famed in hindsight as the festival has gone on to become such a huge event in the summer calendar into the present day and iconic of British popular cultural life. Yet even at the time, it generated a triple album released in 1972 and the film *Glastonbury Fayre*, made by David Puttnam and Nic Roeg, went on general release in British cinemas.

Partridge notes the powerful spiritual dimensions of the early Glastonbury festivals and cites the words of Michael Eavis who owns Worthy Farm which contains the festival's site, who describes the event as 'a kind of utopia, really, something outside of the normal world we all live in' (Eavis, in McKay, 2000: 29). Partridge states that this utopia was definitely not a secular one and reminds us that, as in the case of Stonehenge, Glastonbury was initially chosen as a site of counterculture celebration because of its mythical and spiritual associations (2006: 44).

These associations of the spiritual and the utopian are picked by the novelist John Cowper Powys in his novel *Glastonbury Romance* written in 1933. In the novel, the two protagonists, Philip Drew, an industrialist, and the new mayor, John Geard, have strongly opposing views on the future of the town. Drew wants to destroy what he calls 'an effeminate flower-garden of pretty-pretty superstitions and mediaeval abracadabra' and make the 'idle showplace into a prosperous industrial centre' (Powys, 1975: 230). Geard wants to make the town the 'centre of all the religion in the West' by drawing upon the Arthurian Grail legends and the myths associated with the origins of Christianity in Britain (p. 287). The class conflict in the novel is played out against race stereotypes of the industrialist's love of modernity linked to his Norman ancestry, while Geard is presented as Anglo-Saxon and Celtic with a Romantic's love for a pre-Norman idealized past (pp. xv–xvi). The novel predicts the events that would be played out in Glastonbury after the festival in 1971, and the author reveals himself in the preface to sympathies with British esotericism stating, 'The Grail is older than Christianity as it is older than Glastonbury Tor … the symbolism of the Grail represents a lapping-up of one perfect drop of noon-day happiness.' This esoteric understanding of the Grail would seep into counterculture spirituality, crossing the boundaries of Christianity into esoteric interpretations of religion, and would provide a synergy with Eastern understandings of enlightenment and gnosis.

The forerunners of Glastonbury Fayre

Glastonbury Fayre had been preceded by two smaller events of significance to locate its origin and ethos: Phun City held on the weekend of 24 July 1970 and the Pilton Festival in September 1970. The Pilton Festival was not a free festival as approximately two thousand attendees paid £1 to see Marc Bolan & T. Rex, Al Stewart, Quintessence, Amazing Blondel, Sam Apple Pie, Steamhammer, Ian Anderson and Duster Bennet, along with local blues and folk bands (https://www.efestivals.co.uk/festivals/glastonbury/). The event took place on Worthy Farm and was organized by the owner Michael Eavis who had been inspired by attending the Bath Blues Festival. Eavis's vision was to combine rock festival culture with a more traditional fair and harvest event (https://www.somersetlive) but it remains the original forerunner of the Glastonbury festivals and provided a precedent for the free festival in 1971 that celebrated the summer solstice.

With the exception of the Hyde Park events, Phun City, held on Ecclesden Common near Worthing in Sussex, was the first large free festival in Britain. It was organized by the anarchist Mick Farren and backed by the *International Times*. The event was not fenced and the surrounding woods were used to construct a shanty town for the festival goers and an advert in the Underground press stated, 'There's 20 acres of woodland, partially enclosed in polythene to provide cover for sleeping – and this will be available for copulation, bopping or whatever else you want to use the woods for. Get your end away' (http://www. ukrockfestivals.com/phun-city).

The festival promotion set out to deliberately court the counterculture with a free press advertisement declaring, 'Phun City is attempting to provide a three day environment designed to the needs and desires of the Freak, not just a situation to relieve him of his money' (ibid.). Originally, Phun City was not intended to be a free festival, but funding was lost a few days before the event, so the organizers asked the scheduled bands who turned up to give their services for nothing. Those who played include The Pretty Things, Kevin Ayers, Edgar Broughton Band, Mungo Jerry and the Pink Fairies who were removing their clothes as they played. William Burroughs also appeared and was reputed to have been carried to the medical tent after a drug overdose (ibid.). Most accounts of the festival recall it as 'shambolic' and anarchic. Farren would declare, 'The audience themselves were now in charge, with the organizers just making sure the bands came and went – it was, if somewhat inadvertently, the first large-scale "people's festival" held in the UK' (ibid.).

Phun City can be perceived as an attempt by England's 'freaks' to wrest control of festival culture back to its origins within the counterculture, which was becoming a victim of its own success as the 1960s progressed and the Underground began to merge into popular youth culture. Even as early as the end of 1967, the so-called Summer of Love, a symbolic ritual and funeral procession, was held for the death of the 'hippie' in California. Black-bordered invitations were made available to all announcing, 'Funeral notice. Hippie. In the Haight Ashbury District of this city, Hippie, devoted son of Mass Media. Friends are invited to attend services beginning at sunrise, October 6, 1967, at Buena Vista Park' (Von Hoffman, 1968: 238–9). The coffin is said to have held several false beards, strings of beads and two kilograms of marijuana (McKay, 'The social and (counter)cultural 1960s').

In the previous chapter, the mass success of the rock festival was charted in both Britain and the United States, and no one today would consider the annual summer fixtures as counterculture, although some elements remain.

Nigel Fountain states that 1969 was the year that rock festivals took off in Britain (Fountain, 1988: 76), citing the two Hyde Park free concerts by Blind Faith in June and the Rolling Stones in July, along with Bob Dylan at the Isle of Wight in August as the 'the summer of festivals' (p. 90), but McKay considers that these events in Britain 'signal the start of a new mass(-ish) movement' and in hindsight; 1969 would also 'signal the end of not just the decade but the sense of the decade, the idea of the sixties' (McKay, 'The social and (counter)cultural 1960s').

The Underground Press promotion for the Phun Festival would appear to indicate a yearning for the anarchy and the sense of bacchanalian carnival that had undermined 'straight' society and given the 1960s counterculture its conviction of being underground. David Farber (1992) draws attention to the words of the Motherfuckers: 'We defy law and order with our bricks, bottles, garbage, long hair, filth, obscenity, drugs, games, guns, bikes, fire, fun and fucking.'

The *International Times* would recognize this, albeit in more restrained tone, noting the difference between the late-1960s counterculture and political revolution and also acknowledging the communitas that was developing among participants in 'Freak' culture, declaring,

> We have reached a stage at which it is now possible to talk about a 'we' despite the multi-direction and anti uniformity of our movement ... It is essentially an inner-directed movement – a new way of looking at things. ... [T]he search for pleasure/orgasm covers every field of human activity, from sex, art and inner space, to architecture, the abolition of money, outer space and beyond. ... [It is] post/anti-political – this is not a movement of protest but one of celebration. ... The weapons are love and creativity – wild new clothes, fashions, strange new sounds. (Hewison, 1986: 125)

The problem was that so many under the age of 30 wanted to join the celebration from within the confines of law and order. The sociologists Daniel Foss and Ralph Larkin (1976) define the 'hippie' counterculture as 'walking critiques of bureaucratic rationality' and go on to say,

> By the late 1960s 'freakified' youth were exploring new aspects of self-hood which they had never previously thought existed. Indulgence in drug experiences, sex, communal activities, be-ins, sit-ins, demonstrations, riots, busts, trips with no destination in particular, not only gave subculture members a set of common experiences, but also opened up vast new capacities of self-hood for exploration. (pp. 47–50)

The free festival can be seen as an attempt to restore the counterculture's integrity and this is acknowledged by Mick Farren who affirms that 'to a lot of us Phun City, and Glastonbury Fair a year later, were glimpses of the future. Glimpses of a community sharing possessions, living with the environment, maintaining their culture with whatever is naturally available, consuming their needs and little else. It was a powerful vision' (Farren, 1972: 18).

The choice of bands at Phun City, with the Pink Fairies disrobing on stage and Hawkwind who had confirmed their credentials after the alternative performance on a flatbed truck outside the fences of Isle of Wight, suggests that diehard counterculture events would seek to showcase musicians who were empathetic to the lifestyles of the attendees. The free festival would reduce the growing risk of a performer/non-performer divide and seek the ethos of the early events in California between 1965 and 1967. McKay would claim that Hawkwind were 'the free festival band of the time ... the last "true" underground act' (2000: 18). Nik Turner of Hawkwind would acknowledge the role of the Pink Fairies, stating 'that group put a *lot* of energy into building up the free festival movement in the early days' (p. 19).

The vision of a network of free festival locations throughout Britain to restore the counterculture's model of an alternative society would find a boost in the successful fulfilment of creating the festival at Glastonbury. McKay argues that Glastonbury's origins lay in the 'free festival zeitgeist of the early 1970s' (p. 18). He also considers Glastonbury to be 'emblematic' of festival culture becoming a 'popular form of social pastime and experimentation' during the end of the 1960s and the opening years of the 1970s (p. 17). Yet he is not convinced that the vision of Glastonbury was repeated and extended, at least not in the way that hippie activists envisaged (p. 19). As Glastonbury Fayre emerged as the 'legendary one', a counterculture reclamation of the late-1960s project, the festival would eventually become mainstream and the spirit of the revolution would move to new locations in the 1980s and 1990s.

Glastonbury Fayre may well be renowned for its counterculture credentials and its move away from the mass consumption of large rock festivals attended by hundreds of thousands, for example, Reading or the Isle of Wight, but when it emerged it was far more than a continuation of Pilton, even though the location was the same, nor was it simply a part of the free festival movement as encapsulated by Phun City. Many of the attributes of Phun City were exhibited at Glastonbury Fayre but the festival would also herald a 'new age', a spirituality that was not as centre stage at previous events, with the possible exception of the Mantra-In in San Francisco.

The origins of Glastonbury Fayre

Alister Sieghart, a Glastonbury resident with a long involvement with the festival, is unequivocal that the Fayre was organized primarily by Andrew Kerr with considerable support from Arabella Churchill. He states in an interview with George McKay,

> Looking back at the 1971 event, that's where the mystique of the Glastonbury festival today comes from. You know, acid in the mud, the pyramid, its freedom, the film, all those things ... Michael [Eavis] had nothing really to do with that festival ... it was much down to people like Andrew Kerr and Arabella Churchill ... the seminal early one being put on by some ex-London hippie dropouts. (p. 20)

Neither Sieghart nor McKay mentions the vision that would lead Andrew Kerr to organize the festival.

Andrew Kerr's (2011) autobiography and the early publicity for the Fayre are unambiguous about the motivation for the festival and the possibility of tuning in to the spiritual energies that are to be tapped in Glastonbury as a location. Initially, Kerr had wanted to create a festival at Stonehenge but was put off by the amount of arable land in the area (p. 190). He had attended the Isle of Wight festival in 1970 from outside the fenced area. Bailey (2013: 11) records that Kerr on driving back to London recalls that he said, 'We've got to have a proper festival, one that has some cosmic significance. Let's do it at Stonehenge at the Summer Solstice!' Kerr's disenchantment with the commercialization of festival culture would chime with the mood of the time. Sam Knee (2017) writes that 'by 1969, the festival scene had mushroomed into monolithic proportions, the innocence that had permeated it was morphing into a more complex response to mainstream culture' (p. 22). He observes that the 'dawn of the '70s saw tensions arise between the original, underground musical festivals and a more commercial interpretation of these events' (p. 55). According to Kerr's account, he had not attended Pilton or Phun City in 1970 but it is clear that he experienced the commercialization of the festival scene. His meeting with Michael Eavis would appear to be the result of serendipity. When searching for a site in Stonehenge, he had received telephone calls from friends who told him about the farmer who had organized Pilton on his land. He phoned for a meeting and travelled down to meet Michael in Pilton. He recalls, 'I told him of my wish to stage a festival on his farm, which was to be free, a giving event which sought a spiritual awakening and a demonstration against greed. To my surprise, he said,

'Yes' (Bailey, 2013: 11–12)! Andrew moved into Worthy Farm and established it as the base to organize the festival, where he was joined by various hippie friends and Arabella Churchill.

Andrew Kerr's utopian vision of a more just society is clearly expressed in his autobiography. He states his left-wing utopian view succinctly,

> In recent history, the material changes that have evolved have generated an obsession for plundering to try to satisfy an insatiable greed. The current economy has to be in a state of growth, therefore the division between rich and poor is widening, the rich get richer and the poor poorer … Respect for the natural order is diminishing. Glastonbury Fair attempted to buck the trend. (2011: 235)

Kerr's socialism was inspired by a spiritual vision that he understood to be based on the teachings of the gospels. He writes in an article for *Link*, a parish magazine in Glastonbury on 22 May 1971, in which he attempts to defend the festival, 'If God's laws are observed, His nature respected, and His gift of Life honoured, the new generation will live on a happier Earth. The time is overdue for a genuine spiritual awakening' (p. 356). Allowing for the fact that he was writing for a Christian publication, Kerr's religious sentiments go much further than traditional Christianity and he was convinced that hippies were the people striving for the real awakening (p. 356).

In the early pamphlets for the Fayre, he notes his concern for the environment and this is explicitly expressed in the Glastonbury Fair Manifesto below. Kerr's full vision for the festival and the choice of location are laid out in detail in the Glastonbury Fair Manifesto, the first such document for a rock festival.

> Glastonbury Fair will be held at Worthy Farm, Pilton, near Shepton Mallet, Somerset, from Sunday 20 June to Thursday 24 June, encompassing Midsummer's Day. It will be a fair in the medieval tradition, embodying the legends of the area, with music, dance, poetry, theatre, lights, and the opportunity for spontaneous entertainments. There will be no monetary profit – it will be free. Man is fast ruining his environment. He is suffering from the effects of pollution, from the neurosis brought about by a basically urban environment, and a lack of any spirituality in his life; and a spiritual awakening. Glastonbury is rich in legends. It was here Joseph of Arimathea is said to have brought his young nephew, Jesus, and later to have returned with sacred relics to found the early Christian church in Britain. It was here that King Arthur and the Knights of the Round Table are said to have carried out their quest for the Holy Grail. It was here that the ancient Druids are said to have been initiated into the secrets of the Universe and here

the Priestess of Avalon kept the mysteries of the Earth. It is a magical place. (Bailey, 2013: 14–15)

After a description of the farm, the manifesto returns to describing the site in New Age terminology. Kerr writes about the astrological significance of the site:

Glastonbury Tor stands at the edge of the valley and is clearly visible from all parts of the farm. The ley line between Glastonbury and Stonehenge runs a few yards from the stage site. The hills on the opposite side of the valley go to make up the sign of Sagittarius in the zodiacal plan; the country which lies between the farm and Glastonbury is Capricornus, and the Tor itself is Aquarius. The site lies on the solstice axis of the Zodiac. (2011: 88)

His ideas on the astrological features of the area came from the work of Katherine Maltwood and his occult beliefs had been influenced by John Michell (1933–2009) who he had stayed with in the late 1950s in London (ibid.). Both Maltwood and Michell could be defined as British esotericists, both being early proponents of the Earth Mysteries movement, also known as 'alternative archaeology' (Ivakhiv, 2001: 22, 24, 32). Those who believe in Earth mysteries consider that there are geographical locations of historical or cultural significance that contain sacred or spiritual energy (Hutton, 1993: 118–19, 123, 125, 340). These ideas are often dressed in a pseudo-scientific language that would allow believers to feel that they had transcended religious worldviews or alternatively support spiritual beliefs with scientific discourse.

Michell had been influenced by the ideas of Alfred Watkins (1855–1935), who had proposed the existence of 'ley' lines, after tracking the apparent arrangement of straight lines located along ancient Neolithic landscapes in Britain (Ruggles, 2005: 224). Watkins (1922) had published his findings in 1922 but there is little indication that he applied a supernatural or sacred significance to their existence. John Bruno Hare writes that 'Watkins never attributed any supernatural significance to leys; he believed that they were simply pathways that had been used for trade or ceremonial purposes, very ancient in origin, possibly dating back to the Neolithic, certainly pre-Roman' (Hare, 2004), but he goes on to say that interest in ley lines resurfaced in the 1960s where they were linked to dowsing, flying saucer paths, crop circles, biodynamic farming and even *feng shui* (ibid.). Contemporary ley line theorists claim they can locate esoteric mysteries, reveal ancient sacred places and map spiritual energies of the cosmos and radiate out even to the stars. The sacralization of ley lines can be attributed to the publication of Michell's *The View over Atlantis* in 1969 (ibid.).

Michell had attended a talk on ley lines in 1965 and published an article entitled 'Flying Saucers' in the *International Times* in January 1967 (Screeton, 2010: 5–6). In 1967, he wrote *Flying Saucer Vision* in which he claimed that ley lines were markers for extraterrestrials to navigate spacecraft. He argued that early humanity was helped to develop by alien beings perceived to be gods, but humanity had been abandoned because of its propensity towards materialism and technological development rather than spiritual (Hutton, 2013: 136). Michell would become far more interested in the phenomenon of ley lines than in UFOs and in *The View over Atlantis* he posited that the earth energy latent in ley lines was a magnetic force naturally arising from the ground, which could be focused and channelled for the good of humanity. Michell argued that an ancient spiritual elite had travelled across the world constructing the ley lines and various ancient monuments such as Stonehenge or the Pyramids in order to tap this energy (ibid.). Michell's ideas would dovetail into the developing New Age religious ideas in late-1960s counterculture. He fervently believed that there had once been an ancient and universal wisdom in prehistoric civilizations which had been lost to modernity but would be revived with the dawn of the Age of Aquarius. Michell's belief system was however rooted in theism and he describes such an age as the 'rediscovery of access to the divine will' (ibid.).

Although of a different generation to the post-war counterculture youth movements, Michell was a lifelong marijuana smoker and David Clarke and Andy Roberts (2007) state that Michell's work was 'the catalyst and helmsman' for the growing interest in UFOs among the counterculture (p. 181). Amy Hale affirms that *The View over Atlantis* was 'a smash countercultural success' (2011: 81), and Michell's biographer Paul Screeton states that the book led to the re-enchantment 'of the British landscape and empowered a generation to seek out and appreciate the spiritual dimension of the countryside, not least attracting them to reawaken the sleepy town of Glastonbury' (2010: 16). Michell would be courted by the 'royalty' of the counterculture. He travelled with the Rolling Stones to Stonehenge and hunted for ley lines and UFOs with band members and their inner circle in Herefordshire (Clark and Roberts, 2007: 185). In 1972, he would meet with the Grateful Dead on their European tour impressing Jerry Garcia and Phil Lesh with his ideas (Screeton, 2010: 101). Karl Miller, the editor of *The Listener* to which Michell had contributed an article entitled 'Flying Saucers' in May 1968, would describe Michell as 'less a hippy, perhaps, than a hippy's counsellor, one of their junior Merlins' (Clark and Roberts, 2007: 187). Hale comments that Michell promoted the idea of 'England as a site of spiritual redemption in the New Age' by bringing together 'popular ideas about sacred geometry, Druids, sacred landscapes, earth energies, Atlantis, and UFOs' (2011: 82). Screeton claims that the Pyramid Stage at Glastonbury was built to Michell's specifications and located where he claimed two ley lines met (Screeton, 2010: 30).

Katherine Maltwood (1878–1961) was a writer and artist fascinated by William Morris and the Pre-Raphaelites and with a strong interest in theosophy, Eastern religions, Egyptology and Goddess spirituality. In 1925, she was commissioned to draw a map that would outline the adventures of the knights of King Arthur in their pursuit of the Holy Grail. At some point in the research, she claimed to have discovered that the actual signs of the zodiac were laid out in a large circle within the geographical features of the Somerset landscape around Glastonbury and according to her geography the selfsame area in which the tales of King Arthur were located (1944: 3). She would describe the phenomenon as 'the Temple of the Stars' (1934) in her first book on the subject and over the next twelve years she would publish three more, with the last two written in 1944 and 1946 linking the circle of the astrological signs to the myth of King Arthur's round table. Perhaps less well known than Michell, both figures were esotericists that were British in more than nationality, in that they helped create a spiritual geography that would transform some rural places in Britain into counterculture locations of sacrality.

Kerr also mentions in the manifesto the legends of King Arthur and the tales associated with Glastonbury's place in the origins of Christianity in Britain. Glastonbury Abbey not only is a prominent site of historic Christian pilgrimage but also contains the reputed graves of King Arthur and his queen, Guinevere. The seventh-century abbey was enlarged in the tenth century and destroyed in a major fire in 1184, then rebuilt and by the fourteenth century constituted one of the most powerful monasteries in England. The seventh-century origin of the abbey allows for the development of a number of ancient Christian legends to have developed concerning Christianity's origins and to provide a mythology that links the cathedral to the ancient Britons. From the twelfth century, these two sets of mythology seemed to merge into the legends of King Arthur. Archaeological investigations would appear to reveal evidence that both the Romans and Saxons had occupied the site (Gilchrist and Green, 2016), although Ronald Hutton is not convinced that Glastonbury was a location of religious significance in Celtic or pre-Celtic times (1993: 107) even though contemporary New Age myths associated with goddess worship persist (Bowman, 2006). Christian legends have claimed that the abbey was founded by Joseph of Arimathea in the first century.

The tales recount that Joseph, the uncle of Jesus, whose tomb had been used for Christ's burial after the Crucifixion, travelled to Britain and became the first Christian bishop establishing himself in Glastonbury. In some accounts, Joseph, a wealthy merchant, allows Jesus to accompany him to England, clearly known to William Blake, as it inspired his famous hymn 'Jerusalem' with the well-known lines, 'And did those feet in ancient times, walk upon England's pastures green'. Some time in the twelfth century Joseph is linked to the Holy Grail, the cup in which Jesus celebrated the first communion at the Passover feast before his trial and death (Baring-Gould, 1899: 57). This idea first appears in Robert de Boron's *Joseph d'Arimathie* written in the twelfth century, in which Joseph uses the Grail to collect blood and sweat from Jesus on the Cross.[1] In other versions, he is given the Grail by Jesus who appears in a vision. The Grail is supposedly sent to Britain and is believed to be hidden on Glastonbury Tor. In later romances such as *Perlesvaus*, a French Arthurian romance dating to the first decade of the thirteenth century, Joseph himself travels to Britain with the Grail and other relics. It is said that when Joseph placed his staff on the ground at Wearyall Hill, it miraculously took root and grew into the famed 'Glastonbury Thorn', a type of Hawthorn that blooms twice a year and is only found in the Glastonbury area.[2]

After the rebuilding of the monastery abbey in 1184, the tomb of Arthur and Guinevere was apparently discovered. Gerald of Wales (1146–1223) or Giraldus Cambrensis in his *De principis instructione* ('Instruction of a Prince', c.1193), and repeated in his *Speculum Ecclesiae*, c.1216 (White, 1997: 517–23), states that the abbot, Henry de Sully, commissioned a search and discovered deep in the earth a huge hollowed oak trunk containing two skeletons. Sutton (2001) describes how above it, under the covering stone, was a leaden cross with the inscription *Hic jacet sepultus inclitus rex Arthurus in insula Avalonia* ('Here lies interred the famous King Arthur on the Isle of Avalon'). From this point, around 1190, Avalon became associated with Glastonbury, Gerald making the first connection:

> What is now known as Glastonbury was, in ancient times, called the Isle of Avalon. It is virtually an island, for it is completely surrounded by marshlands. In Welsh it is called *Ynys Afallach*, which means the Island of Apples and this fruit once grew in great abundance. After the Battle of Camlann, a noblewoman called Morgan, later the ruler and patroness of these parts as well as being a close blood-relation of King Arthur, carried him off to the island, now known as Glastonbury, so that his wounds could be cared for. Years ago the district had also been called *Ynys Gutrin* in Welsh, that is the Island of Glass, and from these words the invading Saxons later coined the place-name 'Glastingebury'. ('Liber de Principis instructione')

Both contemporary and historical sources are sceptical of the above accounts. The pilgrimage to Glastonbury was in decline in 1191 and the discovery of King Arthur and Queen Guinevere's tomb recreated an interest in visiting the abbey. It is also asserted that it enabled funds to be raised to rebuild the abbey after the fire (Rahtz and Watts, 2003). The search for Arthur's body is connected to Henry II and Edward I, both kings who fought major wars with the Welsh, and suggests that propaganda may have played a part (ibid.). Gerald, a strong supporter of royal authority, clearly desires to destroy the idea of the possibility of King Arthur's messianic return being used to encourage rebellion:

> Many tales are told and many legends have been invented about King Arthur and his mysterious ending. In their stupidity the British [i.e. Welsh, Cornish and Bretons] people maintain that he is still alive. Now that the truth is known, I have taken the trouble to add a few more details in this present chapter. The fairy-tales have been snuffed out, and the true and indubitable facts are made known, so that what really happened must be made crystal clear to all and separated from the myths which have accumulated on the subject. ('Liber de Principis instructione')

According to Carley and Townsend (2009), John of Glastonbury who wrote *Cronica Sive Antiquitates Glastoniensis Ecclesie* (Chronicles or Antiquities of the Glastonbury Church), a history of Glastonbury Abbey, some time around the middle of the fourteenth century, treated the Grail legend as truth and added a list of direct antecedents through Arthur's mother back to Joseph.

In more recent times, Reverend C. C. Dobson (1879–1960) argued for the authenticity of the Glastonbury legends in 1936 and this is picked up again more recently in 1988 by Gordon Strachan (1934–2010) and the former archaeologist Dennis Price (2009). In 1989, A. W. Smith opposed the view and critically examined Joseph of Arimathea legends and strongly asserted that any oral tradition concerning Jesus' visit to Britain had not existed prior to the early twentieth century (1989: 63, 83).

Kerr knew of the legends surrounding Joseph of Arimathea and the possible visit of Christ to British soil. He would appear to agree with Price concerning the missing years of Jesus and claims that Joseph was awarded a grant of lands in Glastonbury. He also suggests that Jesus visited Glastonbury from Cornwall as it was a great centre of Druid activity (2011: 187). He does not mention Dion Fortune (1890–1946)[3], Nicolas Mann (b.1952)[4] or Geoffrey Ashe (b.1923),[5] who formed theories connecting Glastonbury and Celtic legends of the Otherworld, in attempts to link the location with Avalon, but he does make reference to Paul Ashdown's (2010) *The Lord Was at Glastonbury* (ibid.).

In addition to the Christian and Arthurian legends surrounding Glastonbury, the Tor, a pyramid-shaped hill rising approximately 500 feet above the Somerset Levels and topped by the roofless tower of St Michael, is mentioned by Kerr as part of situating the festival (p. 187). The tower is all that remains of the church destroyed at the time of Henry VIII and also features in the Glastonbury myths. It is claimed that the Tor was a feature in Celtic mythology and known as *Ynys Wydryn*, when it would have been an island rising out of flooded fenland. The rise in interest in Celtic mythology that began with the Celtic revival in the nineteenth century led to connection being made between the Tor and Gwyn ap Nudd, the Welsh supernatural being who is the king of the Tylweth Teg or 'fair folk' and ruler of Annwn, the underworld in Welsh mythology (Bowman, 2008: 251). In earlier myths, Gwyn is associated with Arthur and his knights when he joins in the hunt for the savage boar, Twrch Trwyth ('Culhwch ac Olwen, part 2'). The first link with Glastonbury would appear to be in *Buchedd Collen* (*The Life of Saint Collen*), in which he and his retinue are vanquished from the Tor with the use of holy water (Lindahl et al., 2002: 190). From the nineteenth century onwards, the Tor came to be represented as an entrance to Annwn or to Avalon, the land of the fairies. The Tor is supposedly a gateway into 'The Land of the Dead', also believed to be Avalon (Emick, 2008: 96–7).

In the medley of myths that makes up contemporary belief concerning Glastonbury, the Tor has also become associated with the Goddess, possibly because of its link to Morgan Le Fay. The association may be derived from the unusual visual effect or mirage that the low-lying damp ground can produce known as a Fata Morgana (Forel, 1912: 175–82). The effect is named after Arthur's half-sister and antagonist Morgan Le Fey also known as Morgane, Morgain or Morgana, who appears to have been non-human or fairy, although more recent accounts portray her only as an enchantress (Briggs, 1978: 303). After King Arthur's final battle at Camlann, it is Morgan le Fay who takes Arthur's body to Avalon (Bromwich, 2017: 274–5). Bowman points out that other sites in Glastonbury are associated with the Goddess by contemporary Goddess movements including the flow from the Chalice Well, also known as the Red Spring, situated at the foot of the Tor, being regarded as her menstrual flow, and the Tor itself perceived as a breast of the Goddess. In recent years, an effigy of the Goddess is used in annual processions up to the top of the Tor (2005: 157–90).

Although I have treated the myths that make Glastonbury such an important site of historic and contemporary pilgrimage with a hermeneutic of suspicion, the historicity of the events is not as important as the way in which people accept them. As pointed out by Bowman, 'Glastonbury's past and its present significance have the status of "common knowledge" or "received wisdom."' Bowman notes that in her fieldwork, her informants tended to regard the myths as 'uncontested fact' and if seeking supporting scholarship tended to refer back to writers that include Katherine Maltwood and John Michell. Generally, however, they did not consider such affirmation necessary (p. 158).

Kerr seems to have taken the same approach, and although he might not have been aware of the full bricolage he was certainly instrumental in creating it. Glastonbury was gradually transformed after the Fayre into the town that it is today, where the dominant merchandise in the high street is the paraphernalia of the New Age and the ancient Christian pilgrimage to the town is reinvented to accommodate the multiplicity of occulture that exists around the town and its origins. When Kerr first arrived at Worthy Farm and began to meet with the local people to introduce the idea of the festival he was met with resistance and he reports, 'Many of the pubs and shops in Glastonbury had signs in their windows saying "No Hippies served" and in other places it was "No Shirt, No Shoes, No Service"' (2011: 199). He notes that 'without the festival the rest of the year would not have the kind of shops now prevalent in the town' (ibid.).

Andrew Kerr would borrow from these ideas of Malthouse and Michell, which he mixed with a Christology that rejected Christian dogma and institutions. He created a festival that restored the original vision of the counterculture by drawing upon elements of what Partridge defines as occulture and others as esotericism. Kerr's segment of occulture is rooted in the belief in sacred geometry and geography and the Earth itself is viewed as innately spiritual. He believed that it would respond automatically to the careful placing of the festival site and to the celebrations of a people committed to anti-capitalism and a life not based on materialism and greed. He didn't know what the cosmic response would be to the festival happening but he did believe that something would occur.

Glastonbury Fayre is significant in festival culture because it was the first time that a rock festival was created primarily drawing upon counterculture spiritual beliefs and was located not only because the music could be performed and a crowd gather but also because the site was sacred and the people could be transformed by celebration in a holy place at an auspicious time, the ancient summer solstice. In drawing upon occultural elements and with an expectation of global social transformation, Kerr would unwittingly create the first New Age festival at Glastonbury. This does not mean that any of the other elements of festival culture would be absent. The music, the promiscuity and the drugs, the sense of carnival, the celebration of behaviour that goes against prevailing mores would all feature at Glastonbury Fayre and would aid in the creation of its legendary status. All these elements would together make the Fayre, 'the Legendary One'. As stated by Powys in 1953, 'Nothing more and nothing less than the effect of a particular legend, a special myth, a unique tradition, from the remotest part of human history, upon a particular spot on the surface of this planet together with its crowd of inhabitants' (1975: xi).

The story of Kerr's discovery of Glastonbury concurs with the analysis offered by Irving Hexham (1983). Hexham notes that Glastonbury was occupied by a small number of 'spirituals'. He describes 'spirituals' in the following terms:

> They are united by the belief that Glastonbury is an important spiritual center. Some of them describe it as the religious heart of Britain, while others say it is the most sacred place in the world. Spirituals are comfortably middle class in their dress and way of life and fit very well into the general life of the town. But they do not think like the majority of the population. They believe that modern society is in decline because it has lost its spiritual roots. (p. 3)

He continues by describing the small influx of 'freaks' that took place in the years leading up to Glastonbury Fayre in 1971. He explains the relationship between the 'spirituals' and the 'freaks' as symbiotic. He describes the 'spiritual's sympathy' towards the 'freaks' as 'fellow pilgrims after truth'. Hexham comments that the 'freaks' were not welcomed by the general populace and the 'spirituals' were always

> careful to point out that, while they appreciated the spiritual longings of the freaks, they did not approve of all of their activities … The spirituals gave the freaks a lot of practical help, like allowing them to bathe in their homes. They also told the freaks their own particular views on Glastonbury and its religious significance, as well as suggesting and lending more general books which they believed would help them spiritually. (p. 4)

Hexham's short article helps us to understand the relationship between the earlier generation of gentrified seekers drawn to British esotericism and the new counterculture. Kerr would walk easily between these two worlds of Glastonbury but eventually moved fully into counterculture 'freak' values. Even so, the esotericists would visit and encourage his efforts to organize the Fayre.

In the following chapter, we will see how Kerr's trajectory in pursuing Michell's and Malthouse's theories would succeed in creating a festival that fulfilled his dream of 'We've got to have a proper festival, one that has some cosmic significance' (2011: 188) met with another equally powerful spiritual set of expectations arising from the East occurring from within the same counterculture milieu that had attracted Kerr.

7

Prem Rawat at Glastonbury: Occulture and Easternization?

Introduction

Eastern spirituality had been introduced into festival culture with the Hindu traditions of Krishna *bhakti* (devotion) brought to the United States in the mid-1960s by Swami Prabhupada, acting as the main motivation for the Mantra Rock-In, and the Vedanta guru, Swami Satchitananda opening Woodstock. Alan Ginsberg, the beat poet, would often chant Hindu mantras when performing his poetry on stage and Richard Alpert was transforming into Baba Ram Dass. Easternization was noticeably present in the midst of counterculture music events with even the music itself introducing Indian elements and Ravi Shankar joining the performers. Along with this Easternization, the presence of a whole day dedicated to indigenous North American culture and spirituality at the Human Be-In, along with the location of Glastonbury drawing upon Michell's and Maltwood's ideas of spiritual geometry, would see the intrusion of certain elements of occulture and the celebration of indigenous cultures introduced into the mix.

Even so, Indian religious traditions would be adapted to the normative values of the counterculture, with the exception of those who would actually join the movements being established by the visiting gurus from India or elsewhere in the East. This process of counterculture Easternization would not be without its tensions that would manifest over attitudes towards sexual promiscuity, politics and drug use. Occultural elements could be introduced without necessarily clashing with drug use and even used to justify or promote substance use to enhance psychic/spiritual experience. There were enough historical precedents for drugs used in developing creativity among earlier generations of countercultural Bohemianism as described by Partridge in *High Culture* but Indian spirituality had a more complex relationship with mind-altering substances. Although wandering fakirs and sadhus used marijuana, opium and belladonna to assist spiritual states such as Samadhi, and a substance called Soma is praised in the Vedic literature, many gurus were opposed to the use of such substances in developing a relationship with the divine. Meher Baba had warned his Western followers against drug use from 1962 until his death in 1969. Prabhupada was clearly uneasy with drugs and other elements of festival culture at the Mantra Rock-In and forbade consumption of such substances in the ISKCON temples. Sexuality was equally problematic. Indian culture frowned on sexuality outside marriage and many Hindu movements promoted celibacy as the ideal for spiritual progress (Kent, 2001).

The following chapter will chart the meeting of Glastonbury Fayre attendees with the 13-year-old Prem Rawat in the context of this convergence of Easternization and occultural millennial expectations while positing that by 1971 the Hippie dream was in decline and some individuals were becoming ready to embrace more disciplined spiritual paths after experiencing the consequences of mayhem caused by promiscuity and excessive drug use (Kent, 2001).

The road to Glastonbury Fayre

Andrew Kerr was older than the post-war generation that made up the 1960s counterculture. Born in 1933, he would have been in his mid-thirties at the time of Glastonbury Fayre. Having grown up during the Second World War, he was old enough to be part of the beat generation, and some elements of his lifestyle would suggest a tendency towards Bohemianism. In 1957, he admitted to frequenting 'Bohemian bars' in Soho, especially the haunts of Francis Bacon, Lucien Freud and John Michell and in his words 'other wild characters' (1996: 74). He acknowledged smoking marijuana for the first time in 1959 in the harbour of Palma di Mallorca and indicated that it changed his outlook on life, especially his appreciation of music, a common experience for many cannabis smokers (p. 180). During the 1960s, he was prescribed tincture of cannabis by a Dr Dunbar and took LSD for the first time some time in the late 1960s. He reported that his 'trip' was more than pretty colours and amusing hallucinations but 'the opening of something deep in my awareness that was spiritual' (p. 182). Kerr's experience of LSD would seem to suggest both a transforming of his political awareness and personal enlightenment. He stated that LSD 'changed my outlook, and as Aldous Huxley expressed, opened my Doors of Perception' (p. 180). He argued that the experiences of Cannabis and LSD were valid spiritual experiences and had a 'profound and liberating effect' which removed 'many of his prejudices' (ibid.). Concerning its impact on his political views, he writes that 'it confirmed my earlier thoughts that politics was driving a wedge between rich and poor wider and wider, all being driven by ambitious greed and materialism' (p. 182).

It would appear that in the latter years of the 1960s, he was living a double life. As the personal assistant of Randolph Churchill, ostensibly working with him on the biography of Winston Churchill, Kerr would travel extensively, meeting some of the most famed politicians and celebrities of the era on both sides of the Atlantic. While based at Churchill's estate at Stour, he was also renting a flat from 1966 in Chepstow Gardens, Notting Hill Gate, where he passed his weekends (pp. 180–1). The address was in the heart of hippie activities in London. Kerr admits to living a double life claiming to have had his 'fill of sex and drugs and rock and roll … Yet always returned to Suffolk on time, refreshed and in good shape' (p. 181). The brakes on his hippie existence at weekends appear to have ceased on the death of Randolph Churchill in 1968. He had met with Brian Jones and Jimi Hendrix in London shortly before their deaths and admits to attending the Hyde Park free festivals, frequenting the Roundhouse, UFO, Middle Earth and the Speakeasy clubs in London. His musical tastes would be transformed by the Beatles' *Sergeant Pepper's Lonely Hearts Club Band*, but he was also listening to Buffalo Springfield, Jefferson Airplane, the Doors and Canned Heat. His account of the Hyde Park concerts is religious in tone: 'The sense of collective consciousness when listening to the music reached deep inside those attending. It was a direct spiritual experience' (p. 183). In many ways, Kerr's trajectory into counterculture is typical of the era.

In 1969, he was living in Strand-on-the-Green and attended the nearby Bath Festival of Blues and Progressive Music on 27 and 28 June 1970. Like many counterculture individuals, he entered the festival without paying through a hole cut in the security fence by Mick Farren, the editor of the *International Times*, who sang with the Deviants (also known as the Pink Fairies, when playing without him). He camped without a tent with a car load of friends next to the 20-year-old Arabella Churchill, the daughter of Randolph, whom he had known since she was a small child. He regarded the festival as the highest point of his year (p. 184).

Kerr's developing social awareness of the gap between rich and poor would impact on his awareness that festival culture was becoming commercialized and drawn away from the counterculture by vested interests. He is aware that certain bands such as Hawkwind and the Pink Fairies were not susceptible to the 'commercial scramble' and laments that managers and record producers were earning vast sums of money from successful musicians (pp. 183–4). His ideas on social revolution were also beginning to inform his religious understanding. He began to write *Heaven Is a Planet*. In it, he essentially perceived Jesus as an enlightened soul with a highly developed mystical awareness. He placed him in a pantheon that includes the founders of the world's religions and could not comprehend that any of these enlightened beings would condone war. He stressed that he did not need any institutionalized religion to help him find God but felt an energy that drove him to seek a spiritual path (pp. 185–6).

In August 1970, Kerr attended the Isle of Wight Festival. Although he had a press pass, he refused to use it and instead listened to the music from outside the fenced area. His feelings about the festival were very negative and he comments,

> The crowd was made up of mainly young people, lots of whom would have had a problem affording to pay to get into the arena, itself surrounded by a double corrugated iron fence, with security guards and dogs. It disgusted me. (p. 188)

He commented that the music from Joan Baez, Richie Havens and Jimi Hendrix was brilliant and compares it to church choral music, 'a God-given experience', but reflects that the festival had lost its way. He comments, 'My feelings continued to be with Flower Power – Peace and Love' (p. 188).

Kerr's strong feelings that festival culture was no longer a vehicle for 'Flower Power' were also informed by the violence that had taken place in the crowd when Hendrix played. The sense that the idealism that created the free festival movement was over had begun in December 1969 at Altamont, in Northern California, attended by around three hundred thousand people. The Rolling Stones, Jefferson Airplane, Santana, the Flying Burritos, Crosby, Stills, Nash and Young and the Grateful Dead were scheduled to play. The Grateful Dead refused to perform because of the level of violence including the infamous fatal stabbing of Meredith Hunter by a member of the Hell's Angels. Many were injured as part of the lack of crowd control and overzealous stewarding by the Angels and numerous cars were stolen along with extensive property damage (Grover, 1969). The Altamont festival would stand in stark contrast with Woodstock and commentators would perceive it as the end of the 'hippie' era. Mark Lyttle would claim that 'Altamont became, whether fairly or not, a symbol for the death of the Woodstock Nation' (2006: 336). The rock music critic Robert Christgau wrote in 1972 that 'writers focus on Altamont not because it brought on the end of an era but because it provided such a complex metaphor for the way an era ended' but more significantly he noted what he calls an 'insupportable contradiction', that is, the idea of 'mass bohemia'. More tellingly, Richard Brody declares that Altamont ended 'the idea that, left to their own inclinations and stripped of the trappings of the wider social order, the young people of the new generation will somehow spontaneously create a higher, gentler, more loving grassroots order. What died at Altamont is the Rousseauian dream itself' (2015). The music magazine *Rolling Stone* would identify what Kerr and others were feeling in the scathing critique: 'Altamont was the product of diabolical egotism, hype, ineptitude, money manipulation, and, at base, a fundamental lack of concern for humanity' (Bangs et al., 1970). Although McKay disagrees and cites Arthur Marwick's comment that Altamont 'seemed to signal the end of the magic of rock, particularly British rock, and of love-in pop concerts', he commented that such statements need to be qualified (McKay, 'The social and (counter)cultural 1960s'). McKay's point is that festival culture extends way beyond the 1960s and only became a popular form of 'social experimentation' in Britain at the end of the 1960s and into the 1970s and was continued throughout the 1980s by the 'New Age Travellers' (2000: 17). In either argument, Glastonbury Fayre becomes pivotal, either as a renewal or as a beginning of something new in festival culture.

Yet Kerr is right to feel that 'Flower Power' is under threat. It is not only violence and commercialism that are seen to be the decline of a dream. The late 1960s and early 1970s would see the death of major countercultural icons from substance overdose. Brian Jones, founder of the Rolling Stones, had been found dead at the bottom of his swimming pool following a party at his home on 3 July 1969; Alan Wilson of Canned Heat took an overdose of barbiturates in Topanga Canyon on 3 September 1970; Jimi Hendrix died in London on 18 September 1970 from an overdose of barbiturates, apparently disillusioned with the music industry and experiencing relationship problems (Brown, 1997); Janis Joplin would overdose from heroin in a hotel room on 4 October 1970; Jim Morrison departed on 3 July 1971 in Paris, apparently from a heroin overdose. All were 27 years old. It should also be noted that the drugs were changing. The deaths were caused by opiates and barbiturates, sometimes complicated by alcohol. These are not the psychedelic substances used for consciousness-raising by the flower-power generation. A darker mood was entering the counterculture as the 1960s closed and the 1970s began. Charles Manson and his commune members had committed horrific murders in the canyons outside Los Angeles in 1970, citing the *Bhagavad Gita* as justification for their crimes. The darker turn was noted by Partridge who observes the transformation in music towards Black Sabbath, Coven, Magick and Black Widow's 1970 album, *Sacrifice*. He states, 'As well as the peace, the love and the turning East of the late 1960s and early 1970s, which reflected a certain stream of popular occultural interest, this period also saw the emergence of both Pagan and darker occultural themes' (2004: 149–50).

Mapping the terrain

Kerr had no experience of the music business or organizing events, but word went around that he wanted to organize a festival and in hindsight Kerr would write, 'There was no credible organization, political or religious, which could reach the heart of the ideal' (2011: 190). Kerr's anarchism would bring him allies from the diehards of the countercultural music scene. A chance meeting with Thomas Crimble, who had played bass guitar with Hawkwind, and his current girlfriend, Jytte Klamer, led to a sharing of information on festival organization and a promise of help (ibid.).

Kerr arranged to meet with Michael Eavis, the owner of Worthy Farm, and to his surprise Eavis agreed to his plan to hold a free festival on the land. C. J. Stone writes of his puzzlement at Eavis's acquiescence to Kerr's utopian dream. He states, 'He was a straight-laced Somerset farmer, and a Christian to boot. He didn't even drink or smoke cigarettes, let alone go along with the excesses of the hippies who came with Andrew Kerr to invade his farm house that year' (1999: 193). Eavis's response seems to have been the following: 'I had an affinity with the hippies. I mean, I can have more of a dialogue with these people than I do with a lot of other people' (ibid.).

The farmhouse was up for holiday let, as Eavis was living in Glastonbury at the time. Kerr would move in on 6 October 1970 and was quickly joined by a group of friends. They would include Mark Irons, who had been given a lift as a hitchhiker by Kerr and had civil engineering experience; Jytte Klamer, who had broken up with Thomas Crimble; Crimble would arrive in January 1971; Nik Turner of Hawkwind would also be a regular visitor and helper (Kerr, 2011: 210). The following month, the group was joined by Arabella Churchill. She would arrive with £600 in cash. Kerr describes her as a 'major force in the preparation of the festival' and describes her feelings towards festival culture as experiencing 'a current of energy that was a spiritual experience' that had transformed her life (pp. 194–5). Bill Harkin, who sold whole foods from a van, would also eventually move in as the site architect. Kerr expresses his feelings at the time, 'It was the most blessed thing in my life, the chance to live out a dream, a really crazy dream' (p. 193). He also notes that a rainbow was across the farmhouse when he moved in and asks whether it was an omen or 'a load of hippy nonsense' (p. 194).

Kerr set out to map the spiritual terrain of the site. As a child, he had been taught to dowse or water divine using a hazel wand by Owen Figg, a farm hand on his mother's farm in Oxfordshire. He considered water dowsing to be a divine gift and had noted that cows always calve over a 'blind spring' (p. 191). Utilizing his dowsing skills, he discovered that the alignment of the ley line linking Glastonbury Abbey and St Benedict's Church in the town to Stonehenge and Canterbury went directly through the field behind the location chosen for the festival stage. Using his divining rod, Kerr claims that he found a spiral of energy emitted by the ley line and the stage was built at the centre of this spiral (p. 197). The other ley line, described as 'a remarkable alignment' by Kerr, runs from St. Michaels Mount in Cornwall to Glastonbury Abbey, linking churches dedicated to either St Michael or St George, continuing through to St Margaret's Church at Hopton-on-Sea on the Norfolk coast near Lowestoft. Kerr points out that the two saints 'represent the changing seasons on the feast days of the year, St George at the Spring Equinox (April 23rd) and St. Michael, the autumn equinox (September 29th)' (p. 198). The festival site was located where the two lines crossed. Kerr traces the routes of the first ley line to run from the River Taw in Devon, through Barnstable, Bridgewater, Glastonbury Abbey, Gare Hill on the Somerset-Wiltshire border, Stonehenge, Andover, Maidstone and Canterbury. The other starts at St Michaels Mount, to Glastonbury Abbey, but then runs along the pre-Roman Icknield Way in the Chilterns on its route to Norfolk (p. 199). The festival site thus forms a sacred geography that includes large parts of pre-Christian and Christian Britain. The Pyramid Stage was designed by Bill Harkin aided by dream intervention. Kerr proclaims, 'I believe our stage was the first building in this Country, since the decline of the original Masons and the Reformation, to be built on the lines of Sacred Architecture' (p. 198).

His discovery of Maltwood's Glastonbury Zodiac led him to the ordnance survey map. He states,

> I found that the farm lay between the image of Saggitarius, and the Capricorn (the latter between the farm and the Tor). The line of the Zodiac summer solstice axis running from Summerton, to Park Wood at Butleigh (centre of the Zodiac) to Worthy Farm, to the point of the summer sunrise on the North Eastern horizon. (p. 197)

Having affirmed that his site was positioned according to ancient sacred lore, Kerr began the pragmatic arrangements for the actual festival. He started by a series of meetings to persuade local businessmen, home owners and dignitaries to support the project. He would use Arabella Churchill prominently in this capacity (pp. 195, 199–202). A limited company was set up named Solstice Capers with Kerr and Jean Bradbury as directors. Arabella Churchill and Kerr signed the cheques as they were the only ones financing the event (p. 196). In time, small donations began to appear from those excited by the prospect of the festival, more hippies turned up to help with the work of turning the farm into a festival site and remarkably the bands took no fee for performing (p. 203).

Jean Bradbury, Kerr's co-director, would introduce him to the *I-Ching*, the ancient Chinese book of divination. Kerr would refer to it in order to resolve problems in the organization of the festival. He would also recite the Lord's Prayer as a means of divine protection (p. 212). The occultural elements of Kerr's positioning of the festival would attract a number of visitors with esoteric interests. Andrew Davison, a geomancer, confirmed Kerr's siting of the stage and the positioning of the Glastonbury Zodiac. In one of his letters to Kerr, he offered up an ancient prayer to bless the preparations:

> Sources of Divine
>
> Rejoicings, revolts and sufferings
>
> Direct your actions upon us. (p. 213)

Davison was a member of RILKO (Research into Lost Knowledge Organization), also comprising Michell and Keith Critchlow who had studied the maze at Chartres Cathedral built on top of pre-Christian spirit houses. J. G. Bennett (1897–1974) would visit with his wife. Bennett had been a companion of Ouspensky (1878–1947) and a disciple of Gurdjieff (1877–1949). In addition, he had been influential in the spread of Subud, an Indonesian spiritual movement, studied with the Advaita teacher, Shivapuri Baba, whom he had met in Nepal, also Idries Shah, and the Turkish Sufi, Hasan Lutfi Shushud (Bennett, 1974). Bennett's advice to Kerr was to allow ' "synergy" to rule over their undertakings' (Kerr, 2011: 215).

Kerr's reliance on the esoteric would appear to have been reciprocated by divine assent. He talks of an experience after falling asleep in the bath after a long day working preparing the farm. He describes the event:

> I was aware of a presence in the room. I closed my eyes and 'heard' a soundless voice saying 'there will be a spiritual messenger coming to the festival'. I was generally sceptical about such matters. However, it was very real and powerful. Never before or since had I experienced anything like it. I got out of the bath and dressed feeling a kind of glow within me. I walked into one of the rooms nearby and a helper asked what had happened to me. He said he could see a glow about me. (p. 210)

In the meantime, the word was out on the counterculture grapevine that a festival would happen in Glastonbury over the midsummer solstice. Carol Waters, who drove Prem Rawat to Glastonbury, recalls that the London counterculture milieu was alive with rumours that a special festival was being organized in Glastonbury and that it would be blessed by a visit from an avatar.[1] Kerr reports that the number of visitors attracted by the energy and the possibility of free accommodation and food at the farm was increasing. He wrote, 'We had a high turnover of people staying in the house, many of whom wanted to help. The more smelly ones were accommodated in a room we named the "Dosser's Wing"' (p. 209). Well-known characters such as Sid Rawles, the self-styled 'King of the Hippies', had arrived with the commune members of his Diggers Action Movement (p. 208).

To go or not to go

The festival had also captured the imagination of Suzy Witten, an East Coast American singer with a strong interest in Tibetan Buddhism, and Alice Bailey, who had been in Haight-Ashbury in 1967. Suzy had come to Britain as a student of comparative religion, attending a year at Leeds University. She had seized the opportunity to travel to India when the early followers of Prem Rawat had travelled out in 1970. The seven hippies in a Commer van had offered her a place for £100. Suzi had sold her guitar to raise the money; David Lovejoy remembers her chanting 'Om mani padme om' enthusiastically on the way to India (Lovejoy, 2005: 56).[2] Suzi had ended up in the guru's ashram in Haridwar and returned to London where she was present when Prem Rawat arrived in Heathrow on 17 June 1971. It is clear from the press reports in the national media from someone claiming to be the guru's spokesperson that Glastonbury Fayre was on the schedule along with events in London, Leicester and Exeter. The guru would also visit France and Germany briefly from London before going on to the United States a month later. However, the guru's anticipation of the event was not as keen as some of his followers. Suzy recalls that she told him about the festival and the prophecies associated with it. She travelled down to Glastonbury with Charles Cameron, an early English student of Prem Rawat, a former Christchurch theology student and poet. Charles had invited the beat poets, Gary Snyder and Laurence Ferlinghetti, to visit Oxford after their performance at the Royal Albert Hall in 1965. He would write the book *Who Is Guru Maharaj Ji?* published in 1972.[3] Along with them was an Indian mahatma, Ashokanand, recently sent to help Charnanand with the increasing counterculture interest in the teachings of Prem Rawat. Ashokanand and Suzy had returned to London while Charles had remained at Worthy Farm to introduce the idea of the guru speaking at the festival.[4] Mike Finch, another early follower, who had gone to India in 1970 to attend the Peace Bomb festival in Delhi, suggests that he opposed the idea and attempted to dissuade the guru from going. Mike remembers that there was considerable discussion from the time of Prem Rawat's arrival until the start of the festival. He writes, 'Everybody was in favour of him going, but I was against it, pointing out the drug and hippie culture of the event. It seemed that he was taking my advice, and I was not very popular. Everyone else felt I was a spoilsport' (1996: 20). Certainly the author's experience was that Prem Rawat was ambivalent. His view was that people had not gathered to listen to him and would be fully involved in the music. It should be noted again that Prem Rawat was 13 years old and had no experience of counterculture life other than the hippies who had been meeting him in India or travelling out to visit him in 1969–70. His mother had permitted him to come to England during his school holidays with the presence of the two Indian mahatmas and a personal guardian and trusted family retainer, Behari Singh, who had accompanied the guru from India to ensure some level of insurance that he would be safe in the new Western environment. However, it was the new counterculture followers, numbering no more than one hundred individuals, who would organize the guru's tour and personal care. Throughout the four days leading up to Midsummer's Day, Prem Rawat refused to make up his mind concerning Glastonbury but he did accept the telephone calls that were increasingly coming in from Glastonbury and listened carefully to the pleas of those who wanted him to attend. Foremost among these was Charles Cameron. He had found an old chair in the farmhouse to place on the stage. The festival was very anarchic and the challenge would be finding a space between the bands for the guru to speak without him waiting around at the festival for hours, even all night. The schedule was famously loose. David Bowie, who was due to play Midsummer's night, did not perform until dawn the following morning ('David Bowie at Glastonbury'). Charles Cameron would pen the following poem and hand it out to people arriving:

> Glastonbury centre of all stars
> perfect purity is the child seated
> upon the throne of all our hearts
> for in purity alone, all hearts are one.
> Children of the hedgerow wayfaring children
> perfect purity takes human form

to water flowers of his children's
hearts with dew of his divine tears.
Upon the hearts throne
shines glory's face
which by the crown of grace
alone to man is shown
children of the heart, rose hip
children, come to his feet, for
all rainbows are within your
eyes watering your hearts with
his gracious glory in the shyness
of his dawning.
Come amid summer, it is morning.
peace is not a state of affairs
Peace is a prince
The Prince of peace walks today
We have seen his glory.
(SHRI SANT JI MAHARAJ IS PEACE)

The handwritten texts were completed with a drawing of the Tor and a rising sun appearing out of the ocean with a Sanskrit symbol of OM in the sun (Ringrose, 1996: 20).

The Special edition of the *Divine Times* published to celebrate the twenty-fifth anniversary of Prem Rawat's arrival in the West also acknowledged the sudden departure to Glastonbury. It reports, 'The Glastonbury festival, the English "Woodstock", was a very important event in the alternative calendar of that summer. People were really urging Maharaji to go in. But he stood aloof from it all. Then at the very last minute he decided to go' (Winter, 1996). Mike Finch recalls, 'Then Maharaji said he would do a programme at Exeter, and asked me to go down and prepare. I did, but as soon as I had left for Exeter, Maharaji went with everyone else to Glastonbury!' Mike's account makes it appear as if Prem Rawat had already made up his mind and departed as soon as Mike's negative influence had been removed. However, the author's memories are different. I recall that Prem Rawat made up his mind only at the last minute and I felt that he responded to the sincerity of the calls coming from Glastonbury rather than Suzy's tales of prophesies to be fulfilled, Ashokanand's attempts at persuasion based on the numerical strength of the audience or Mike Finch's warnings about drugs and wild behaviour. This is also supported by Susan Radcliffe Beauquier, who wrote,

There was to be a big pop festival at Glastonbury at the time of the Summer Solstice, and lots of predictions had been made about what would happen. Premies were there, preparing and hoping that Maharaji would come. Maybe he knew he would go, but in the residence all day he kept saying, 'Yes, I'll go. No I won't'. And finally he left at the last minute to drive fast to Glastonbury. (1996: 2).

At the last minute he had asked the author if the car was ready with a driver. I responded that Carol Waters was available in her red Ford Cortina. He asked me to accompany him along with Behari Singh and Charnanand. We left promptly as time was short for the Glastonbury festival evening session and the schedule given to us by Charles Cameron, factoring in the journey back to London. Carol recalls that even on the way to Glastonbury we had to convince him to go, after he had changed his mind a couple of times in the car.[5]

On arrival at the Pyramid Stage, after negotiating a very muddy track down the hill, we were greeted by some very excited and mud-bedraggled premies who had been waiting for Prem Rawat's arrival. A number of people remember the occasion. Ricardo of the Rainbow Gypsies had taken LSD. He recalls a car pulling up by the side of the stage and a small child getting out dressed in spotless white Indian clothing. He noticed many people dressed in Indian-style clothes running towards the car and throwing themselves in the mud at the guru's feet. He had no idea what was going on but left the next day with the Gypsies to find the guru in London.[6]

Thomas Crimble took us onto the Pyramid Stage. Brinsley Schartz was playing at the time. The stage was invaded by premies and Thomas requested Prem Rawat to ask everyone to leave. Suddenly, the band stopped playing. A chair was placed in front of the microphone and Prem Rawat addressed the crowd, who were all chanting 'Hare Krishna, Hare Rama'. Only Charnanand, Behari Singh and the author were on stage with him. He spoke in his very thick Indian-English accent and it must have been hard for the crowd to distinguish his words. His speech went as follows:

I have come to tell you of that yoga which is not physical, that yoga that generated your mind. In that yoga you must give up your mind and you will obtain the place that you are seeking. There is a Word. There is a Knowledge. There is a thing. I have got that Word. I have got that Knowledge. I have got that thing, and I tell you that I can help all mankind – every one of you – by giving out that Knowledge. Every one of you.

And if somebody comes to me I might refuse him. Only if he has pure devotion for me, pure love for me and for the true Knowledge will he receive it. If you come with true devotion and true love and ask for true Knowledge of the true self, which you are seeking through relative forms, I can give it to you. The Knowledge is within you, God is within you. And I can show you God, if you want to see Him. I can show you your Father, and I can challenge, if you please, millions of people that I can show them that God which they are seeking in forms. If someone comes to me with pure devotion, I can show them that thing. But they must come with pure devotion.

I have that Knowledge and I can give you that Knowledge. That is the only service I can do. My age is so little, my body is so small, I can't serve you as a military officer. I can't serve you as a police constable. The only service I can do is to help you by giving that Perfect Knowledge that you are now seeking in materialism. All materialistic things are perishable. You too will perish one day. So how are you going to find God? You should know such a thing that will never perish and that is the Holy Word, the Holy Knowledge of God, and that is inside you. You only need to discover it. Isaac Newton only discovered the Law of Gravity, he didn't invent it, did he? In the same way, the Knowledge is within you. I can reveal it. I cannot give it to you from somewhere else. I will tell you who you are and what is the purpose of your coming into this world. If somebody comes to me, I am sure I can give him the Knowledge and he will be satisfied.

There are many devotees who are saying I preach a religion. No. Not that. I am not a religious man. I am only saying that I am a spiritual man. I never believe in religions, because I believe religions divide men and men's ideas into separate sects. But if the True God is equal for everyone (like we say Bhagwan in Hindi, God in English, Khuda in Urdu), God is the same thing and Knowledge of Him is always the same. If the formula H_2O is the formula for water everywhere, it means that the flavor and taste of water is the same. So if God is equal, if God is one, if God is the same, then the Knowledge of Him must also be equal. And so it cannot be attained by going into different sects and religions. It is within you. You can commit your body to different sects and religions, but Knowledge is not there.

To go anywhere you need some money, some dollars. To go to the picture hall you need some money for the tickets. The same anywhere. You need dollars. Now my dollars are love and devotion dollars that can only be obtained by Knowledge. I have a bank and in it is the money of love and devotion. I don't like materialistic money – pounds, shillings, pence and dollars – because they are perishable. The only thing that is imperishable you already have within yourself and that is love and devotion for Knowledge. Give it to me. It's alright. I am very sure that I can give you what you are really seeking and what you are becoming tired of seeking in the materialistic forms of the changeable world. You can't find spiritual Knowledge in material things. Materialistic things can be attained by materialistic forms and spiritual things by spiritual forms only. So please want the Holy Knowledge. Remove all the sects, be pure and be above all sects. Fly over them, just as a plane breaks through the clouds and flies above them. If you want to reach Holy Master, Holy God, you have to escape from all sects and religions and come to me. I can show you the right path for you to follow, I will give you that Knowledge. Come to me with devotion and love.

Tomorrow I have to leave for Germany and I will be preaching there, too, and giving this same discourse. 'Know your Master, know your Holy God.' G for Generator. O for Operator. D for Director. Generator, Operator, Director.

Have you given Him something? No. What can we give Him? Only pure devotion and pure love. Everybody has it – an old man, a young man. Everybody has it.

I won't keep you longer. Thank you very much. ('Midsummer Night at Glastonbury')

Prem Rawat's brief invitation to the audience of Glastonbury to 'come to him' for the knowledge they were seeking in so many diverse outlets demonstrates a total lack of awareness of the lifestyle of the audience. The choice of 'military officer' and 'police officer' as examples of a service he cannot offer shows his naivety at the time. Stephen Kent also comments on Prem Rawat's choice of examples as inappropriate to countercultural norms. He describes meeting the guru in 1974 and being disappointed that he used an analogy comparing an aircraft with spiritual knowledge (2001: xvi).

Many could not hear him properly. Thomas Crimble thought he said 'sex' rather than 'sects', again unlikely to hold much appeal for many at the time, for whom 'free love' was part and parcel of the counterculture. Nick Lowe of Brinsley Schartz mistakenly felt that Prem Rawat was 'touting' for money rather than using money as an analogy for devotion. Parts of the crowd were angry at the sudden loss of music from the band. Certainly, Brinsley Schartz was not pleased. However, Nick Lowe was not positive about the experience of the festival either. He complains,

I played the Glastonbury Fayre with Brinsley Schwarz to about 1,500 people in a field. It's heresy to say this, but I couldn't bear it – it was so cold and muddy. My abiding memory is of Maharaji, the teenage guru, turning up in a flower-bedecked Ford Zephyr, followed by all these weird Americans. He wanted to address his people while we were in the middle of a really good gig. There was no security in those days, and when we wouldn't get off, the flower children became more and more nasty. We'd finish a tune, and they'd say 'The master is here!' Then huge chunks of metal started being dropped on us from the pyramid by his more enthusiastic followers, and eventually they drove us off the stage. He got on, asked the audience for money, got back in his car and cleared off. (*Daily Telegraph*, 1971)

Nick Lowe had every right to feel disgruntled. The author cannot remember any metal being thrown onto the stage or 'weird Americans'. Suzy Witten had disconnected the band, and while they ran around trying to figure out what was happening to their sound, Prem Rawat was taken to the microphone. He was brief. On his departure from the Fayre, Quintessence played their set. Andrew Kerr sums up the sense of disgruntlement:

> Another favourite band were Brinsley Schwartz playing on Midsummer's Day, June 21st. Half way through their set followers of the fourteen year old Indian boy, Prem Rawat, known to his devotees as Guru Maharaj Ji flooded the stage, ejected the band and set up a very ancient chair from the farmhouse, which Michael had bought from his neighbour Teddy Stone. The Guru removed his shoes, sat in it and addressed the audience below. I was horrified and left the stage. He was dressed in a white suit that seemed to glow as I passed him. I heard that it was not a very good experience for the boy Guru, who had only been in the country a few days and his first public experience anywhere outside India. Walking through the crowd I heard him say that should be an end to all sex. It made me laugh as there were copulating couples all over the place. I have found no record of how many souls were generated as a result. Later, I discovered that he had in fact said 'sects'. (Kerr, 2011: 222)

In a later article written in 1996, Kerr has modified his tone. He still admits his disdain and notes, 'At the time the whole episode seemed to me to be quite out of order. Not a very auspicious beginning to something that was to completely alter my life. I was blind and disdainful' (1996: 21).

Kerren Ringrose's experience was very different. She was transformed by the experience:

> One day, I was down by the pyramid stage when a young man walked on and started to speak. I didn't know who he was but I could hear the power and clarity and peace in his voice and I knew he was 'there' where I wanted to be forever. He said something like 'come to me and I will give you peace' and when he left the stage I started to walk towards him but some people were shouting and heckling so I turned and went the other way'. (1996: 20)

The differences in experience are not unusual. Kent also reported that he was underwhelmed by meeting the guru in 1974 and was totally surprised that his companions 'spoke glowingly' of the guru's words, to the point that they wanted

Figure 9 Prem Rawat speaks from the Pyramid Stage. Copyright RKV Delhi.

to return the next day (2001: xvi). Kent's dismay would leave him pondering for twenty-five years as to why so many of his peers reacted to the guru so favourably and was part of the reason that he sought to find the answer and interpret 'the crucial decisions of my generation' (ibid.).

We would leave Glastonbury to return to London. In my memoirs, I have written an account of the departure. I remember that the car stuck in the mud on the way out, climbing above the brightly lit pyramid. The premies, led by Charles Cameron, pushed the car up the hill. Charles was puffing and panting and joking with the guru through the open window. We left Glastonbury and its revellers to continue their experience of the Fayre for the next two days. Prem Rawat did not comment. On the way back, we stopped for tea. I recall that he said to me that he did not think many people would have heard his words, but in spite of that, we should be prepared at the ashram for an influx of seekers who would proclaim that they had first seen him at Glastonbury. His words were borne out over the following weeks and, in some cases, years later. The short introduction to the Glastonbury visit in the *Divine Times* twenty-fifth anniversary special edition confirms this influx of counterculture individuals immediately after the Fayre. It states, 'On the pyramid stage premies hastily erected a small podium amid the amplifiers and drum kits and then Maharaji told the crowd that they could receive Knowledge. From the very next day, the London residence was crowded with those who had heard him speak on that summer solstice' (Winter, 1996: 20). Prem Rawat's life was about to be transformed by the unlikely appearance at Glastonbury.

Andrew Kerr was not so convinced of the success of the Fayre. He had staked his personal financial assets into the festival and pledged to repay the outstanding debts. More significantly, he had hoped for a spiritual transformation to take place from the Earth itself. He writes, 'The whole process of Glastonbury Fayre had been a cathartic episode for me. I had staked all my material assets in order to achieve a spiritual awakening and the need to draw attention to the need of changing our way of life so that we can survive on earth' (2011: 235). It would take until 1973 for him to be able to assert that 'the feeling that the Glastonbury episode was a complete failure gradually melted away' (p. 269).

Kent's question as to explain the success of the guru among his countercultural peers remains an unsolved enigma to many. However, in spite of the apparent out-of-context examples and Prem Rawat's apparent unawareness of counterculture norms, he would go on to become over the next few years the most successful of the Indian gurus to attract counterculture individuals. The following chapter will explore the aftermath of Glastonbury, especially focusing on the success of Prem Rawat in the early 1970s and the consequences for several of the prominent figures who had organized the Fayre as a result of that early meeting with the guru. It will explore the years immediately following Glastonbury Fayre up to end of 1973 when the countercultural acceptance of Prem Rawat would culminate in the Millennium '73 Event in the Houston Astrodome and lead to a radical break with his Hindu-orientated family and eventually with the counterculture and its utopian hopes of a New Age.

8

The aftermath of Glastonbury Fayre: Prem Rawat and counterculture

Glastonbury Fayre was one turning point in the history of the post-Second World War baby boomers' experience of counterculture. The numbers attending were relatively few but they represented the committed among the 'hippies', which by 1971 had morphed into popular youth cultures. In Britain, it was one of the markers of the shift away from political activism and drug culture to the acceptance of Eastern religious practices or the developing emergence of New Age spirituality with its medley of occultural beliefs. The Fayre would also emerge as a symbol of authenticity for later revivals of counterculture, for example, the Rave movement and the New Age travellers of the 1980s and 1990s, and would maintain their enthusiasm for the free festival as a site of resistance and the sacred. It would also accelerate the creation of the town of Glastonbury as new centre of contemporary spirituality in Britain, having an enormous impact on the town itself.

The line in Charles Cameron's poem, when he calls upon the 'children of the hedgerows' to take note of Prem Rawat's impending arrival at the festival, is almost prophetic. The end of the 1960s had marked the end of 'flower power', just as the latter had challenged political activism with its 'drug-fuelled' opposition to the mainstream. By the early 1970s, the counterculture was turning sour. The festivals and the music had become commercialized. The 'hippies' were moving away from psychedelic substances to opiate use, sometimes mixed with alcohol. New drug laws had permitted the creation of a drug market that belonged to criminal gangs, and the purity of the narcotics and the psychedelics could no longer be trusted. Utopian ideals were becoming dystopian nightmares as counterculture individuals experienced addiction, early death, drug-related psychosis and physical illnesses. Heavy metal replaced the softer psychedelic music as the decade of the 1970s progressed. The disillusionment created fragmentation. Zablocki (1980) notes that other options competed with drug culture and anti-war activism, including ecology, rural living, communes and gay and gender rights (pp. 48–57). In Britain, where the counterculture was essentially an urban movement, many of the survivors of the 'flower power' dream fled for the hills of Wales, the rural backwaters of Somerset or Cornwall and Devon, seeking to live out their vision of a transformed society in cottages and communes. On both sides of the Atlantic, thousands would 'participate in a "rush for salvation" leading to the acceptance of mystical based Eastern religious movements' (Kent, 2001: 7).

Andrew Kerr would head for Scoraig Peninsula on the extreme north-west of Scotland only one month after Glastonbury. He departed with his partner Jytte and two dogs in an Austin Gypsy, staying at campsites on the way. They would squat in a disused croft, gradually restoring the house and trying to live by subsistence farming. Before leaving, they visited Wales to stay with friends who had been with them in Worthy Farm (2011: 243). Andrew's move would be duplicated by many over the next few years. A considerable number would remain in Glastonbury and the surrounding area, drawn by the spiritual energy of the location. As Kerr points out, most of the people who attended the Fayre knew something about ley lines (p. 233). In an article written after the Fayre,

Figure 10 The audience listen to Prem Rawat on Midsummer's Night. Copyright Ron Geaves.

Kerr elaborated on the choice of the festival site and still maintained that the link between sacred geometry and human well-being was real. He speculated that ley lines 'correspond to the nervous system' and therefore 'connect all the energy points' (ibid.). He claims that Glastonbury Fayre was an experiment in healing the 'tired Earth' wearied by people's inability to live in peace with each other and in harmony with nature (pp. 233–4). Kerr still hoped that people departed the festival 'feeling a lot better for the experience, more creative, happier and more appreciative of the Universe' (p. 234).

Transformations in counterculture

Kerr also identified two important interlinked elements of the next two decades of counterculture when he decided to create the Fayre. Both were concerned with lifestyle choices. The first is political in that Kerr argued that our choice of consumer capitalism is destroying the planet and eroding human self-worth. He claimed, 'In recent history, the material changes that have evolved have generated an obsession for plundering to try to satisfy insatiable greed ... Greed is giving grief to the have-nots in all societies and it is always the have-nots that suffer ... Glastonbury Fayre attempted to buck the trend' (p. 235). The second would suggest that one of the options open to human beings would be to learn the ways of 'ancient people' who had respect for the environments in which they lived (ibid.). He affirms that Glastonbury had taught him that 'ancient peoples, who built Stonehenge and edifices with similar objectives the world over, had a proper respect for their environment. They lived within the rules set by nature and used the seasonal forces as the basis of their cyclical lives' (ibid.). The attempt to live according to the natural cycles would be more than a material choice imposed by ecological concerns. It would be a spiritual reconciliation with the Earth as those who follow such lifestyles would 'understand that some of these forces are hidden' (ibid.). They would know 'how to tap them and live in harmony with them' (ibid.). Kerr's words are a prediction of the concerns and solutions sought by later generations of counterculture manifestations who would seek powerful locations of Earth energy to form communes and off-grid living, including in the surrounds of Glastonbury. Indigenous people and shamans would replace the gurus of the East and the more sophisticated religious systems that had in the main been the product of urban civilizations. Ecology and the environment would replace the threat of nuclear destruction as the primary fear of later counterculture manifestations in the final decades of the twentieth century and the early decades of the twenty-first.

But these would be later choices. In the immediate aftermath of Glastonbury, as some would escape to remote rural and Celtic regions of the nation, as Kerr would do in Scoraig, others were offered a different choice for peace that looked away from counterculture anti-war movements or harmony with the Earth forces and were opened up to the possibility of peace within themselves. Kent would note,

> By the late 1960s, tension existed between mystically-flavoured drug culture and the politically driven antiwar movement. This tension was radically reshaped in the 1970s, as both sides participate in a rush for salvation. On the one hand, many former drug users came to believe that they could acquire similar insights and visions through the adoption of religious practices that required renunciation of drugs. On the other hand, many former activists came to believe that the adoption of these same religious practices would lead to the social revolution that they had failed to initiate through political activity. (2001: 7)

Kent explored in extraordinary detail the impact of the new Eastern movements (and Western-based spirituality) on the counterculture's activists in the 1970s. He noted the presence of important male and female activists in ISKCON, HHH, TM and among the followers of Meher Baba but observes that 'nowhere was the new prioritizing of religion or spirituality over politics more dramatic than among followers (called "premies") of the adolescent Guru Maharaj Ji' (p. 48). This major shift in the counterculture is described by Kent as 'Gods came alive as the 1960s movement withered' (ibid.).

Prem Rawat was insistent that peace could only be found by a rigorous inner journey aided by the tool of Knowledge, a gift offered by the kindness of a master, and given throughout the ages to those who longed for transformation. He was outspoken and direct in his claim that he was the master of the age and those who had found such peace through his message should band together to help him secure inner peace across the globe. Activists would be attracted to the organization-building ability of the premies and their former allegiance to the counterculture, including many prominent US anti-Vietnam campaigners such as Rennie Davis.[1] Davis would become a high-profile 'convert' to the message of inner peace in 1973 and would tour the United States promoting Prem Rawat and his organization. He would state, 'We can do what the street people sought in the sixties – abolish capitalism and other systems that oppress' (p. 49). It is highly unlikely that Prem Rawat saw his teachings, especially the practice of Knowledge, as a means to a left-wing utopian world revolution.

In Britain, political activism had not been the same force as in the United States, and arguably the counterculture's manifestation here remained more influenced by 'drug culture' and psychedelia as the main opposition to the mainstream culture. However, many North American and British members of the counterculture would buy into a millennial dream of world peace led by a messiah who transcended any one religion.

The success of Prem Rawat's Glastonbury visit

While Andrew Kerr called on the occult and sacred geography to create a new ecological politics and disappeared to rural Scotland, others who had been at Glastonbury responded to Prem Rawat's call in his short speech delivered at the festival. On his arrival in London only four days before his appearance at the Fayre, Prem Rawat had attended one public event in Conway Hall, London. Approximately one hundred people attended, mostly existing premies who had met Charnanand in London. The day after the Fayre Prem Rawat would leave for Heidelberg in Germany, where he attended a small event in the university. Lena Zieschang who organized his visit recalls that fifty leaflets were printed and five posters were put up in the city. She remembers with fondness that he stayed in her house, sleeping in her father's bedroom for three days. After the public programme, five people were instructed into Knowledge. On his return, he attended programmes in Exeter University. A much larger crowd attended filling the lecture hall to capacity. Word had got out that this was the guru who had spoken at Glastonbury. The growth in numbers would encourage the small band of followers in London, and after the event in Exeter a tour of England was organized, utilizing the services of the University of Exeter Student's Union minibus driven by Mike Finch (1996: 20). Events would take place in Leicester, Birmingham and London that would include Hindu temples and a Sikh Gurdwara. On returning to the capital, the guru spoke in Porchester Hall, Paddington. The hall has a capacity of approximately five hundred. The author did not think that it would be filled and recalls standing nervously awaiting Prem Rawat's arrival and watching the hall slowly fill. Hippies were notoriously last-minute but the hall was filled to overflowing with counterculture men and women. The grapevine was working and everyone wanted to see the young guru. Many had seen him for the first time at Glastonbury.

In the meantime, a handful of followers in the United States were trying to persuade Prem Rawat to visit. It should be remembered that he had been given permission by his mother to come to the UK for one month only. In addition, he was expected back in India by mid-July to attend a large gathering in Bihar where tens of thousands were expected to attend. His mother (Mata Ji) had not been happy with her son departing to the West in the first place. Charnanand describes the encounter between the son and the mother in the following words:

> 'I heard that you are going to go to England. Is this really true?' Maharaji answered, 'Yes'. She said, 'No, I don't feel comfortable to allow you go abroad at this tender age (13). First you need to complete your education.' Maharaji said, 'I don't want to waste my time any more sitting in a classroom. Those teachers have nothing to teach me. I simply wanted to learn English which I can now speak. I know what my purpose on this earth is.' (1996: 5)

Mata Ji was not convinced that her youngest son should leave for the West and originally refused permission. She would ask Charnanand if he felt it was the right time for her son to visit England. On receiving an affirmative answer from the mahatma, she gave her permission but only for three weeks (ibid.).

The requests coming from the United States and the success of the British tour would test the resolve of the guru. On the one hand, his mother wanted him back and on the other hand, the small number of British and North American followers were begging him to stay. Charnanand describes the dilemma:

> Many premies were writing and calling him to come back to India for the festival in July. And from the United States, Joan Apter and other premies were imploring him to come there. Maharaji's feelings were going back and forth; he knew how much Indian premies loved and wanted to be with him on that special occasion [Guru Puja], but he could not resist the American premies' invitation either. (ibid.)

According to the mahatma's account, the guru asked him. He would reply, 'As far as my feelings are concerned, I know that if you go back to India, Mata Ji will definitely send you back to school. I heard you saying that you don't want to waste your time there. So let's go to America' (ibid.). According to this account, the guru agreed and replied, 'You are right, it feels good.' On 17 July 1971, they would both depart with Behari Singh for Los Angeles. In Prem Rawat's account of this life-changing decision, he confirms the above version of events. He explains,

> It wasn't that I decided to not to go to school. What I decided was to continue doing what I was doing. That's a little bit different. I was just really awakened to the fact that something was happening here. I was away from my family, and I loved it. At first, I thought that it was going to be hard, but then I realized it

was just wonderful. It was the best of all worlds. Here I was, doing what I really wanted to do, what I loved to do. And when I saw the response and the love and the feeling, I just knew this was what I wanted to do. (1996: 13)

The guru describes a difficult telephone conversation with his mother in which she asks him if he is going to return to school. He says that he told her, ' "Well look. I'm doing what I'm doing and this is what I want to be doing." Then there was silence. And that was it' (p. 13).

The response in the United States would confirm the Guru's decision was right. The flower-power generation flocked to him in California, the East Coast and Colorado, joined by some notable peace activists. Gary Girard, one of the first Americans to discover Prem Rawat in India, describes how only a handful of individuals organized the first US visit. He says,

One day there were three of us sitting in a house talking about Maharaji in India to people who really thought we went over the deep end. Then the world changed … On 17 July 1971, there were hundreds of people at Los Angeles International Airport. There were hundreds of people at a house that Maharaji was to stay at. There were hundreds of people at a reception held in health food restaurant in Maharaji's honour. And there were hundreds of people in my house! (1996: 3)

The first American to meet the guru in India, Joan Apter, exclaims, 'People were literally hanging off the ceiling' (1996: 15). In his own words, Prem Rawat recalls,

In England a base had been established which had a chance to grow and stabilize a little bit. Then, once I came to America, things really picked up. The enthusiasm was fantastic and grew quite rapidly. Support was available, the halls were inexpensive, and interest was high, it became obvious there would be no point in going back to India at that time. (1996: 13)

Prem Rawat does not mention Glastonbury in his recollections but his followers in England certainly thought that his attendance at the Fayre was significant. Sue Ratcliffe describes his visit to Paris and on his return a trip to Leicester. She goes on to reflect on how much everyone wanted Guru Puja (lit. guru veneration) in London; 'Everyone really wanted that programme, we felt so little compared with the huge, intense Indian pull for Maharaji' (1996: 2). Prem Rawat did not go back to India and the celebration was held in Hampstead and attended by British premies who expressed their gratitude for the visit. Glastonbury was still at the forefront of everyone's minds. A velvet-covered scroll was presented to Prem Rawat in which he was thanked for turning England into 'Albion'. Reference was made to the double rainbow that had appeared across the Vale of

Avalon the morning after the solstice. It is clear from these references that the prophecies associated with Glastonbury had been fulfilled by the guru's visit, at least in the minds of his British counterculture students. They would have been meaningless to his British Indian followers and it is not known how much relevance he would have given to them himself, especially as they were outside his frame of reference.

On his return from the United States, Prem Rawat would speak at Westminster Central Hall, the headquarters of Britain's Methodists, next to the Houses of Parliament. The magnificent grand hall in the building holds over five hundred people. The event took place on the 2 November 1971. The streets of central London were packed with counterculture youth making their way to the event. In a conversation with Robert Heywood, at the time a road manager for Caravan, a well-known counterculture folk-rock band, he explained to me, 'It was the place to go, it was out on the grapevine. He had spoken at Glastonbury.' I was told by someone that the 'Lord had appeared at Glastonbury and he was only thirteen'. The next day, a Boeing 747, chartered by the newly created Divine Light Mission (DLM), would take North American and British followers to attend a large gathering in Delhi to be held on Prem Rawat's return to India where they would stay on for a month in Premnagar Ashram.

By the following year, it was estimated that the guru had fifty thousand followers in the United States. Exactly one year later, seven Boeing 747s would transport around 2,500 followers on the same journey. During the early years of the 1970s, DLM experienced phenomenal growth. The teachings of Prem Rawat, or Guru Maharaj Ji as he was known at the time, spread quickly to Britain, France, Germany, Holland, Switzerland, Spain, Italy, Scandinavia, Japan, South America, Australasia, Canada and the United States (Geaves, 2006a). He would receive the keys to several US cities for his humanitarian activities, primarily because of the number of American youth who would cease their drug use after experiencing inner peace and self-knowledge as a result of his teachings; these would include New York City, New Orleans, Oakland, Miami Beach and Detroit. In 1973, he would appear on the Merve Griffin Show shortly after 'Millennium '73' was held in the Houston Astrodome, which attracted around twenty thousand counterculture youth. Many parents would also attend and Prem Rawat was described as 'a rehabilitator of prodigal sons and daughters'. The festival was called the 'youth culture event of the year' (Foss and Larkin, 1976). By the end of 1973, DLM was active in fifty-five countries (Downton, 1979:5). Tens of thousands had been initiated, and several hundred centres and dozens of ashrams had been established. Around eighty of these were in the cities and towns of Britain. The year of 1973 has been called the 'peak of the Mission's success' (Aagaard, 1980).

Glastonbury after 1971

Glastonbury Festival would not occur again until 1978 when the arrival of 'New Age' travellers washed out by rain from Stonehenge were led to believe that a festival was taking place at the site. A small event took place with around five hundred attendees. There was little organization and few facilities. This became known in the annals of the event as the 'impromptu' festival (https://glastonburyfestivals.co.uk/history/history-1978). In 1979, Arabella Churchill and Bill Harkin would join with Michael Eavis to hold a charity event in aid of children. The Children's World Charity which still works in special schools throughout Somerset and Avon was established. Twelve thousand attended and Peter Gabriel, Steve Hillage and the Alex Harvey Band played, but once again the event left the organizers with large debts in spite of the numbers, and in 1980 no one would dare risk organizing another festival (https://glastonburyfestivals. co.uk/history/history-1979). In 1981, Michael Eavis took control of the event and renamed it Glastonbury Festival. It was held to raise funds for CND (Campaign for Nuclear Disarmament). The Pyramid Stage was built as a permanent structure and New Order, Hawkwind, Taj Mahal and Aswad played to around eighteen thousand people and £20,000 was given to CND (https://glastonburyfestivals.co.uk/history/history-1981).

Synergy

Despite their divergent fortunes, there was a synergy between the 1971 festival and the first students of Prem Rawat. This synergy would have direct consequences for the organizers of the Fayre. The early students of Prem Rawat believed passionately that peace could be established in the world. They were optimistic believers in a new era to marshal in a transformation that would begin from a purification of each human heart. Kent argues that the 'primary *political* [my italics] word that Maharaj Ji and his organization used to attract disaffected activists and radicals was "peace"' (Kent, 2001: 49). This may have been true in the United States, but British followers appeared more interested in the spirituality on offer seeing the possibility of psychedelic experience by inner transformation and mystical awareness than the opportunity to pursue leftist goals by another means. Although they were not committed to Andrew Kerr's idea of change by tapping the forces of the cosmos through sacred geometry, there was certainly among them believers in the Glastonbury myths and prophesies that foretold a 'once and future king'. The Grail legends were open to esoteric interpretations that chimed with Prem Rawat's insistence on an inner perfection attained through a special knowledge.

Andrew Kerr's sincerity was also shared by Prem Rawat's first Western followers. Kerr writes of this passion in describing the way that Glastonbury Fayre was brought to fruition. He states, 'This was a chance to try out altruism on a shoestring! Small amounts of cash and cheques came in from time to time from generous hearted souls. These sparks made it turn into something amazing. Others gave their energies' (2011: 203). This description could easily have been applied to the beginnings of DLM and Prem Rawat's arrival in London. In his own words, the guru reflects on the decision to come to England,

> One day I came back from school and there was a green van parked in the driveway. I went and looked at it, and there was a bunch of hippies sitting in the back … They had driven all the way from Europe to see me. Then people began to ask me, 'Will you come to the West? Please come to the West!' But it was still like dream that would happen some day. (1996: 11)

Later on, in the same interview, he reflects, 'I think that it was a very sweet time because of the simplicity that existed' (p. 12). He elaborates on his affection for that time, 'That smoothness or sweetness of things – that's what is very special. It was there at that time, and everybody made a little bit of effort' (ibid.). Those who were present at Prem Rawat's first visit to the West also shared Kerr's 'shoestring and a prayer' attitude. There was little in the way of financial resources. Prem Rawat arrived with a return ticket and little money. Charnanand had arrived in 1969 with £3. The *Divine Times Special Edition* produced in 1996 states that although a Rolls Royce, bedecked with flowers, collected the guru from the airport, it was hired only for a few hours by Michael Cole. After that Prem Rawat was driven around the UK in Carol Water's Ford Cortina and then by Mike Finch in the University of Exeter's minibus. A house was rented in Lincoln Street, off the King's Road, but when the money to pay the rent ran out after only a week, Prem Rawat shared with the dozen or so inhabitants of the ashram, a rented three-bedroomed house in Golders Green. Glen Whitaker recalls that many slept in the garden as it was a hot summer (1996: 2).

The lack of money would in no way dampen the sense that everything would happen according to a divine or cosmic plan. Kerr's trust is affirmed in the gospel references to the Sermon on the Mount, especially the teaching that creation is looked after by a benign Creator, stated by Jesus in his reference to birds that neither 'weave or spin' but are cared for, and he also mentions how Jesus asked his disciples to 'leave everything behind' (2011: 203). The first students of Prem Rawat also referred everything to the grace of a benevolent divinity. Kerr is disappointed that he was left in debt after Glastonbury. He seeks to rediscover altruism in the communal values he hopes to find among crofters in Scotland. Many of the first two hundred Western students who would greet Prem Rawat at Heathrow and leave for India with him the following November would enter the ashrams in the UK and the United States, renouncing all personal possessions to work towards bringing peace to others.

The other synergy was the 'word of mouth' method of communication that would be used to organize Glastonbury and also to communicate the benefits of the guru's message to the counterculture. In an age before mass or social media, the grapevine was the main vehicle for passing on information about a festival or a new drug experience. This would be achieved primarily through counterculture friendship networks that shared good or 'cool' experiences. Roy Hollingsworth captures this networking in an article for the *Melody Maker* on 19 June 1971. He writes, 'Thousands of people will converge on this mysterious site – prompted by no ads, no promise of big bands. The event has been passed on by word of mouth throughout the length and breadth of the country.' For several decades before the advent of the World Wide Web and the opportunities it offered for instantaneous communication, Prem Rawat's message was passed on by word of mouth, replicating countercultural networks.

A final synergy is expressed by Kerr when he sums up Glastonbury Fayre as the first large-scale event 'pleading for respect for the lovely planet we have been given and the seeking of a spiritual awakening' (2011: 220). One of Prem Rawat's consistent themes is for the person to feel an appreciation for the gift of life combined with a state of gratitude. Prem Rawat would use the term 'spiritual' as opposed to 'religious' in his short Glastonbury address asserting, 'There are many devotees who are saying I preach a religion. No. Not that. I am not a religious man. I am only saying that I am a spiritual man. I never believe in religions, because I believe religions divide men and men's ideas into separate sects' ('Midsummer night at Glastonbury'). Kerr had come to the same viewpoint along with thousands of other counterculture individuals on both sides of the Atlantic. Institutionalized religion was not trusted as a vehicle for spiritual development and possibly for the first time in history, spirituality was about to be separated out from mainstream religions.

Another cluster of synergies might help to explain the counterculture's attraction to Prem Rawat. Elizabeth Nelson (1989) identifies four important characteristics of British counterculture from 1966 to 1973. The first is 'playfulness'. Nelson cites Richard Neville as saying 'counter-culturalists were relearning how to play', to have fun (p. 85). She explains this to be a reaction to dehumanization and the boredom of work (p. 85). The counterculture was essentially a movement of youth and Prem Rawat was only 13 when he arrived in the UK. His Indian followers would often play with him and commented on the guru's mischievous nature. In Hindu understandings of the world this would be compared to *lila*, the cosmic playfulness of divinity, usually associated with the childhood exploits of the avatar Krishna. The British and US media would mock the guru's playful exploits, rarely taking into account that it is normal for 13-year-old boys to play. Prem Rawat had a host of counterculture rebels rediscovering playfulness as companions in his games. On their part, they incorporated the Hindu doctrine of *lila* into their reaction against the prevailing Protestant work ethic.

The second element was drugs. Nelson identifies the new psychedelics as explaining and providing insight into the workings of consciousness and these experiences were allied to the concept of 'self' as central in the struggle to obtain social or political liberation (p. 93). It does not take much analysis to realize how close such ideas were to Vedantic thinking. Prem Rawat offered a similar view of life's purpose but transposed drug use for the practice of inner exploration through his revealed techniques of Knowledge.

Her third feature is the importance of festivals and concerts. Nelson makes the point that 'festivals were an important means of developing and maintaining a commitment to alternative lifestyle. They provided entertainment, an illusion of togetherness (even if not the reality), a *kind of ritual where the believers could worship* [my italics], almost fetish-style the new consciousness' (p. 97). A central element of Prem Rawat's *sadhana* (path or discipline) was *satsang*, loosely translated as 'company of truth'. Premies would gather every day in large or small numbers to listen, communicate and celebrate the experience they had discovered. Events with Prem Rawat would duplicate many of the features of the counterculture festival. There may not have been the same emphasis on music, but as observed at the time by *IT* music only provided the excuse for getting together not the reason for doing so (p. 97).

Figure 11 Prem Rawat in London, late 1971. Copyright RKV Delhi.

Finally, Nelson notes the importance of building communities, based on the idea of revolution by exemplary lifestyle 'inherent in the counter-culture from its beginning'(p. 103). The most committed lived in communes. The idea of exemplary lifestyle was central to DLM's approach to mission and the most dedicated premies would join the ashram communities where they would commit to vegetarianism, a life arranged around meditation, satsang and service and to celibacy. In all of these elements of premie life, the counterculture's understandings of being different and superior to 'straight society' was not jeopardized but possibly even enhanced. None of these synergies would be very apparent to the attendees at Glastonbury on the guru's visit, but they would become an integral part of their acceptance of Prem Rawat.

This synergy of ideas and the friendship networks would create another meeting of minds between Kerr and Prem Rawat. Two years later, when Kerr and Jytte were living together on Scoraig, they were visited by Thomas Crimble and his partner Lorna who had recently been attending 'meetings of people who were followers of Guru Maharaj Ji' (Kerr, 2011: 266). Against his better judgement, Kerr is persuaded to go to Aberdeen to meet an Indian Mahatma who was going to hold a 'Knowledge session'. Jytte and Thomas wanted to attend and suggested that Andrew stayed behind to look after the dogs. Lorna had already received 'Knowledge'. Andrew described his negativity towards the

Guru as 'high resistance' based on his Glastonbury experience. Lorna chided him and argued, 'If you do not go, you will never know if it is any good' (ibid.). These words would chime in with those of Prem Rawat in 1996 when he would respond to an interviewer's question, 'When you came to the West, you were 13 years old. Didn't a lot of people have a problem with that?' After addressing the question, Prem Rawat says, 'And that takes us to an even more fundamental issue. What is the proof that the Knowledge is real? The proof is in itself. You feel, you experience, you enjoy. That is the proof' (1996: 14).

Despite his apprehension of not wanting to get involved in a cult, the small group left for Aberdeen in Thomas's van. In his memoirs, Kerr described the experience of receiving 'Knowledge' (2011: 266) and in 1974 he would attend a festival with Prem Rawat in Copenhagen, working on an oil rig to raise the money for the family to travel. In the early decades of Prem Rawat's activities in the West, his events would have parallels to festival culture, complete with music, dancing, spontaneous expressions of joy, free food, child care and often held outside over several days. Certainly, this would continue until the 1990s when these elements were toned down in favour of a more lecture-style occasion where Prem Rawat would address the audience. Andrew would certainly have recognized these elements of festival culture in Copenhagen but without the drugs and bacchanalian features. This festival experience would bring him to say that 'going to the Maharaj Ji programme the Knowledge was slowly beginning to make sense. The feeling that the Glastonbury episode was a complete failure gradually melted away. My spirit became a little happier' (ibid.). For Kerr, the principal inspiration for the Fayre, the convergence between Glastonbury and Prem Rawat, was complete. In the *Divine Times Special Edition*, he declares, 'He changed my attitude. He continues to teach me what life is about and how to enjoy it' (1996: 21). He was not the only organizer of the Fayre to become a student of the guru. Along with Jytte and Thomas Crimble, Mark Irons and Andrew Tweedie who photographed the Fayre would also receive Knowledge in the early 1970s. Arabella Churchill would see Prem Rawat in Manchester in the 1980s after George Blodwell, an early follower of the guru who had also been at the Fayre, met her in the city. She would become a student soon after.

Others would experience the synchronicity so much loved by the 1960s counterculture individuals as proof of a conscious-benign universe. Kerren Ringrose describes how she wrote Charles Cameron's poem in her diary when she left the Fayre and set off to India to find a master. She would have two chance encounters in Afghanistan and then in India where she would meet students of Prem Rawat with 'a look in their eyes that would fascinate me. She would attend his event in November 1971, joining those who had travelled on the chartered Boeing 747 (1996: 20). The Rainbow Gypsies who describe themselves as 'a theater troupe, a traveling commune, a band of pilgrims ... dancers, poets, musicians, hipsters, hustlers, mystics and freaks' had left California in 1969, danced and performed their way across Europe, Africa and Asia fuelled by 'a vast quantity of pure Owsley LSD' ('About the Rainbow Gypsies'). They had entertained the crowd at Glastonbury and next morning departed to meet Prem Rawat in London. They would receive Knowledge and continue across land to India performing on their way. Their final destination was Prem Rawat's ashram in Haridwar.[2]

By 1972, Prem Rawat and the Fayre were inextricably woven together in counterculture myth-making. When Nicolas Roeg would release his film *Glastonbury Fayre* on general release to cinemas in the UK, the distribution poster would have the name 'Guru Maharaj Ji' headlining over the rock bands that played in the festival. At the end of his memoirs written in 2012, Kerr summarizes his spiritual position. He remains apocalyptic and calls for the vision of 1971 to be restored to save the planet from greed. He affirms,

> I have come to the conclusion that what I have learned from the Knowledge and the teachings of Jesus, Gnosticism, Krishna in the Bhagavad Gita, and the Buddha, who sat beneath the Bodhi Tree for 49 days in meditation until he saw the Light, that same Eternal Light. The practice of Knowledge (the Gnosis) reveals that it is simple but not at all easy. (2011: 349)

Kerr's perennial wisdom expressed in 2011 is echoed by Charles Cameron in 1972. The book *Who Is Guru Maharaj Ji?* is infused throughout with a sense of an eternal transmission of Knowledge or Gnosis revealed by an unbroken chain of masters; on the way, it refers to prophesies of a final moment when the greatest master of all will appear to bring enlightenment to all living human beings. It also affirms the techniques of Knowledge through an investigation of quantum physics, health benefits and its ability to free the human mind from addiction. The book is openly messianic and apocalyptic and certainly chimes with *senso stricto* definitions of New Age but it is not in any sense advocating the bricolage that makes up later *senso lato* forms of contemporary spirituality. It is inclusive in that it includes all cultures and religions as having had a master but exclusive in the sense that it calls everyone to follow the master of the time rather than the religions that developed from masters of the past. Rennie Davis was openly millennial, declaring at Berkeley University that 'the Perfect Master teaches perfection, and will bring perfection on Earth – not after the

Millennium, but right now, in three years' (Kent, 2001: 48, 49). Prem Rawat would appear to accept that peace was possible in a very short time. He would declare at the Millennium '73 event in Houston, 'I will establish peace in this world.' ISKCON devotees would also be convinced that Krishna Consciousness would occur globally within decades. It is hard to determine to what degree either Prabhupada or Prem Rawat bought into these utopian visions for the near future. It is more likely that their respective encounters with countercultural hopes would fuel their own sense of mission and their respective reasons for leaving India.

Twenty-five years later, Prem Rawat was more cautious. He refers to the well-being and meditation industry as something completely different to the aims of his message. He points towards motivation and asserts, 'Sometimes people receive Knowledge for other reasons – to make their blood pressure go down, or make their head hurt less. Or something else. But Knowledge doesn't work for that' (1996: 12). In the same interview, he also states, 'I wasn't trying to offer people a better lifestyle or a substitute for religion' (ibid.). On the topic of messianic expectations among his followers, he declares, 'Some people had a concept that I was some kind of messiah or prophet, and that wasn't really acceptable to a lot of people. But I was saying right from the beginning "I am not a messiah; I'm not a prophet; I'm not any of those things." Those are just concepts' (p. 14).

Prem Rawat's apparent divergence from the views of his followers who had flocked to him from the counterculture is important to the central thesis of this book. The next chapter will explore this discrepancy in the context of countercultural expectations and in the process attempt to throw a more nuanced light on understanding such concepts as Easternization, occulture, New Age and festival culture and in the context of the disintegration of the late-1960s counterculture from the early 1970s.

9

Counterculture, occulture and Easternization revisited

Throughout I have argued that Prem Rawat was an unlikely candidate to appear at Glastonbury Fayre and emerge as the leading counterculture Indian guru in the early 1970s. Nothing in his outer appearance or upbringing suggested an affinity with Western counterculture, although Morgan points out that Divine Light Mission (DLM) was the most westernized of all the Eastern-based movements and that Prem Rawat would normally dress in a suit as opposed to the Indian garb of other gurus (1973: 94). He also notes the male followers dressed similarly (ibid.), even though Kent observed that the women wore the typical clothing of counterculture styles of the period (2001: xv). Prem Rawat was not a long-haired bearded yogi in the vein of Maharishi Mahesh Yogi or a monk of an established devotional Hindu sampradaya such as Bhaktivendanta Swami, who had both preceded Prem Rawat to the West. In both these two gurus who attracted counterculture individuals in both the United States and Britain, there was arguably an affinity with countercultural spiritual interest in India. The playful bhakti of Krishna in which mischief, dance and music interacted with a sexuality implicit in the Gopi tales and the love between Krishna and Radha would have struck a chord with the playfulness and the erotic inherent in the 'flower-power' generation. Mahesh Yogi looked the part of an Eastern sage and had attracted the Beatles and other celebrities to his teachings.

Prem Rawat, on the other hand, was a child of a middle-class Indian family, living in a bungalow of the former British garrison town of Dehradun, attending a well-known British-founded Roman Catholic school when he came to London in 1971 and conventionally dressed in North Indian white pyjama and kurta. He would quickly adopt a suit and tie when addressing Western audiences and it is highly unlikely that he was aware of the music that was being created by the 1960s counterculture. However, Charnanand, the mahatma who had been sent to the West, had lived with counterculture individuals and had been in close association with the geographical concentrations of counterculture in London. Charnanand would joke that the inner sound reached through one of the four techniques taught by Prem Rawat sounded similar to Pink Floyd, and he would comment on his audiences in West London that 'they were called "hippies" but I would call them "happies"' (1996: 4).

There was only a slight affinity between the festival culture developing within the counterculture and manifested at Woodstock, the Isle of Wight and Reading in the late 1960s and the events in India in which Prem Rawat or his father would speak. In these Indian events, tens of thousands would gather to sit under large colourful canopies, all would be fed free of charge from giant outdoor kitchens, musicians would sing traditional Hindu and Muslim devotional music and speakers would address the gathered crowds with Prem Rawat's message, including references to love, inner peace, self-realization and the nature of God. The mood of these events was joyous and would rise to ecstatic when Prem Rawat would address the audience in the late evening. Many would stand and dance or shout greetings of praise to the young guru. The first individuals from Britain and the United States had attended these events and brought back with them eye-witness accounts to counterculture audiences in London and, later, Los Angeles and Boulder, Colorado.

In the early 1970s, Prem Rawat would address thousands of Western premies gathered together for three-day festivals that would incorporate elements of festival culture combined with the traditional elements of the Indian events. These occasions lacked the Dionysian hedonism of Western rock or folk venues and there was definitely an absence of mind-altering substances. Consciousness transformation was achieved by meditation, listening and intense bhakti (devotional love). Arguably, the early counterculture devotees would notice the parallels to festival culture; they had attended psychedelic music venues in London, free concerts in Hyde Park and returned home to Britain in 1969 and 1970 to hear about the Isle of Wight, and they made comparisons with what they had experienced in India. Early events with Prem Rawat were organized by them and the increasing number of countercultural individuals flocking to the guru in the early 1970s, with elements drawn from festivals of the era.

The changes in dress codes observed by Kent in 1974, where he notes 'as a twenty-two year old hippie, I noticed that many others in the audience looked like "freaks" (as we called ourselves) … the male devotees looked like business school aspirants – but I realized that, not long before, they probably had been scruffy and long-haired like me' (ibid.). Kent's observations arise from changes that took place from 1973 and are key to understanding the tensions inherent

Figure 12 Rainbow Gypsies at Glastonbury. Copyright The Rainbow Gypsies.

in Easternization. The reasons for the transformation were not superficial and require analysis. Ironically, they were initiated by Prem Rawat's mother and the Indian mahatmas, both of whom remained essentially Hindu in lifestyle and dress codes.

The case study of Prem Rawat and his changing relationship with the counterculture throughout the decade of the 1970s has provided a real-life scenario that permits a more nuanced reflection on Easternization and occulture in the context of late-1960s and 1970s hippie subculture. In the case of the former, I have argued that it requires a degree of uncoupling from occulture, especially in regard to the complex and changing relationship between Easternization and Western esotericism from that which existed pre-Second World War or even in the 1950s. To further complicate matters, 'Easternization' as a categorization urgently needs to be assessed in the light of recent scholarship on the breadth and depth of what is labelled 'Hinduism' with all of its many offshoots, some that even refuse to be defined within that spectrum of belief and practice and offer themselves up as opposition to such categories. Occulture, too, has its problems. In the medley of beliefs and practices that Partridge labels 'occulture' and also defined as '*senso lato*', it may be the case that particular tropes of belief come together to form a fit with certain new religious movements (NRMs) or groupings within New Age to create a bridge across to particular subgroups without embracing the full bricolage or even rejecting large parts of the bricolage.

The relationship between occulture and Easternization can even be fraught, and, in some cases, the mix of the two can supply meaning that is far from that desired by the founder figure. In such instances, constant negotiation and transformation became the norm, undermining the usual sociological processes of institutionalization. In the 1970s, the 'flower-power' counterculture was fragmenting, developing new forms, reassessing radical politics, festival culture, high culture, gender and the full range of technologies of the self. Prem Rawat arrived in the UK and visited the United States, rapidly established a movement at the fulcrum of these changes taking place and, in part, was instrumental in the direction that such transformations took. I have argued that attending Glastonbury Fayre was pivotal in his decision making.

Easternization and essentialism

It is clear that Eastern ideas infiltrated the Western counterculture, picking up speed as the decade of the 1960s progressed and introducing NRMs transported by Indian gurus, providing an impetus to already existing beliefs such as karma or reincarnation introduced earlier through colonial encounter with the orient or influencing the direction of popular music. However, the label of Easternization to this phenomenon risks essentializing a very ancient and diverse set of traditions that comprise Hinduism and Buddhism, already oversimplified by the World Religion's model that has held sway for decades over the academic study of religion. It has been posited that Hinduism requires analysis as 'Hinduisms' as opposed to a discrete bordered entity with a common set of characteristics. Richard King describes the creation of Hinduism as a discrete world religion as a 'Western inspired creation' (1999: 98). Buddhism's spread across Asia developed spiritual worldviews as diverse as Tibetan tantra or Japanese Zen schools. Even as far back as 1966, Robert Slater was warning against such essentialism. He states, 'Umbrella terms such as Christianity and Buddhism are deceptive as they tend to obscure the rich diversity of belief and practice to be found within these and other traditions' (Lewis and Slater, 1966: 2). I have argued against the 'world religions' construct as failing to recognize the complexity of religions or recognize how such labels have been framed in the history of colonial domination of the East (Geaves 2005b). The essentializing of Islam as a single homogeneous entity has been particularly difficult for the Muslim presence in the West where the heterodox complexity of Islamic belief and practice has been placed at risk by both right-wing rhetoric and revivalist movements trying to establish themselves as orthodoxies in the Muslim world. This tendency to essentialize also applies to Eastern teachings arriving in the West, especially those introduced by a number of Indian teachers arriving in the late twentieth century, who were often demonized as cult leaders.

I have drawn heavily on scholars who challenge the essentializing of Indian religions including my interventions in 1998 and 2005. Sutcliffe would bring these critiques of method in the study of religions to the study of New Age spirituality, arguing that problems of definition were a 'fresh and pressing example of how our concepts (continue to) construct our data' (2013: 17). He makes the case that New Age studies have been guilty of understanding the clusters of spirituality as marginal exoticisms only because the World Religions paradigm has been accepted as a normative reality rather than a constructed scholarly convention. Sutcliffe asserts, 'Read against the grain of the World Religions paradigm, new age phenomena show continuities with a level of popular belief and practices expressed within and across a range of different religious traditions' (ibid.). Sutcliffe's argument is compelling and enables Easternization to be assessed not as a given reality of tendencies within counterculture but instead as a problematic label that fails to grasp the complexity of how Eastern religious ideas and movements have entered into Western comprehension of transcendence.

Gilhus takes Sutcliffe's critique further and notes a number of terminology problems. She agrees with Sutcliffe that terms used in categorizing 'New Age' or 'New Religious Movements', 'spirituality' or 'alternative spirituality' posit a relationship where the objects of study are perceived as secondary or subsidiary to established religious tradition (2013: 35). She also affirms Sutcliffe's point that these terms began as emic but were translated into the etic without a sufficient analysis of their intellectual baggage (p. 36). In addition, she notes that the terminology tends to turn a 'huge diversity into one unity' and also fails to recognize that these entities are fluid, a project in the making (p. 37). A final observation recognizes that all too often language categories such as 'spiritual' or 'New Age' refer predominantly to the narrative and mythic dimensions of religion and are therefore 'reductionistic in a way that is not especially fruitful in relation to the multi-layered formation which they aim to describe' (pp. 36–7). All of these problemizings of terminology and method are relevant to comprehend the changing relationship of Prem Rawat to the counterculture.

One of the challenges for sociologists of religion or even scholars of contemporary manifestations of religion in the West is constructing the full history or complexity of religious movements that have arrived in the West in recent times. Otherwise, assessments that treat this phenomenon as the impact of Easternization on contemporary spirituality will fail to recognize that these teachers represented a diversity of traditions that had historically arisen over millennia in India.

These religious groupings created by Indian gurus and their followers demonstrate differing strands of Indian religious life but may have historical oppositions to each other, combined with remarkable diversity of individual negotiation of the beliefs and practices once transported to the West. Robert Jackson has argued that the tradition may be a reference point but that the individual, although influenced through membership of the group, is nevertheless unique (1997). In addition, the Indian subcontinent is characterized by pluralism and diversity which does not conform easily to systematized patterns of religious data and conceptual frameworks imposed by Western scholarship (Geaves, 1998). Richard Eaton's observation that there is a need for contextualized study of particular religious and explanatory discourses is pertinent to this debate on Easternization.[1]

Counterculture critique of Easternization

Timothy Leary had realized the superficiality of counterculture's appropriation of the East and had become wary. Writing from Fulsom Prison in 1973, he advises people to 'reject the "Hindu trap" he had earlier embraced, with its "soft, sweet, custard mush" of unity' (Davis, 2015: 644). The American historian Theodore Roszak comments on the eroticization of Eastern traditions, especially the embracing of tantric traditions by counterculture, arguing that 'nothing is so striking about the new orientalism as its highly sexed flavour' (Roszak, 1969: 135). Jeffrey Kripal notes that ISKCON combined asceticism with 'rich emotional-devotional orientations' (2007a: 14) and argues that Eastern traditions were appropriated not to reproduce them in the West but rather to utilize them to 'encode and entextualize a new democratic-erotic body no longer bound to a traditional religious register' (p. 26). Kripal calls this a 'religion of no-religion' and claims that 'it sparkled at the heart of the countercultural experience' (ibid.). Kripal disagrees with Roszak's view that the asceticism at the heart of Vedanta popularized in the first half of the twentieth century had been replaced by Hindu and Buddhist tantra in the second half of the century with a new emphasis on the sensuous (p. 14). Instead, he observes that the argument is too simplistic as asceticism would remain in many Indian movements arriving in the 1960s, a point that is valid for the early DLM whose Indian origins lay in Vedanta. The point here is that each movement requires individual analysis of why it would prove popular among countercultural elements. There is considerable difference between the intense personal devotion to Krishna that was advocated by Swami Prabhupada and had its origins in the teachings of Chaitanya Mahaprabhu (1486–1534), a Bengali ecstatic, and the mass consumption of a mantra promoted by Mahesh Yogi, whose own origins lie in Advaita Vedanta. Similarly, the tantric elements that combined so effectively with the Human Potential Movement in the teachings and practices of Rajneesh differ substantially from the iconoclastic antinomianism of the solitary sant, the closest 'fit' that, I have argued, works to categorize Prem Rawat's place in the history of religions.

Sant iconoclasm

I have drawn upon Rawlinson's (1997) categories to begin the process of avoiding essentializing the Easternization that arrived with the Indian gurus relocating their traditions primarily among Western countercultures in the 1960s. Rawlinson's categories have the benefit of being developed to explore counterculture manifestations of Eastern spirituality, but the downside is that they were created to correspond to Western teachers who taught Eastern spirituality rather than the gurus or masters who originated the practices and beliefs. In the case of Prem Rawat, it could be argued that he transcended these binaries as he left India when only 13 years old, married a member of the West Coast counterculture at 16, raised four children in London and Los Angeles and never returned to India as a national.

Prem Rawat would appear to cross several of Rawlinson's categories, including 'embodiment of the truth' (p. 30), 'authorisation from a teacher' (p. 18), 'setting up on their own' (ibid.), 'living in accordance with a transcendental source' (p. 28) or even 'belonging to a Hindu sub-tradition' (p. 17). Some of these would appear to be in opposition to each other and might better describe different stages of Prem Rawat's life and teaching. Yet from an early age, he exhibited signs of accepting the authorization given his father while simultaneously setting up on his own. Early DLM exhibited signs of being a Hindu subtradition and most followers accepted wholeheartedly that their teacher 'lived in accordance with a transcendental source' or even incarnated such a source. Yet the degree to which this was constructed out of a mix of Hindu ideas of an avatar combined with messianic return borrowed from Christianity, rather than Prem Rawat's understanding of his place in the world of Indian spirituality, is complex to unravel. I was tempted to turn towards Rawlinson's category of the followers of Eastern gurus as 'those who travelled on the inner path' (p. 29) as this is how he frames DLM. The problem is that Rawlinson also falls into the error made by many – that is, Prem Rawat's organizational forms were part of the modern phenomena of Sant Mat, epitomized by Radhasoami offshoots.

To develop a more nuanced understanding of Prem Rawat, I have moved towards Gold's (1987) and Vaudeville's (1987) studies of sant phenomena as a way of avoiding the more simplistic 'inner Hinduism' described by Rawlinson (1997), which may have described some of the beliefs of early DLM members but is not adequate to situate Prem Rawat. Gold has the benefit of categorizing various stages of sant development and these are helpful to burrow down deeper into what occurred when Prem Rawat came to the West and DLM was established around the time of Glastonbury Fayre and the later deconstruction of both Indian and counterculture values simultaneously existing side by side in DLM. Gold posited three stages in the life of a sant lineage. It begins with a solitary figure such as Kabir, Nanak or Ravidas where authority is derived from personal charisma, and it is highly unlikely that there is any intention of beginning a *panth* (sectarian institution). In this scenario, the followers of an individual sant are not part of an overarching formal organization but are united with their teacher in being committed to the value of personal experience. A lineage is created by disciples who became noteworthy sants in their own right; usually, a disciple is chosen to continue as the guru by the original sant. A sant lineage is called a *parampara* as long as the dominant focus of spiritual power is still contained in a living holy person who has succeeded the original sant master. The term *panth* is used for the final phase of a sant lineage, when it has become a sectarian institution which claims to spread the teachings of the past sant(s), but the dominant focus of spiritual power now resides in ritual forms and scripture often developed from the writings or speeches of the founder sant(s). A *panth* is usually headed by a *mahant* (religious functionary, normally a celibate monk) and a committee that looks after the ritual and administration (p. 85).

In this analysis of India's sant tradition, DLM manifested some of the elements of a parampara as the young guru had been chosen by his father to continue his mission and take it to the world. However, because Prem Rawat was a minor when he inherited his father's work, his mother and senior mahatmas had developed an institutional structure with some panth characteristics, ostensibly to assist the child-master until he reached adulthood (Geaves, 2004a, 2007). This interpretation of events would hold together if it is assumed that Prem Rawat was merely a hereditary successor to an established *parampara*. His departure from India ruptured any sense of continuity from the past and provided the door for the young sant to proclaim his own authority and establish his work as he wanted it to manifest.

If Prem Rawat is understood as a 'solitary figure' as described by Gold, it becomes necessary to understand the type of authority that these sant masters invested themselves with. Although Gold speaks of 'personal charisma', this needs elaboration.

Sant iconoclasm as counterculture

Charlotte Vaudeville describes a sant as

> a holy man of a rather special type, who cannot be accommodated in the traditional categories of Indian holy men – and he may just as well be a woman. The Sant is not a renunciate ... He is neither a *yogi* nor a *siddha*, practices no *asanas*, boasts of no secret *bhij mantras* and has no claim to magical powers. The true Sant wears no special dress or insignia, having eschewed the social consideration and material benefits which in India attach to the profession of asceticism ... The Sant ideal of sanctity is a lay ideal, open to all; it is an ideal which transcends both sectarian and caste barriers. (1987: 36–7)

When such sants chose to promote their worldview to a wider public in India, they appeared to both Hindu and Islamic orthodoxies as spiritual countercultural figures who denied the religious constructions that the elite members of such orthodoxies believed to be time-honoured truths. Such sant missionary activity tended to be people's movements in that they drew upon vernacular language to transmit their message, reached out to both women and the dispossessed in Indian society and proclaimed a form of egalitarianism based upon God's immanent presence within the human being. This is true of Prem Rawat who attracts thousands of rural people including those of low caste and women.

Juergensmeyer describes sants as regarded by all Hindus as 'innovators, religious radicals, rebels against prevailing orthodoxies and the social institutions related to them' (1991: 23). Sant spirituality affirms an interiority that, at best, believes that exterior forms of religion are irrelevant or even counterproductive to the realization of truth. In Indian religious history, the sants have been critical of the Hindu pantheon, caste systems and most forms of religious hierarchy including yogis and Brahmins and have condemned asceticism as having no impact on realization.

I have defined Prem Rawat as a 'solitary Sant' as a way of drawing together Gold's 'solitary figure' and Vaudeville's understanding of a 'holy man' outside of the usual parameters of Indian religious and social life and have called this particular twentieth-century manifestation of the sant phenomena 'the de-traditionalized "religion" of Prem Rawat' (2009). In my understanding, a sant is someone who has realized the ultimate truth within creation, with particular reference to the presence of the divine within the human being and therefore experiences a higher reality in daily life and as such are more often found in opposition to the variety of Hindu worldviews.

Various Eastern-origin movements that formed in the West would challenge Leary's perception of a '"soft, sweet, custard mush" of unity', as they would to varying degrees rival each other's worldview. They would often perceive each other through the lens of Hindu-origin sampradaya (sect) construction, modified in each case by the individual vision of the respective teacher and Western adaptations. ISKCON devotees would criticize Prem Rawat's premies for their dismissal of Hindu avatars as objects of contemporary veneration, and premies would consider the ritual temple worship of the Krishna devotees pointless. Yet each would emphasize experience as primary in the quest for the divine, even though their respective attitudes towards the ritual and mythic dimensions of religion would vary. In the teachings promoted by DLM, the authority of the master was paramount and the 'solitary sant' typology was regarded as divinity. Juergensmeyer states that the sant considers all religious authority as invalid with only one exception, that is, that of the 'devoted follower of the Lord, whose own achievements in spiritual matters enable him or her to serve as a model for others' (1991: 23). Gold points out that in sant discourse the 'holy man' of the sant tradition is considered to outshine even the major gods of the Hindu pantheon (1987: 86). In sant terminology, this type of teacher is given the title 'satguru' (the true guru) and has extraordinary transformative powers, primarily expressed as the ability to qualify his devotees for knowledge of the formless divine (ibid.). The guru in India is generally regarded as more accessible and trustworthy even than the gods (1987: 175) but can lead to the conviction among sants that the satguru is the highest incarnate being. This intense *gurubhakti* had resulted in many in India regarding Prem Rawat as an avatar of Krishna or Ram. These views were prevalent among the mahatmas and the family members of Prem Rawat and were inculcated by the early premies, especially those who visited India to meet the guru there, but there were very early signs that Prem Rawat wanted to focus on the experience on offer rather than Indian hagiographical and mythological interpretations of guruship.

Figure 13 Prem Rawat with American followers, 1971. Copyright RKV Delhi.

After his appearance at Glastonbury Fayre and his subsequent visit to the United States, Prem Rawat's fame would spread through the counterculture like wildfire. Michael Finch disputes the figures but agrees that the growth was phenomenal. He notes that the small handful of followers who had sat 'around Maharaji's feet only two or so years earlier [1971] had mushroomed into a multi-million dollar enterprise, with perhaps 100,000 premies in 480 centers in over 30 Western countries' (2009: 110). The word would spread through the same networks or clusters of counterculture that also told each other about the latest batch of LSD. Helen recounts how she lived in Boulder and attended Swami Satchitananda's Integral Yoga Institute. One day she stopped by there and she noted that about twenty people who had previously lived there had disappeared. She recounts that almost 'everybody had gone to follow Guru Maharaj Ji' (Downton, 1979: 38).

On her journey to Prem Rawat, she also consults the *I-Ching* and *Be Here Now* by Baba Ram Dass for advice on accepting a guru, attends meetings of Rinpoche Trungpa, reading his books *Meditation in Action* and *Born in Tibet*, and practiced Johrei, the channelling of divine light taught by the Japanese movement, the Church of World Messianity (pp. 38–43). Shortly after this, she would meet 'Sam and Julie who are both deeply into meditation' (p. 42). Julie's language is surprisingly Christian. She speaks of Prem Rawat as the 'same spirit as the Christ' (p. 43). This blending of Eastern and Christian language requires investigation. We have already mentioned Paul Schnabel's claim that the divinity of the guru is a standard element of Eastern religion, but when removed from its cultural context, and combined with the 'Western understanding of God as a father', what the difference between the guru's person and that which the guru symbolizes is lost and can result in a limitless personality worship (1982: 142). When Schnabel's observation is combined with Stewart's understanding that receiving cultures first accommodate terms and concepts from another tradition and appropriate them (2003: 586–8), a more complex picture emerges than Downton's view that Eastern understandings of God replaced Judeo-Christian ones.

David Smith points out that there is no 'thorough academic study of the Hindu aspect of what is often called the guru phenomenon' (2003: 168), and he goes on to list a number of characteristics, shared by some but not all gurus:

1. The guru requires submission from the disciple, whose limited powers of reason might inhibit understanding of superior truth.
2. A standard procedure in guru/disciple relationships is a process of initiation (*diksha*) in which a disciple is given a secret Sanskrit phrase (*mantra*) for either internal remembrance or external chanting.
3. A guru may either assert his authority by simply convincing people through his charisma or alternatively lay claim to authenticity through a recognized lineage.
4. Gurus are commonly held to have special powers, at least the ability to read their disciples' thoughts or possibly healing powers.
5. Gurus are often renunciates belonging to one of Hinduism's principal renunciate orders.
6. Gurus may claim to be an *avatar* of a deity, the supreme being or an *avatar* of a previous guru or at least the direct and immediate representative of God (167–73).

Smith's characteristics are useful to describe the treatment of gurus in many Hindu movements but Daniel Gold's in-depth study of the sant tradition focused on the sophisticated theology that has developed around the sant master and his/her relationship with the divine is more useful. He states, 'North Indian devotion, then, presents holy men and singular personalities as substantial beings who manifest channels of grace in the world' (1987: 25). The devotee gains access to such channels. Gold continues his analysis by arguing that the antinomian outlook of the 'solitary sant' leaves devotees only with the option to find the source of the divine in the holy man alone (p. 31). He says, 'The disciple, moreover, could also recognize hidden links to the guru, knowing the guru as a being who manifested within him – a being finally one with the Formless Lord. The Sant could then stand as a channel of grace independent of both Hindu and Islamic heritages' (p. 31). In sant traditions, a focus develops on purifying, controlling or negating the 'mind stuff' through a yogic outlook towards spiritual life but it is combined with an intense devotion to the sant master that does not depend on a system of ritual (ibid.).

Sant synergy with 1960s counterculture

Prior to the 1960s, some countercultural elements would have been familiar with the poetry of some Sufi mystics who had expressed something of the sant's iconoclasm and numinous sense of immanence as opposed to Islam's outer ritual forms. Others would have come into contact with the revival of Sant Mat found in Radhasoami groups. George Harrison would introduce the music and lifestyles of the Bauls of Bengal in 1971 to counterculture audiences attending his concert in aid of Bangladesh. It is not clear to what degree Western counterculture individuals at the time were aware of the synergy that existed between their own relationship with prevailing social order and that of the sants, but it is likely that they would have been attracted to the Prem Rawat's brand of 'religion of no-religion' (Kripal, 2007a) or as I have described it 'traditionless tradition' (2009: 25), without realizing its roots in Indian spirituality. It could be posited in Prem Rawat's case that the initial acceptance of Western counterculture travellers to the East arose from the sant propensity to accept the downtrodden and alienated within society and this was responded to by encounters with the guru by counterculture individuals as he toured Britain and North America. All this has to be placed within the context of the spiritual move eastwards within counterculture and the move towards the globalization of Eastern traditions that began with Vivekananda.

Prem Rawat's personal charisma owed itself to a combination of factors. His young age, his ability to speak spontaneously drawing upon real-life experiences, anecdotes and his own experience, rather than scriptural interpretation, and the intense devotion of his following based upon their own inner experiences combined with an already developing hagiography led to the conviction of an individual master, uncluttered by tradition or acknowledgement of any outer authority. It is the emphasis on experience over faith that marks out Prem Rawat's message. As he says in an interview in 1996, 'The proof is in itself. You feel, you experience, you enjoy. That is the proof' (p. 14). I have described this emphasis on experience as 'charisma relating to the experiential dimension' (Geaves, 2005a). Prem Rawat and his father before him were known in India for their emphasis on experiential knowledge and its transformative qualities and the lives of counterculture individuals who accepted him as their teacher were, in many cases, undoubtedly transformed.

It is this emphasis on seeking the primacy of the present moment as the only opportunity to grasp the reality of the divine within that would possess appeal to the counterculture's desire for immediacy and tapping the limits of experience. Yet they are different. Spontaneity can often be an act of desire fulfilment in the immediate now, whereas Prem Rawat would be more inclined to advise caution in pursuing the mind's desires. Checks would be placed on the hedonism of the counterculture. In addition, Prem Rawat's teaching emphasized an 'embodied theology', one in which the divine was literally enveloped within and throughout the living human being, rather than found in churches, temples or sacred texts and places. The source to discover this divinity was the 'here and now' rather than in an afterlife. An analysis of the primary encounters between counterculture individuals who became students of Prem Rawat reveals little emphasis on the discursive. It has already been shown that the meeting that took place in Glastonbury Fayre was not perceived in terms of understanding but feeling. It is this dichotomy of feeling and understanding, heart and mind, that would baffle Stephen Kent and lead him to describe the message as 'banal' (2001: xvi) but Andrew Tweedie, who photographed the Fayre, when asked if he had 'a Glastonbury experience' answered, 'Yes, but I don't know what it was' (Midsummer Magic, 1996: 20). David Lovejoy comments on the young Prem Rawat's stillness. He describes his first encounter, 'I only recall the stillness emanating from the form of Maharaji himself. I can't say I noticed his physical being very much. All the energy and activity in that place seemed to depend upon him, started and finished with him, while he never moved at all, wrapped in this profound stillness' (2005: 71–3). Peter Lee also comments on his stillness (1996: 19). The *Divine Times Special Edition* contains a number of accounts of first encounters with Prem Rawat that comment on his presence of being, his brightness and a powerful presence. The language to describe the moment is affective. Richard Profumo, an early American student, declared that 'this young man knew and spoke from a place of experience. He came from the heart and he spoke to the heart' (1996: 15). Transformation could take place after these encounters with Prem Rawat. Access to the young guru was relatively easy in these early years but most counterculture individuals would access the message first through the grapevine. Many would be impressed by the transformations that they would see manifested in the lives of close associates. Rennie Davis would describe how he encountered many leftist veterans in DLM, and it was their presence in the movement which persuaded him to explore the guru's message (Kent, 2001: 49–50).

Occulture and Easternization

If Eaton's work warns us to take note of particular religious and explanatory discourses, Tony Stewart's (2003) work reveals how a receiving culture first accommodates terms and concepts from another tradition and appropriates them (pp. 586–8). He argues that this is not evidence of syncretism or identity construction but rather different conceptual worlds meeting each other. Stewart's critique of syncretism is vital to understanding how the counterculture embraced the East and highly pertinent to the tensions that would create and ultimately destroy DLM. For example, Rennie Davis, as a former radical peace activist, had worked frustratingly in many organizations. Michael Rossman would describe this as 'despair' caused by 'their outer impotence, their inner conflicts and ego games and wasted energies' (1979: 22). He would describe Davis as seeking the same ends by different means and this would lead Davis to herald DLM as a 'perfect organization' where the 'ideals of peace and justice' could be achieved not by 'struggle and conflict' but by its 'perfect working' (Kent, 2001: 49). It is highly unlikely that Prem Rawat saw it that way or even considered DLM as the appropriate vehicle for his message. Nor was the practice of Knowledge a means to a leftist utopia.

Stewart's understanding of 'different conceptual worlds' needs to be borne in mind when assessing the thesis that posits occulture as a continuing stream of development from the late nineteenth century through to the present day and providing an ever-shifting bricolage of Eastern ideas and practices within Western esotericism. This is certainly true when assessing the counterculture of the early 1970s. Earlier movements that arrived from the East, for example, Radhasoami, and the Sufi Order of the West attracted a Western upper-middle-class membership, some of whom had travelled in the East or had been influenced by theosophical ideas or were interested in spiritualism. Arguably, both these movements offered a more authentic contact with Eastern spirituality than the East-West occulture manifested in theosophy but they also permitted a fusion of Indian spirituality and Western esotericism. In Roszak's view, an eroticized tantra had replaced an ascetic Vedanta. He writes about late-twentieth-century counterculture as being a new departure from earlier manifestations. In somewhat eloquent terms, he describes the difference:

> One always has the feeling in looking through its literature that its following was found among the very old or very withered, for whom the ideal swami was a kindly orientalised version of an Irish Jesuit priest in charge of a pleasant retreat … But the mysteries of the Orient that we have now have broken entirely from this earlier Christianized version. (1969: 135–6)

Certainly, it would appear that these older-generation followers of earlier arrivals from the East found countercultural interest in their movements problematic. This conflict between two generations is described by Aziz Deukasis, a teacher in the Sufi Order of the West.

> There were two types of murids – the dopeheads who were getting high and singing Allah and the old people who had met Murshid (the title given to Hazrat Inayat Khan) and they were very different. The old ones were establishment with money. The old people were really insulted by the long hair, the dirt and the barefootedness of the hippies. (Geaves, 2000: 76)

In view of these apparent differences between the generations, it would be useful to examine the spectrum of previous beliefs, both from Eastern influences and Western esotericism, that had developed among counterculture individuals that would discover Prem Rawat.

A number of narratives of transformation describe the literature being read leading up to meeting Prem Rawat. David Lovejoy states that 'naturally I was devouring books related to religion and cosmic consciousness, from William James to Gurdjieff and from Huxley's *Perrenial Philosophy* to the *Upanishads*' (2005: 47–8). He also mentions Timothy Leary's and Richard Alpert's edition of the *Tibetan Book of the Dead*, although this seems to have been more utilized as a guidebook to developing mystical states through LSD usage (ibid.). Mike Finch was first influenced by the books of Yogi Ramacharaka, who he believed to be an 'Indian Yogi' but in reality was an early-century American theosophist. He would go on to explore Paul Brunton and then quickly moved on to attempt to live a spiritual life in an Anglican Benedictine monastery and later a Thai Theravada Buddhist temple (2009: 15–17). Downton's study of DLM in the early 1970s provides a number of such narratives. Literature emerges as one route towards countercultural spirituality and transformation, with mentions of *Siddhartha*, *The Aquarian Gospel*, *The Tibetan Book of the Dead*, *Be Here Now*, Ouspensky's *In*

Search of the Miraculous and the writings of Carl Jung. My interviews with early students of Prem Rawat reveal that they were reading not only the *Bhagavad Gita* and the *Upanishads* but also the works of medieval Christian mysticism, notably *The Imitation of Christ* by Thomas à Kempis (1380–1471).

Downton considers that 'religious books played a surprisingly strong role in the spiritual awakening of these premies, as nearly all of them had become acquainted with spiritual literature through their friends and relatives' (1979: 119). Others had spent time in a variety of Eastern spiritual movements including TM, the Integral Yoga Institute, practising Hatha Yoga or trying by themselves to meditate. The revealing factor about such accounts is that it becomes clear that Eastern spirituality was the dominant influence with little reference to Western esotericism, but it is apparent that the writings of the earlier generation were influential. Christian teachings are not dismissed completely even though most are negative towards Christian institutions. When this literature is surveyed, it reveals a strong interest in mysticism rather than esotericism, and the interest in Huxley shows a strong tendency towards perennialism, the idea of a common mystical experience underlying all of the world's major religious systems. Although these books do play a role, there were more important factors at play in forming counterculture spirituality.

Immediacy and high culture

Downton's study of Prem Rawat's students in the early 1970s revealed the impact of psychedelic drug use in the formation of their spirituality. Downton provides a comparison with ISKCON devotees who show slightly less use of psychedelics and among those who have used the drugs, less reported religious experiences as a result of their drug use. Downton concludes that ISKCON followers were more likely to have been influenced by social factors in their life histories but goes on to say that with regard to Prem Rawat's counterculture followers, 'there is little doubt that psychedelics were an aid in the spiritual awakening of these premies, for they changed their religious outlook, replacing their Judeo-Christian conception of a personal God with an organic view of God as energy'. Typical of comments made concerning psychedelic spiritual experience were the following: 'I guess drugs started me on a search for unity'; 'Ok, God I know that I have to be one with you'; 'when I tripped my heart just opened up'; 'you really have this sense of a higher order of existence'; 'we are all one' (1979: 102–13).

One possible reason for the spiritual experiences might have been that LSD was being taken as a 'sacrament'. Individuals who had read Leary, for example, were trying to create an environment in which the potential of psychedelics was harnessed to induce such experiences. David Lovejoy describes such occasions. 'We would start with Indian sitar music and sit meditatively in a room provided with some interesting and beautiful objects until the effects became too strong. Then we would adjourn to the garden and study flowers, cracks in the wall, and sky' (2005: 341). Downton sees these processes as more compatible with Eastern spirituality than Judeo-Christian worldviews and suggests that their experiences 'acquainted them with a view of God which was quite compatible with Eastern spiritualism. They came to see God as the force holding the universe together and animating all living things' (1979: 111).

The dramatic success of Prem Rawat may be attributed to other sources in which the large-scale use of psychedelics played a vital part. Robert Masters and Jean Houston would appear to confirm that approaches to psychedelic usage as described by Lovejoy would reap spiritual rewards. They state that 'in a setting providing religious stimuli, from seventy-five to ninety percent [of psychedelic subjects] report experiences of a religious or even mystical nature' (1966: 255). This is confirmed by Jane Dunlap who wrote of the 'sudden partial lifting of the veil between what we usually call consciousness and a mental state in which such great unity and completeness is felt' (1961: 8–9). It would seem from an analysis of Downton's cohort that their reading and their LSD experiences were shaping an awareness of perennial philosophy drawn more from the mystical traditions of the world's religions than Western esotericism. Partridge identifies this process succinctly when he states, 'A number of influential thinkers within the modern history of psychedelic mysticism have argued that a perennial philosophy can be established on the basis of pure experience, unmediated by conceptual frameworks' (2018: 18).

The intense use of psychedelics among counterculture individuals on both sides of the Atlantic may have predisposed them to 'psychedelic immediatism' that is 'spontaneous, direct unmediated spiritual insight into reality (typically with little or no prior training) … a "pathless path" to religious enlightenment' (Versluis, 2014: 2). In such instances, direct spiritual awakening or enlightenment appears to be possible immediately. Versluis states that the 'immediatist says "away with all ritual and practices"' (ibid.). If this proposition is accurate, the impact of Knowledge and the usage of the sant message that cuts away or critiques both traditional and orthodox paths of religion by Prem Rawat may well have echoed 'psychedelic immediacy' in the counterculture milieu. DLM's promotional literature would also appear to announce 'direct, unmediated insight'. For example, the poster announcing the guru's appearance at Oakland City Auditorium on 9 September 1972 would proclaim, 'Imagine what is peace/ come and realize the practical experience' (Kent, 2001: 49).

Partridge has pointed out that the immediatist position or, for that matter, perennial wisdom is not concerned with the means by which mystical states are arrived at but rather the universal and spontaneous nature of the experience (2018: 18). This was not Prem Rawat's position on the matter. Charnanand would cite drug use as an unlicensed 'back-door entry' to the divine within, citing Ramakrishna's words in Calcutta.[2] Prem Rawat rarely addressed the issue of alternative methods, whether drugs or religious paths, but he did assert the unique nature of the Knowledge experience as incomparable but not necessarily incompatible with the practice of religion. He would usually urge interested seekers to make their own judgements after experiencing what was on offer. In that respect, he may not have been as judgemental as other Eastern teachers. We have seen that a number of gurus were uneasy with hippie drug culture including Meher Baba and Prabupada. In 1972, Prem Rawat answered a direct question concerning why he did not advocate drug use. On being asked the question, 'Why do you want us to leave these drugs?' he replied, 'You used to take drugs, and you say that apparently these drugs brought you to a point. But then you took Knowledge and that was beyond them. So now leave the drugs and proceed purely, proceed naturally' (Downton, 1979: 119). Instant enlightenment did not appear to be an element of the guru's teachings as he advocated a rigorous daily regime of practising withdrawing inwards, combined with service (*saiva*) and participating in *satsang* (lit. company of truth), usually taken to mean regular attendance at gatherings of premies.

Messianism, occulture and new age

The title of Gold's book *The Lord as Guru* could equally have been the 'Guru as Lord', and it is not surprising to find early Western initiates making comparison with the life of Christ. David Lovejoy describes some early students in India asking Prem Rawat if he was Christ (2005: 75–6). It has to be recognized that any answer would carry with it the sant understanding of Jesus as a master similar to the 'solitary figure' described by Gold rather than orthodox Christian interpretations of Christ's role in the Trinity. In other words, it is Stewart's assertion that appropriation is about different cultural worlds rather than syncretism that is at play here in the above encounters between countercultural individuals and Prem Rawat.

A closer look at developments in the early 1970s would find much of the above becoming problematic in the Western environment. We have already seen that early British and American followers persuaded Prem Rawat to attend Glastonbury to fulfil prophesies concerning the advent of the New Age and that rumours of an avatar visiting the Fayre were prevalent in the counterculture grapevine. This tendency would reach its apex two years later at the aptly named Millennium '73 Festival at the Houston Astrodome in Texas.

New Age expectations abounded in the counterculture. Michael Finch recalls, 'I did take the Golden Age seriously' (2009: 111). Tina, one of Downton's informants, describes taking LSD with friends as she had heard that the Aquarian Age had begun that night. She says, 'We wanted to see what would happen. That night I realized that my only reason I was alive was to realize God' (1979: 112). Michael Finch described the festival in Houston as 'the event that would usher in the New Age, a thousand years of peace, and the recognition by this jaded world that the Lord, Guru Maharaj Ji, was indeed here' (2009: 119). Rennie Davis would declare from the stage constructed in the Astrodome, 'If America wants to know what is happening it must first understand the main thing that is happening, the Lord is on the planet, he is in a human body and he's about to usher in the greatest change in the history of human civilization' (Downton, 1979: 121). The author does not remember being overtly millennial but when on the Pyramid Stage at Glastonbury, dreams of an 'Albion' replacing the British social and cultural 'straight' world were foremost in my mind.

It would appear from this millennial language that any sense of Prem Rawat's 'solitary sant' origins had been lost by these counterculture students. The sants were not promoters of a futuristic utopia or an afterlife of bliss in paradise, but rather they focused on the possibility of fulfilment in the present. Prem Rawat would sometimes refer to the Hindu concepts of *kal yuga* (Age of Darkness) and its antithesis *sat yuga* (Age of Truth), but these have much longer durations of time than the astrological ages used in New Age discourse. Generally, he would also focus on this life as the opportunity for realization. Downton remarks that ideas were developing among premies who considered 'Guru Maharaj Ji to be so spiritually perfect and powerful that he could do no wrong and that no obstacle was big enough to stop him from reaching his goal of ushering a new age of peace' (p. 178). To what degree Prem Rawat actually saw his goal as ushering in this 'new age' is debatable but Western counterculture individuals who came to the guru in 1971 seemed to differ from their Indian counterparts over their motivations for renunciation. Downton reports one person as saying, 'When I received Knowledge in 1971, the general feeling was that soon the whole world would have peace, so to hold anything, like money, job, education, or family, was a sign of a weak level of devotion' (p. 189). These ideas seemed to have reached their apex in November 1973 and there is no doubt that the festival was seen among American counterculture followers as the fulfilment of their dreams of social change. This would result in considerable speculation and prophesies concerning what would take place in the Astrodome.

Michael Finch describes the speculation as focusing around the belief that there would be 'visitations from extraterrestrial believers' (2009: 120).There were wild rumours abounding that Prem Rawat would use the Astrodome itself as a kind of spacecraft which, similar to Noah's Ark, would save the chosen remnant (ibid.). Sophie Collier, who was involved in the lead-up to the festival, describes an interview with a reporter from *Village Voice* who she could not divert from the interest in visiting aliens. The article would include the following paragraph: 'Balbhagwan Ji (Prem Rawat's eldest brother) said that a lot of strange things are going to happen in Houston. All of those UFOs that people've been seeing are around the Gulf Coast waiting for the Millennium.' The aliens are described as 12 feet tall and having round gleaming eyes (1978: 177). The article is accurate on one point. The source of the speculation did appear to be Prem Rawat's older brother. Collier describes the speculation as 'Millennium fever' and labels the Guru's brother as the 'fever's carrier'. She writes, 'Between the present time and the time of the festival, according to BB's [Bal Bhagwan Ji] predictions, there would be a series of major disasters, natural and political (including the collapse of Wall Street on November 18th). To augment this would also be a series of extraterrestrial phenomena. All of these things would lead people to seek the return of the messiah' (p. 157).

Sophie Collier's view of the festival's name is more mundane. She replies to one person's claim that after the festival no one will worry about anything because 'after the festival is the New Age'. Her answer is to assert that 'when we decided to call the festival "Millenium" I thought it was because our vision of one peaceful world based on spiritual values was evoked by the word, "Millenium" – not because the hoped-for Millenium will begin on November 8th' (p. 152).

It is unlikely that Prem Rawat would have shared his brother's views or understood the cultural baggage that arrived with the label 'Millenium'. For him, it would have been one more event in a very busy tour schedule – one that was much more ambitious in scope than anything undertaken so far. The event would leave the mission $600,000 dollars in debt but more significantly it would create a sea change in Prem Rawat's relationship with the counterculture and its attempts to forge a new world order. Although Thorne Dreyer would write that the 'Maharaj Ji has fused the New Left and the flower children' (1974), Downton felt that the festival left 'ruined dreams [that] were hidden under their exuberance' (1979: 189). These 'ruined dreams', however, were more to do with the counterculture's expectations of a New Age.

The accounts of the American followers' religious milieu at the time and the expectations created around Millennium '73 reveal the existence of *senso stricto* depictions of New Age among countercultural followers from both the political and flower spectrum, fitting precisely to Hanegraaff's definition of an 'esotericism based upon the 1950s interest in UFOs and apocalyptic expectations' (2001). Sutcliffe expanded this understanding drawing upon emic understandings of a millennialistic transformation on a global scale in which a spiritual awakening would take place following the collapse of the capitalist, militaristic and material exploitation of the world (2014: 41). But New Age, *senso lato*, that is, a broad cluster of esoteric activities that include channelling, healing, spiritual growth and neo-paganism (Chryssides, 2012: 247), was also evident in the milieu that would flock to Prem Rawat in the early 1970s.

The parting of the way with counterculture

The explanation for the millennialism may lie in the myths of Christianity being closer to the surface in the American psyche than the much more secularized North Europeans. Whatever the reason, the relative failure of the Astrodome event to match expectations of attendance, leaving the mission in considerable debt, was seen by academics as one of the principal reasons for the decline of the movement. In addition, the failure to fulfil prophesies created disillusionment in some North American followers. After Millennium '73, Prem Rawat would radically transform and overhaul the vehicles used for the transmission of the message, picking up momentum during the decades following his arrival in the West in 1971, while simultaneously striving to maintain the central message that peace is possible. He would move the emphasis away from global peace to individual fulfilment arguably consolidating his empathy with the 'good news' central to sant discourse (Geaves, 2004a: 45–62). He would begin a process of rooting out the more obviously Eastern beliefs and practices that were culturally embedded in a message that had originated in India, although it should be noted that the global vision of peace was not an Indian export but rooted in

Figure 14 'Soul Rush' processions to announce Millennium '73. Copyright RKV Delhi.

countercultural expectations. In the 1980s, he would also begin to critique the 'New Age' beliefs of his followers. Both sets of meaning constructions would be combined together as 'concepts', a term taken to include all constructions of reality that would include religions.

Prem Rawat's attempts to transform the organizational structures and to eradicate the more overtly Indian cultural and religious aspects of his teachings set up the possibility of a conflict between his efforts to balance his own commitment to the ideal of a fluid organization and his desire to continue teaching globally. Especially after his experience of religious-building during the DLM stage, Prem Rawat would seek out organizational forms that would work to deal with changing circumstances, often experimenting and dissolving structures that were put in place. Price would argue that DLM transformed itself into a 'sect' marked by a degree of 'epistemological authoritarianism' throughout the early 1970s, although she acknowledged that this was never total and, in reality, a high degree of 'epistemological individualism' existed (1979: 247). However, in spite of this 'epistemological individualism', many followers had begun to take on a very strong exclusivist claim to salvation, combining an epistemology developed from certain devotional forms of Hinduism which contained ideals of monasticism, celibacy and vegetarianism and a range of Hindu-based customs and Christian expectations of a return of Christ at the end time. Together, these would create a powerful emotive epistemology of incarnation in regard to Prem Rawat. Hindu classical *avatar* (incarnational descent) doctrines with the common attribution of divinity to the guru and strong millennial hopes arising out of a countercultural wish for an end to 'straight society' would merge with Christian hopes of a messiah figure that had little to do with Indian traditions. All these developing practices and beliefs arising out of Hindu worldviews were encouraged by the senior members of Maharaji's family, especially his mother and eldest brother, and the visiting Indian mahatmas, who had taken on the leadership of the mission during Prem Rawat's childhood and had been endowed with varying degrees of divinity and holiness by followers. It is difficult to ascertain the degree to which they encouraged the occultural elements creeping in from the counterculture, and it is also difficult to ascertain Prem Rawat's feelings towards the powerful religious movement developing around him except that it is possible to surmise that he had a degree of ambiguity concerning what was unfolding in his name. Now reaching adulthood, he was beginning to assert his own vision to the consternation of some family members and the Indian mahatmas.

Three key events between 1973 and 1975 hastened the demise of DLM and the beginning of the deconstruction of the Indian heritage that had accompanied Maharaji from India. The three significant events were the impact of the event in the Houston Astrodome in November 1973, the marriage of Prem Rawat to an American follower named Marolyn Johnson in 1974 and the subsequent departure of Prem Rawat's mother and two eldest brothers for India from where they announced that Prem Rawat had been 'corrupted' by his stay in the West and that the eldest brother was taking over as the new satguru and leader of DLM. However, the reality of the apparent decline was more to do with a period of rebuilding that was required as the young adult Prem Rawat took on the actual leadership after the departure of his mother and brothers. For several years, there was a liminal period in which he experimented with organizational forms, closed down the ashrams, removed the Indian accretions and set up new channels to communicate his vision to remaining followers (Geaves, 2006b).

So soon after the original counterculture success that began at Glastonbury, Prem Rawat would begin to dismantle the cluster of beliefs and practices that made DLM an Indian movement. In addition, he would distance himself from the counterculture and its millennial hopes and the attempt to link him with countercultural syntheses of Eastern beliefs and Western esotericism. Throughout the 1980s and 1990s, new directions were to weaken counterculture identification with the guru, although the considerable following that had developed in the West during the 1970s remained alongside him as staunch supporters of his work. Their definitive worldview that included both the hope of inner transformation and outer revolution, combined with Eastern philosophy and Western esotericism, would be diffused into a watered-down New Age set of beliefs and practices, mainly confined to holistic or alternative medicine. The need to discover other resources to counteract the psychic damage done to individuals as a result of drug use and excessive hedonism was over as premies raised families and moved into middle age. New forms of counterculture would remain focused on Glastonbury and Stonehenge as sites of sacredness throughout the 1980s but would rarely discover Prem Rawat or be aware of his impact on their predecessors.

1971 to 1973 marks the peaking of the counterculture's involvement with Prem Rawat, an encounter that flourished between Glastonbury Fayre and Millennium '73. To Andrew Kerr and the small group of hippies who worked with him, Glastonbury Fayre was to be the renewal of the countercultural dream that had appeared to have gone sour through commercialization. With hindsight, it is apparent the Fayre was the beginning of the end for the mass manifestation of counterculture that marked the late 1960s. Certainly, as far as the United States was concerned, many counterculture individuals found a way of continuing the dream by transporting both their *senso lato* and *senso stricto* understandings of New Age into a NRM built around the message of a 'solitary sant'. Yet they were not to know that there was an innate contradiction in building a perfect organization around such an individual. The dream was to effectively die at Millennium '73, more or less ending Prem Rawat's encounter with Western counterculture which would go its own way creating diverse manifestations in the decades that followed the 1970s. In these new manifestations, the earlier flirtation with Eastern mysticism would continue only as a weak undercurrent among the bricolage of beliefs and practices that would flourish in the final decades of the century and into the twenty-first.

Prem Rawat would catch a *zeitgeist* on his arrival in the West. A generation had created the first mass counterculture based around 'high culture' and festival culture but by the beginning of the 1970s many had taken their drug experiences to the limit. Downton argues that before the advent of spiritual movements there were few ways out of counterculture that were deemed acceptable, without appearing to 'sell out' and return to 'straight' society (1979: 118). By the beginning of the 1970s, word was spreading through the counterculture that spirituality, especially Eastern mysticism, could replace the drug experience with a 'natural' or 'permanent high'. Downton described this as 'a mass exodus out of drugs and into mysticism' (p. 118). It is difficult to ascertain to what degree Prem Rawat's message was instrumental in transforming the lives of thousands of countercultural youth or to what degree they had already tired of the negative consequences of the lifestyles they had chosen and were ready to participate in a transformation that provided an escape that was even more meaningful than counterculture life. The reality is probably a combination of both. Either way, Prem Rawat has to be credited with playing a significant role in the eclipse of the counterculture.

I began this book with the question to what degree can Prem Rawat be described as a 'New Age' guru? The degree to which counterculture individuals took with them a 'fairly rigid set of ideas about his divinity and the coming of the new age' (p. 199) and appropriated a 'solitary sant' worldview to their own in the early 1970s would suggest the answer would appear to be affirmative. Yet Downton also notes that Prem Rawat's teachings were marked by an emphasis on giving up or challenging pre-existing religious beliefs and concepts (p. 199). The history of the sant phenomena in North India shows this to be one of the trademarks of the solitary sant's role in Indian spiritual life. Downton also noted that during 1971 social forces encouraged millenarian beliefs within the counterculture. He is right to point out that after 1973 there were two sets of concepts that required challenging: those that arose from earlier countercultural socialization and those they had picked up from within the movement.

Prem Rawat's struggle as the first 'solitary sant' to move out of India would see him challenge the concepts and beliefs introduced from the East in the early 1970s, spurred on by the differences that he had with his family and most of the mahatmas whose religious and cultural worldviews were reinformed by their Hindu upbringing. The two elements identified by Downton, that is countercultural norms and those picked up in DLM, would come under the guru's scrutiny, and in time, so would the Eastern construction of 'guru' come under the 'solitary sant' radar for deconstruction. It is interesting to observe that in Prem Rawat's public discourses of recent decades he has been as critical of the new popular usage of 'spiritual' as he is of conventional religion. His critique of 'spiritual' as a contemporary category of identity marks him out as critical of New Age, perceiving the bricolage of practices and beliefs as just another mindset. Downton makes an important observation that it was only after 1973, when millenarian beliefs declined, that Prem Rawat's counterculture students were 'ready for an assault on their ideology' (p. 200). If Downton is correct, he is confirming that the popular perception of Indian gurus as maintaining an autocratic control over their devotees required an overhaul. It would seem that when the gurus came to the West in the late 1960s, their teachings were just as much appropriated and made to fit into existing countercultural ideas on reality and thus undermined ideas of 'autocratic control'.

In the final analysis, I return to the theoretical considerations that inspired me in part to write the book. I hope that I have demonstrated that Easternization is a complex, multifaceted phenomenon. I remain unhappy with analyses that perceive it as part of the bricolage that makes up New Age in the *senso lato* form, creating what Christopher Partridge names 'occulture'. In a diffused form, not very recognizable to its Hindu or Buddhist origins in the East, it can be appropriated by those drawn towards the esoteric or the occult and reordered in the image of these Western beliefs. The 1960s counterculture further diffused it, far more than those who embraced it through theosophy or other movements in the early twentieth century. Some elements of Easternization would embody cherished and time-held traditions of India or elsewhere, and these would insist upon transforming countercultural beliefs. This was no more apparent than in the teachings of Prem Rawat, who I have categorized as a 'solitary sant', even though he may not agree with the label. He does not see himself as 'Hindu' or 'Buddhist' and refuses most definitions of where he fits in the religious/spiritual spectrum, usually denying that he belongs to either. As the 'solitary sants' defined by Gold (1987) would be equally unhappy with pigeon-holing, it is the closest fit I can find. It would appear to me that that attempt to understand Easternization in the period under investigation would require the type of approach used by naturalists to identify tigers living in their natural habitats. Bruce Kukele uses the technique of photographing a section of the tiger's stripes and reimposes the image over that of another tiger caught by the camera in the same area. Although tiger stripes are similar, just as human fingerprints they are never identical ('Tiger stripes, 9 May 2013'). The reimposed images reveal whether the tiger is the same animal or different. I would advocate that any attempt to understand the similarities of Eastern transplants with each other or their synergy with counterculture spiritualities requires such an approach. I have tried to do this with the case study of Prem Rawat and his encounter with Glastonbury Fayre. It reveals a very complex intermingling of worldviews with various players adding to the construction and deconstruction of beliefs, ultimately leading to the destruction of DLM in the early 1970s. An Indian teacher in the West is influenced by the new environment but does not necessarily commit himself or herself to the worldview of new followers.

Prem Rawat does not associate the practice or experience of Knowledge as religion. Drawing upon Jonathan Z. Smith's (2003) model of religion as *there* (civic or state-sponsored), religion *here* (domestic or customary) and religion *anywhere* (pragmatic or apotropaic), it would be reasonable to agree with the decision to place Knowledge outside of religion, for it is certainly none of these, and Prem Rawat's message is either critical of the above categories or treats them as irrelevant. However, he is no longer happy with spiritual either. His encounter with the counterculture has made more dismissive of the term. Ulrike Popp-Baier prefers the term 'self-controlled religiosity' to the contemporary usage of spiritual. She defines this as where 'people select and combine elements from different belief systems, practices and organizations to meet their own specific needs and practices' (2010: 34). Premies may do this to a large degree, and in the years following Glastonbury, purists went along with their guru and disowned most of such practices. Others held that Knowledge was superior but practised a number of elements from different belief systems to meet specific needs and practices. There is no sign that Prem Rawat ever did so himself. He remained committed to the path of the 'solitary sant' who dismisses all such efforts as a non-negotiable failure to achieve the goal of fulfilment.

Each case study is different. Prem Rawat's 'stripes' are unique and do not match any other Indian guru nor provide a perfect fit to the beliefs of contemporary spiritualities, even though there may be some matches. These apparent 'fits' can confuse but should not lead us as scholars to oversimplified conclusions.

10

Postscript

Both Prem Rawat and the organizers of Glastonbury Festival have striven for almost half a century (1971–2019) to find a format that responds to the time, circumstances and their respective objectives. Prem Rawat remains unchanged in his mission to promote peace encapsulated in his often repeated maxim 'the peace that you are looking for is inside of you'. Glastonbury Festival cannot any longer be described as an exercise in spiritual geometry that would revolutionize Britain as envisaged by the counterculture of the late 1960s. Both have struggled with various organizational identities. In 1990, Glastonbury changed its name to Glastonbury Festival for Contemporary Performing Arts to reflect the range of attractions now on offer (Bailey, 2013: 61). The label of 'Fayre' had been officially given up in 1981 when the new name of Glastonbury Festival was coined by Michael Eavis (p. 24).

Glastonbury Festival

Throughout the 1980s, the festival struggled with how to balance its image as the foremost counterculture event on the summer schedule while distancing itself from, in Eavis's own words in 1978, 'too many hippies and too many drugs'. However, the real problem was the losses incurred by a free festival primarily aimed at the counterculture, now morphed into New Age Travellers moving on to Glastonbury after celebrating the solstice at Stonehenge (p. 17). The solution was to hand the organization of the festival over to CND (Campaign for Nuclear Disarmament), a cause dear to Michael Eavis and an organization with counterculture credibility. Throughout the 1980s, the festival grew in size, with numbers attending increasing from twenty-five thousand in 1982 and to sixty-five thousand by the end of the decade. Donations to CND and local charities would average around £100,000 per annum in the final years of the decade. The festival would begin to attract the top bands of the era to play from the Pyramid Stage. Van Morrison (2), Jackson Browne, Echo and the Bunnymen, Aswad, Style Council, The Boomtown Rats, The Cure, Madness, Simply Red, The Waterboys, The Pogues, Level 42, Elvis Costello, Suzanne Vega and Pixies would appear throughout the decade. Land was purchased adjacent to the farm in order to accommodate the rising numbers and improve facilities ('The History of Glastonbury Festival').

The early 1990s saw continuing trouble with travellers, security issues and complaints from the local councils. Perimeter fences would be added with increasing effectiveness to keep out those who felt that the ideal of the free festival should be maintained. In 1992, Michael Eavis would begin to donate to Greenpeace and Oxfam. He felt that the era of the Cold War had ended and that environmental issues were more urgent than nuclear disarmament ('The History of Glastonbury Festival'). Numbers had risen to seventy thousand and the donations given to the charities reached £250,000. By the end of the decade, over half a million pounds were being donated to the charities and attendance had exceeded one hundred thousand for the first time. The festival was being broadcast on BBC2 and Channel 4 and transmission was global (https://www.glastonburyfestivals.co.uk/history/1995). In 1997, the site was expanded to 800 acres (https://www.glastonburyfestivals.co.uk/history/1997). The music acts over the decade still reflected the counterculture origins of the festival with Velvet Underground, Lenny Kravitz, P. J. Harvey, Massive Attack, Bob Dylan, The Levellers and the Chemical Brothers featuring, but the festival was now the foremost music venue in the world and could also attract the most famous stars of the era, for example, Oasis, Blur, Simple Minds, Portishead, Radiohead, Sting and Robbie Williams (https://www.glastonburyfestivals.co.uk/history).

The first and second decade of the twenty-first century would see the festival consolidate its position as the foremost music festival in the world. TV coverage would take place on every day of the festival. Numbers attending would rise to around 150,000. By 2003, the amount given to Greenpeace, CND, Oxfam, Fairtrade, Wateraid and local charities had risen to one million pounds (https://www.glastonburyfestivals.co.uk/history/history-2003/). The festival would encourage green causes sponsoring the I Count campaign, which highlighted the need to address climate change, and signed up seventy thousand people to the campaign over the weekend (https://www.glastonburyfestivals.co.uk/history/history-2007/). In 2015, for the first time since 1971, the festival was visited by a major spiritual leader. The Dalai Lama arrived at the Green Fields for a morning address to a huge crowd in the King's Meadow, took lunch with the monks in the Greenpeace Field and then made an impromptu appearance on the Pyramid Stage in the afternoon in the middle of Patti Smith's set (https://www. glastonburyfestivals.co.uk/history/2015-2/). The festival's liberal credentials would be further enhanced in 2017 when Jeremy Corbyn would address the audience from the main stage (https://www.glastonburyfestivals.co.uk/ history/2017-2/).

By the second decade of the twenty-first century, the festival's tickets would sell out within twenty-four hours of their release. There would be over thirty areas, one hundred stages, over two thousand artists and performers and the BBC film coverage would go out to over thirty countries (https://www.glastonburyfestivals. co.uk/history/2015-2/). The stars would get bigger but more eclectic. The Rolling Stones would play in 2013 along with other major counterculture figures from the same era. Joan Baez and Leonard Cohen performed in 2008 but the introduction of rap stars, Lionel Ritchie, Shirley Bassey and Neil Diamond, would offend the traditionalists who felt that Glastonbury should remain true to its origins in rock festival culture. The festival would incline towards pop as well as rock, seeking out major stars of several genres, many of them far from counterculture. However, huge amounts of money were generated for green charities, and the visits by the Dalai Lama and Jeremy Corbyn would ensure that the world's most successful music festival would retain at least liberal credibility.

Prem Rawat

Prem Rawat would face the challenge of presenting an ancient wisdom in a contemporary Western setting, facing up to the challenges that were brought to him by the cult controversies among some NRMs in the 1970s, throwing off the Indian guru label that no longer worked in a global context and, as with Glastonbury, moving to a larger playing field than that presented by the counterculture. He had always expressed that he wanted to bring his message of peace within to all human beings, regardless of nationality, gender or religion. We have seen that the worldview of the counterculture presented a barrier as much as Indian spirituality or the Hindu religion. Like the Fayre, he would also change his appellation, moving away from Guru Maharaj Ji to the plainer and less baggage-laden 'Maharaji' to finally settling upon his given name, Prem Rawat. Divine Light Mission (1971–82) was abandoned to be replaced for several years by Elan Vital from 1982 to 2002 (Geaves, 2004a, 2006a, 2006b.

I have argued that in spite of forces such as globalization, Prem Rawat's message as a narrative of transformation appeals because it provides some people with a more appropriate way of existing in the world. Each organization created over the years has been an evolving attempt to produce a closer match between Prem Rawat's vision and this appropriateness in order to produce a more effective resource (Geaves, 2006a, 2006b).

Prem Rawat has never ceased to travel around the world speaking to audiences that range in size from 100 (Hapuna, Hawaii) to 325,000 (Gaya, India). An accomplished pilot, he flies himself, encircling the world at least once a year. His website states that he 'regularly clocks up 100,000 miles and attends two events a week, in an average year' ('About Prem Rawat'). Since his advent to the West in 1971, he prides himself that his events are not advertised and have no ticket price, paid for by voluntary donation. In recent years, he has been asked to speak as a guest at a variety of formal gatherings where dignitaries interested in peace or conflict resolution might gather. Examples include Australia's Parliament House in 2005 and the Italian and Argentine Senates in 2006. In the same year, he was awarded the title 'Ambassador of Peace' by the rector of the International University of Peace (Unipaz) in Brazil (ibid.). Today, his addresses are broadcast on television channels around the world and are available through a wide range of media, both online and offline. As a result, his message is now available in ninety-seven countries and seventy languages.

These invitations stem from his humanitarian work. In 2001, Prem Rawat founded The Prem Rawat Foundation (TPRF), which focuses on the fundamental human needs of food, water and peace so that people can live with dignity, peace and prosperity. The foundation's model food program, Food for People, provides hot nutritious meals for children in poverty-stricken areas, now including Bantoli, India; Tsarpu, Nepal; and Otinibi, Ghana. The TPRF Peace Education Program is an innovative educational program with a curriculum that fosters personal strength and positive life skills. The foundation also provides relief for survivors of natural disasters ('Humanitarian Efforts'). TPRF has relationships with the other humanitarian organizations with a strong presence in the field: Friends of the World Food Program, the Red Cross, the Houston Food Bank, Action Against Hunger and Oxfam, among others. These partnerships have proved to be successful and to date the foundation's relationship with Friends of the World Food Program has enabled them to provide food for one month to 9,000 Indonesian tsunami victims, 2,000 famine victims in Niger, 4,500 school children in Guatemala, 6,000 earthquake victims in Pakistan and thousands of earthquake victims in Peru. Through the Red Cross, the foundation provided food aid to mudslide victims in the Philippines, and through Oxfam, TPRF helped to provide drinking water to war victims in Lebanon and Israel. In partnership with the Houston Food Bank, TPRF provided three meals a day for three months to eight thousand victims of Hurricane Katrina (ibid.).

Perhaps the most successful initiative has been the PEP (Peace Education Programme), consisting of ten sessions, each focusing on a particular theme. These customized, interactive workshops are non-religious and non-sectarian. The content of each theme is based on excerpts from Prem Rawat's international talks. The themes are Peace, Appreciation, Inner Strength, Self-Awareness, Clarity, Understanding, Dignity, Choice, Hope and Contentment. The programme has been particularly successful in prisons and is on offer in nearly five hundred correctional facilities globally (www.tprf.org/programs/peace-education-program).

Prem Rawat's success globally matches that of Glastonbury Festival, although arguably far less known. The charitable causes reflect the humanitarian activities carried out by the festival, albeit Prem Rawat remains primarily committed to the message that he arrived with in 1971. His words that introduce his website show his commitment to the teachings that first drew his attention to the counterculture: 'What I offer people is not just talk, but a way to go inside and savor the peace that is within.' Experience, embodiment and immediacy still prevail and remain central. In this respect, there are parallels with the festival, although both have moved far from their counterculture origins. Prem Rawat's challenge remains the same as in 1971; how to convince a sceptical or disinterested public that his message is relevant to their lives? Glastonbury struggles with balancing its counterculture origins with its present-day standing as the largest commercial rock festival on earth.

Notes

1 Introduction

1 'Guru Maharaj Ji' is used by most devotees of a guru in India. It refers to the respect given to a spiritual master who is considered higher than any temporal authority. David Smith notes that 'he is often addressed as "Maharaj" (Great King)' to indicate this hierarchical ranking in Indian spirituality (2003: 172).

2 Presumably the informant was Ashokanand, an Indian mahatma who had arrived in the country some weeks earlier and was helping to establish Prem Rawat's activities in the UK.

3 Surprisingly, Prem Rawat's various online presences do not mention Glastonbury. Ex-members have focused on the event, tending to trivialize the occasion, for example, see 'Prem Rawat at Glastonbury Festival 1971' at prem-rawat-bio.org/glastonbury.html or 'Glastonbury Fayre 1971'—prem-rawat-bio.org prem-rawat-bio.org/videos/glastonbury_fayre.html. The words of the guru's speech can be found at Words of Love—Glastonbury 1971—Prem Rawat Fan Video www.wordsof.net/peace/fv/?p=204, which appears to be more sympathetic.

4 Nick Lowe opinions of Glastonbury Fayre are very negative and his view of Guru Maharaj Ji is not complimentary. 'He got on, asked the audience for money. Got back in his car and cleared off.' The actual words used by the guru were 'the money of love and devotion' (Nick Lowe, 'The Best of Glastonbury Moments').

5 Considerable academic energy has been given to the insider/outsider debate in the study of religion. Key texts are the collection of essays edited by Russell T. McCutcheon (1998), The *Insider/Outsider Problem in the Study*, and George D. Chryssides and Stephen E. Gregg (2018). An anthropological position can be found at Kate Aston's response to George Chryssides (2012).

6 The Dutch Provo movement of the mid-1960s recognized that boredom and alienation were powerful forces that could be harnessed for social change. The Provos used provocative direct action ('pranks' and 'happenings') to arouse society from political and social indifference. They were well-known for their 'White Plans', particularly 'White Bicycles Plan' that provided 20,000 free-use white bicycles to replace cars in the centre of Amsterdam ('Learners, Dreamers and Dissenters').

7 *Freedom* remains a London-based anarchist production published by Freedom Press, which was formerly a monthly newspaper. The newspaper was the oldest anarchist medium started in 1886 by volunteers including Peter Kropotkin

and continued until 2014 as a regular publication when it transferred its news production online, publishing irregularly until 2016, when it became a biannual. Originally, the subtitle was 'A Journal of Anarchist Socialism'. The title was changed to 'A Journal of Anarchist Communism' in June 1889. Today, it simply labelled 'Anarchist Journal' (Rooum, 2008).

8 Rudi Dutshke (1940–1979) was the foremost leader of German revolutionary movements in the 1960s. He survived an assassination attempt by Josef Bachmann in 1968 but died twelve years later as a result of the injuries. Radical students blamed an anti-student campaign in the papers of the Axel Springer publishing empire for the assassination attempt. This led to attempts to blockade the distribution of Springer newspapers all over Germany. Daniel Marc Cohn-Bendit (1945–), a student leader during the unrest of May 1968 in France, also known during that time as *Dany le Rouge* (Danny the Red), supported Rudi Dutshke. He entered Britain to lead demonstrations against the *Daily Mirror*, which was supporting the Axel Springer newspapers in Germany (https://www.revolvy.com/main/index.php?s=Rudi+Dutschke&item_type=topic).

9 The cult and anti-cult literature would be ignited by the mass deaths in Jonestown on 18 November 1978, when 918 followers of Reverend Jim Jones, founder of the Peoples Temple of the Disciples of Christ, elected to commit suicide by drinking 'Kool-Aid laced with poison' (Lusher, 2018; 'Jonestown Massacre'). From the early 1970s, American parents were becoming concerned about dramatic changes of behaviour in their children on joining what was to become coined as 'New Religious Movements'. The first organized opposition to new religions appeared in 1972 with the formation of FREECOG (Parents Committee to Free Our Sons and Daughters from the Children of God). Eventually, this opposition polarized into the various anti-cult movements mainly driven by ex-members who espoused a 'brain-washing theory to account for member and a number of prominent sociologists who have appeared in multiple court cases arguing that there is no empirical evidence for "brain-washing"'. These include David Bromley, Thomas Robbins, Dick Anthony, Eileen Barker, Newton Maloney, Massimo Introvigne, John Hall, Lorne L. Dawson, Anson D. Shupe, J. Gordon Melton and Marc Galanter (Bromley and Shupe,1981a, 1981b, 1994; Robbins and Zablocki, 2001; Wilson, 1994).

2 Theorizing New Age and contemporary spiritualities

1 R. A. Geaves, (May 30–1 June 2003), 'Globalisation, Charisma, Innovation, and Tradition: An Exploration of the Transformations in the Organizational Vehicles for the Transmission of the Teachings of Maharaji', Alternative Spirituality and New Age Studies, Joint Conference, Association for Alternative Spirituality and New Age

Studies and the 11th Annual Contemporary and New Age Religions Conference, Open University: Milton Keynes, UK.

2 Foremost among such bodies are CESNUR (Center for Studies of New Religions) and INFORM. CESNUR was founded by the Italian sociologist, Massimo Introvigne in 1988 as a neutral think tank to investigate NRMs. CESNUR consists of a number of European and North American scholars who study the field (www.cesnur.org). INFORM was founded by Eileen Barker, a British sociologist, also in 1988 and describes itself as 'an independent charity providing information that is as up-to-date and reliable as possible about what many call cults, sects, New Religious Movements (NRMs), non-conventional religions' (www.inform.ac.uk).

3 The Lobsangrampa.net website proclaims Lobsang Rampa to have been a Buddhist monk and medical doctor, born in Tibet, who settled in Canada near the end of his life and 'experienced life in both the East and the West'. The website proclaims Rampa to have been a revolutionary of his time, one of the first of the Eastern teachers to bring Buddhism and metaphysics to the West in a popular fashion (http://www.lobsangrampa.net/). The identity of Lobsang Rampa is controversial and investigations by several sources including the British media revealed him to be Cyril Henry Hoskin, a native of Plympton, Devonshire, the son of the village plumber and a high school dropout. Hoskin had never been to Tibet. When confronted with these allegations, he did not deny that he had been born as Cyril Hoskin but claimed that his body was now occupied by the spirit of Lobsang Rampa. Whatever the truth of Rampa's identity, his book *The Third Eye* published in 1956 by Secker & Warburg remains one of the most popular works claiming to represent life in Tibet. It is the book's focus on the occult that raised suspicions (Dodin and Rather, 2001: 196–200; Lopez, 1996; Tibballs, 2006: 27–9). Lopez (1999) assesses the influence of *The Third Eye* on the Western interest in Buddhism.

4 Written by Levi H. Dowling in 1908, *The Aquarian Gospel of Jesus the Christ: The Philosophic and Practical Basis of the Religion of the Aquarian Age of the World and of the Church Universal* was adopted by New Age groups. Dowling claims to have accessed the text of the book from the Akashic records. The contents describe the eighteen years of Jesus's life missing in the Bible (ages 12–30). Like Nicolas Notovitch did before in his *The Unknown Life of Jesus Christ: By the Discoverer of the Manuscript* (1887), the *Aquarian Gospel* describes these missing years as a time when Jesus travels in India, Tibet, Persia, Assyria, Greece and Egypt. He demonstrates that he is 'God's chosen one' and eventually returns to Galilee and Judaea with the wisdom he has developed in the East. There are a number of attractions of the book for New Age spirituality. Time is separated into astrological ages which last approximately two thousand years. The information on Jesus's life was revealed because humanity is entering the Aquarian Age. Jesus is depicted as human who achieves a 'Christ' nature, more akin to the Buddha's enlightenment.

Reincarnation and karma are promoted rather than eternal reward and
punishment. Humanity has forgotten God and is currently working its way back.
All souls will evolve to perfection (Goodspeed, 1956; Pement, 1988; Watson, 2009).

5 In particular, Jack Kerouac's *On the Road* published in 1957 and *The Dharma Bums*
in 1958. In a contemporary review, Nancy Wilson Ross (1958) writes that *On the
Road* was 'a chronicle of the hitch-hikers, hipsters, jazz fans, jalopy owners, drug
addicts, poets and perverts of the Beat Generation' but *Dharma Bums* shows the
same strata of dropouts 'trying to learn to meditate in Buddhist style, their new
goal nothing less than total self-enlightenment, the *satori* of the Zen masters of
Japan and China'.

6 Alan Watts was a British Buddhist and philosopher who became known for
interpreting Eastern religions to a Western audience. Watts studied Zen in
New York and moved to California in 1950 where he joined the Faculty of the
American Academy of Asian Studies in San Francisco. Watts (1961) popularized
the counterculture viewpoint that Buddhism is not a religion, presenting it instead
as a form of psychotherapy. He wrote more than twenty-five books and articles
on Eastern and Western religion but his most influential work was *The Way of
Zen* published in 1957, which was instrumental in introducing Buddhism to
the counterculture youth movement in the United States. It remains one of the
bestselling books on Buddhism (Snelling and Watts, 1990).

7 D. T. Suzuki was arguably the most influential scholar able to translate Zen
Buddhism to a Western readership. Suzuki spent several lengthy stretches teaching
or lecturing at Western universities in addition to being a Zen practitioner. As a
university-educated intellectual familiar with Western philosophy and literature,
Suzuki was successful in captivating a Western audience. But his work carries a
warning note. A member of the Theosophical Society, Suzuki created the popular
image that 'Zen refers not to a specific school of Buddhism but rather to a mystical
or spiritual gnosis that transcends sectarian boundaries' (Sharf, 1995). Sharf
argues that 'Zen apologists have been forced to respond to secular and empiricist
critiques of religion in general, and to Japanese nativist critiques of Buddhism as
a "foreign funerary cult" in particular. In response, partisans of Zen drew upon
Western philosophical and theological strategies in their attempt to adapt their
faith to the modern age.' His written works include *Essays in Zen Buddhism: First
Series* (New York: Grove Press, 1927); *Essays in Zen Buddhism: Second Series*
(New York: Samuel Weiser, 1933); *Essays in Zen Buddhism: Third Series*
(York Beach, Maine: Samuel Weiser, 1934); *An Introduction to Zen Buddhism*
(Kyoto: Eastern Buddhist Soc., 1934), republished with foreword by C. G. Jung
(London: Rider & Company, 1948); *The Training of the Zen Buddhist Monk*
(Kyoto: Eastern Buddhist Soc., 1934; New York: University Books, 1959); *Manual
of Zen Buddhism* (Kyoto: Eastern Buddhist Soc., 1935; London: Rider & Company,

1950, 1956; New York: Random House, 1960; and subsequent editions). After
the Second World War, he wrote *The Zen Doctrine of No-Mind* (London: Rider
& Company, 1949; York Beach, Maine: Red Wheel/Weiser, 1972); *Living by Zen*
(London: Rider & Company, 1949); *Mysticism: Christian and Buddhist: The
Eastern and Western Way* (Macmillan, 1957); *Zen and Japanese Culture*
(New York: Pantheon, 1959); and *Zen Buddhism and Psychoanalysis.*

8   *Siddharta* was originally published in Germany in 1922 but the English edition
appeared in the United States in 1951. The narrative recounts the spiritual travelling
of the protagonist named Siddharta and a fictional contemporary of the Buddha.
Siddharta's journey mimics that of the Buddha and eventually leads to him.
Siddharta will not follow the Buddha, as he does not consider the teachings to
account for the individuality of the self or the distinct experiences that make up
each individual. He dismisses the Eastern need for a spiritual guide in the process
of enlightenment and argues that He the individual has to find a personal meaning
that cannot be revealed to him by a teacher. His subsequent travels take him to
wealth, lust, fatherhood and other experiences only to find peace by the side of
a river as a ferryman (McClory, 1998: 1–42). *The Glass Bead Game* published in
English in 1949 was Hesse's last novel and influential in the award of the Nobel
Prize for Literature. The novel is set in the future and describes an arcane order
where austere intellectuals run boarding schools for boys and play the Glass Bead
Game, an elusive and indescribable game whose rules are so sophisticated that they
are only alluded to in the narrative. As the novel progresses, with some parallels to
Siddharta, the protagonist Joseph Knecht, the Magister Ludi of the Order, questions
his loyalty to the order and gradually comes to the conclusion to leave and become
of value to the wider society. This conclusion begins a personal crisis and a spiritual
awakening (Ziolkowski, 1994).

9   Carlos Castanada's *The Teachings of Don Juan: A Yaqui Way of Knowledge* (1968)
was published as a contested work of anthropology. It claims to document
Castanada's apprenticeship with a Yaqui Indian shaman/sorcerer. The book is
divided into two sections. The first part, *The Teachings*, is a first-person narrative
that recounts Castaneda's first interactions with Don Juan. He speaks of his
personal experiences with Mescalito (a teaching spirit inhabiting all peyote plants),
divination with lizards and flying using the *yerba del diablo* (lit. 'devil's weed';
Jimson weed), and turning into a blackbird using *humito* (lit. 'little smoke'; a
smoked powder containing *Psilocybe mexicana*).

10 Robert Pirsig (1974), *Zen and the Art of Motorcycle Maintenance*
(New York: Bantam). In an obituary on the death of the author, the book is
described by Todd Gitlin as being written in the last throes of the counterculture
and appealing to those 'who wanted to seek to reconcile humanism with
technological progress, and had been perfectly timed for a generation weary

of the '60s revolt against a soulless high-tech world dominated by a corporate and military-industrial order' (https://www.nytimes.com/2017/04/24/books/robert-pirsig-dead-wrote-zen-and-the-art-of-motorcycle-maintenance.html. The book would hit a mid-1970s zeitgeist and sell millions of copies. It describes a fictionalized account of a motorcycle road trip across the US that Pirsig took in 1968 with his 11-year-old son, Christopher, and two friends. The narrative alternates between accounts of their seventeen days on the road, from the Pirsigs's home in Minnesota to the Pacific Coast, and long interior monologues. The narrator focuses on what he calls 'two profound schisms': the 1960s culture war, in which 'hippies' rejected the values of modernity that had been embraced by the 'straight' mainstream society and the narrator's own mind, as he struggled to comprehend his recent mental breakdown (ibid.).

11   Located on 125 acres of Pacific coastline near Big Sur, California, the Esalen Institute was founded by Stanford graduates Michael Murphy and Dick Price in 1962 to support alternative methods for exploring human consciousness. Until 2016, Esalen offered over five hundred workshops annually in areas including personal growth, meditation, massage, Gestalt Practice, yoga, psychology, ecology, spirituality and organic food. In 2016, about fifteen thousand people attended its workshops. Within a few years of its foundation, Esalen established itself as the centre of practices and beliefs that make up the New Age movement. In its early years, guest lecturers and workshop leaders included many leading thinkers, psychologists and philosophers who influenced counterculture or contemporary spirituality, including Erik Erikson, Ken Kesey, Alan Watts, John Lilly, Buckminster Fuller, Aldous Huxley, Linus Pauling, Fritz Perl, Joseph Campbell, Robert Bly and Carl Rogers (Krieger, 2017; Ollivier, 2012). For a longer and more complete version of the Esalen story, read Kripal (2007).

12   The Findhorn website claims that the community began as a fortuitous 'accident' when the three founders Peter and Eileen Caddy and Dorothy Maclean originally come to North-Eastern Scotland in 1957 to manage the Cluny Hotel in Forres. After the hotel owners ceased their employment, they began to grow vegetables in the sandy soil of the Findhorn Bay Caravan Park. They grew huge plants, herbs and flowers, most famously the now-legendary 40-pound cabbages, and the word spread. The garden became famous. Dorothy claimed that she was able to intuitively contact the intelligence of plants – which she called angels and then devas – that gave her instructions on how to make the most of their garden. Other people came to join the Caddys and Dorothy in their work and soon the original group of six grew into a community, committed to their spiritual path and to developing the garden in harmony with nature. The community published a small volume of Eileen's guidance *God Spoke to Me* in 1967, and the word spread further. Significant friends and supporters of the community included English New Age

pioneer, Sir George Trevelyan, Scottish esotericist, R. Ogilvie Crombie, and Richard St. Barbe Baker, 'the man of the trees'. In the late 1960s, Peter and community members, in accordance with Eileen's guidance, built the Park Sanctuary, a meditation sanctuary, and the Community Centre, where the community still meets and eats. In 1970, a young American spiritual teacher named David Spangler arrived in the community and with his partner Myrtle Glines helped to define and organize the spiritual curriculum, and a programme of learning was established at The Park. In 1972, the community, the Findhorn Foundation, was formally registered as a Scottish Charity and in the 1970s and 1980s grew to approximately three hundred members. In 1975, the Foundation purchased Cluny Hill Hotel (which had declined after the Caddys' departure) as a centre for workshops and for members' accommodation and in 1983 purchased the caravan park in Findhorn (https://www.findhorn.org/about-us/). Findhorn has received thousands of residents from more than forty countries. The Foundation runs various educational programmes for the Findhorn community; it also houses about forty community businesses such as the Findhorn Press and an alternative medicine centre (Parker, Valerie and Patrick, 2007: 100). For an academic treatment of the significance of Findhorn to contemporary spirituality, see Sutcliffe (2000: 215–31; 2003).

13 Gandalf's Garden rose to prominence in late 1960s as a place for members of the counterculture to meet with each other, exchange ideas and listen to teachers, gurus, monks, and so forth, from every spiritual tradition. The shop was based in World's End, at the then unfashionable end of Chelsea. Gandalf's Garden was directly opposite the World's End pub. The centre promoted getting high without drugs through spiritual practices and its clientele sat around on large cushions drinking herb teas. The basement included a shrine room where meetings were held in the evening and homeless street people rested during the day. The members of the founding team have mostly gone on to be deeply involved in various aspects of the New Age movement, including shamanism, Sufism and alternative medicine. Muz Murray is known in India as Ramana Baba and teaches mantra yoga and Advaita Vedanta globally. Gandalf's Garden had disappeared by 1972 but is remembered on the website (http://www.users.globalnet.co.uk/~pardos/GG.html).

3 Easternization: Indian gurus and the West

1 Mata Hari was the stage name taken up by Dutch-born Margaretha Zelle when she became one of Paris's most popular exotic dancers on the eve of the First World War. Although details of her past are sketchy, it is believed that she was born in the Netherlands in 1876. She was executed in 1917 by the French for espionage. It was in Paris where she reinvented herself as an Indian temple dancer thoroughly versed

in the dance traditions of the East. She attracted audiences in their thousands
(http://eyewitnesstohistory.com/matahari.htm).

2 Ruth St Denis (1879–1968) was an American contemporary dancer particularly
interested in the East. In 1906, after studying Hindu art and philosophy, she offered
a public performance in New York City of her first dance work, Radha (based on
the milkmaid Radha who was an early consort of the Hindu god Krishna), together
with such shorter pieces as *The Cobra* and *The Incense*. A three-year European tour
followed. She was particularly successful in Vienna, where she added *The Nautch*
and *The Yogi* to her program, and in Germany. Her later productions, many of
which had religious themes, included the long-planned *Egypta* (1910) and *O-mika*
(1913), a dance drama in a Japanese style (https://www.britannica.com/biography/
Ruth-St-Denis).

3 Weightman states that the transcendental complex is so named because it refers to
a number of spiritual paths whose principal motivation is to take the individual to
a state of being that transcends 'both the world of caste and every level of existence'
(1978: 39).

4 Roger Ballard in his analysis of Punjabi religious life renames the pragmatic
complex as Kismetic. He defines the term as 'those ideas, practices and behavioural
strategies which are used to explain the otherwise inexplicable, and if possible to
turn adversity in its tracks' (1996: 18). Thus, the supernatural world is called upon
to relieve the host of problems that can arise from the vagaries of fortune, the lack
of control of the natural world and the belief that the living space of the villagers is
shared with a panoply of supernatural beings.

5 George Gurdjieff's *Meetings with Remarkable Men* was first published in 1963.
Gurdjieff, born in Alexandrapol, was an important contributor in the development
of occulture, influencing both early-twentieth-century occultists and later
counterculture figures such as Alan Watts and Timothy Leary. Gurdjieff taught
that most people live their lives in a state of 'waking sleep', but that it is possible
to transcend to a higher state of consciousness and achieve full human potential.
According to Gurdjieff, his method for awakening one's consciousness unites the
methods of the fakir, monk and yogi, and thus he referred to it as the 'Fourth Way'
(De Penafieu, 1997: 214).

6 According to a variety of sources, Brahmachari Mahesh left Uttarkashi in 1955
and began publicly teaching what he stated was a traditional meditation technique
learned from his master Brahmananda Saraswati, and that he called Transcendental
Deep Meditation (Rooney, 2008; Williamson, 2010: 97–9). Later, the technique
was renamed Transcendental Meditation (TM) (Russell, 1977: 25). It was around
this time that he was first publicly known as 'Maharishi', an honorific title meaning
'great sage'. According to William Jefferson, in 1958, Maharishi went to Madras
to address a large crowd of people who had gathered to celebrate the memory

of Brahmananda Saraswati. It was there that he spontaneously announced that he planned to spread the teaching of TM throughout the world (1976: 7–21). He travelled around India for two years interacting with 'Hindu audiences' in an 'Indian context' (Gablinger, 2010: 76). In 1959, Maharishi Mahesh Yogi began his first world tour. The Maharishi's 1986 book, *Thirty Years around the World*, gives a detailed account of his world tours, as do two biographies, *The Story of the Maharishi* by William Jefferson (1976) and *The Maharishi* by Paul Mason (1994).

7   Maharishi met the Beatles in London in August 1967 and the band went to study with him in Bangor, before travelling to Rishikesh in February 1968 to 'devote themselves fully to his instruction' (Kozinn, 2008). Following the Beatles' endorsement of TM, during 1967 and 1968, the Maharishi appeared on American magazine covers such as *Life*, *Newsweek*, *Time* and many others (Needleman, 1970b: 139). He gave lectures to capacity crowds at the Felt Forum in New York City and Harvard's Sanders Hall and also appeared on *The Tonight Show* and the Today TV shows (Goldberg, 2010: 362).

8   Maharishi came to the United States in 1959 when his Spiritual Regeneration Movement was called Transcendental Meditation. That same year, he began the International Meditation Society and other organizations to propagate his teachings, establishing centres in San Francisco and London (Hunt, 2003: 197–8). In 1960, the Maharishi travelled to many cities in India, France, Switzerland, England, Scotland, Norway, Sweden, Germany, the Netherlands, Italy, Singapore, Australia, New Zealand and Africa (Mason, 1994: 52–4). While in Manchester, England, the Maharishi gave a television interview and was featured in many English newspapers such as the *Birmingham Post*, the *Oxford Mail* and the *Cambridge Daily News* (Maharishi, 1986: 305). This was also the year in which the Maharishi trained the first Transcendental Meditation teacher in Europe (p. 302). In 1961, the Maharishi visited the United States, Austria, Sweden, France, Italy, Greece, India, Kenya, England and Canada (p. 199). While in England, he appeared on BBC television and gave a lecture to five thousand people at the Royal Albert Hall (p. 199). In April 1961, the Maharishi conducted his first Transcendental Meditation Teacher Training Course in Rishikesh, India, with sixty participants from various countries (p. 328). His 1962 world tour included visits to Europe, India, Australia and New Zealand. The Maharishi again toured cities in Europe, Asia, North America and India in 1963 and also addressed ministers of the Indian Parliament (Mason, 1994: 66–7). The Maharishi's fifth world tour, in 1964, consisted of visits to many cities in North America, Europe and India (pp. 71–5). During his visit to England, he appeared with the Abbot of Downside, Abbot Butler, on a BBC television show called *The Viewpoint* (p. 72). During this same year, the Maharishi finished his book *The Science of Being and Art of Living*, which sold more than a million copies and was published in fifteen languages (van den Berg, 2008).

In 1967, the Maharishi gave a lecture at Caxton Hall in London which was attended by Pattie Boyd, George Harrison's wife. He also lectured at UCLA, Harvard, Yale and Berkeley (Bainbridge, 1997: 188). Sean McCloud also reported that traditional Indian sages and gurus were critical of the Maharishi, for teaching a simple technique and making it available to everyone and for abandoning traditional concepts of suffering and concentration as paths to enlightenment (2004).

9   From the 'Houseboat Summit' panel discussion, Sausalito, California, February 1967:

Ginsberg: So what do you think of Swami Bhaktivedanta pleading for the acceptance of Krishna in every direction?
Snyder: Why, it's a lovely positive thing to say Krishna. It's a beautiful mythology and it's a beautiful practice.
Leary: Should be encouraged.
Ginsberg: He feels it's the one uniting thing. He feels a monopolistic unitary thing about it.
Watts: I'll tell you why I think he feels it. The mantras, the images of Krishna have in this culture no foul association. ... [W]hen somebody comes in from the Orient with a new religion which hasn't got any of these [horrible] associations in our minds, all the words are new, all the rites are new, and yet, somehow it has feeling in it, and we can get with that, you see, and we can dig that! (Cohen, 1991: 182).

10 An avatar (*descent*) is perceived in Hinduism as an incarnation of a deity into a human or animal form. The main human avatars are Rama and Krishna, but Vaishnavite traditions within Hinduism regard the Buddha as an incarnation, and some also accept that Jesus may have had the same status. There is an avatar to come known as Kalki. The classical doctrine of avatars of Vishnu upheld by Vaishnavites has been extended to Shaivite traditions who believe that Shiva also incarnates but more significantly to those who follow the teachings of a guru, who are likely to claim that their respective teachers are avatars (Geaves, 2006c: 6).

11 Meher Baba's teachings can be found in his two principal writings: *God Speaks* (Walnut Creek, CA, 1997): Sufism Reoriented; and *Discourses*, 7th edn. (Myrtle Beach, SC: Sheriar Foundation).

12 Juergensmeyer states that 175 Americans were followers of Sawan Singh, 70 more were followers of his successor Jagat Singh, but between 1951 and 1974 the numbers increased to 5,000. Since then, the number has tripled (1991: 206, footnote 17).

13 Roy Wallis introduced the distinction between world-affirming and world-rejecting new religious movements. *World-rejecting movements* view the prevailing social order as deviant and a perversion of the divine plan. Such movements see the

world as evil or at least as materialistic. They may adhere to millenarian beliefs. The ISKCON, the Unification Church, the Brahma Kumaris and the Children of God are considered as *world-rejecting* movements, whereas *World-affirming movements* might not have any rituals or any formal ideology. They affirm the world and merely claim to have the means to enable people to unlock their 'hidden potential'. As examples of world-affirming movements, Wallis mentions Werner Erhard's EST and Transcendental Meditation. Wallis also provided a category of *World-accommodating movements* which draw clear distinctions between the spiritual and the worldly spheres. These movements adapt to the world but they do not reject or affirm it (Wallis, 1984).

4 Prem Rawat and contextualizing Indian religions in the West

1 Estimates of the number of Rawat's adherents have varied widely over time. Petersen stated that Rawat claimed seven million disciples worldwide in 1973, with sixty thousand in the United States (1982: 146). Rudin and Rudin gave a worldwide following of six million in 1974, of which fifty thousand were in the United States. According to these authors, the adherents had fallen to 1.2 million for Prem Rawat's personal worldwide following in 1980, with fifteen thousand in the United States (1974). Spencer J. Palmer and Roger R. Keller published a general DLM membership of 1.2 million worldwide, with fifty thousand in the United States in 1990 and 1997 (p. 95). All these estimates are based on Latter Day Saints publications. According to Prem Rawat's official website in the eight years prior to May 2008, Key Six sessions were attended by 365,237 people in sixty-seven countries. These are the video sessions where the techniques of Knowledge are taught by Prem Rawat ('The Keys, by Maharaji').

2 The full quotation is as follows: 'The major focus of Prem Rawat is on stillness, peace, and contentment within the individual, and his "Knowledge" consists of the techniques to obtain them. Knowledge, roughly translated, means the happiness of the true self-understanding. Each individual should seek to comprehend his or her true self. In turn, this brings a sense of well-being, joy, and harmony as one comes in contact with one's "own nature." The Knowledge includes four meditation procedures: Light, Music, Nectar and Word. The process of reaching the true self within can only be achieved by the individual, but with the guidance and help of a teacher. Hence, the movement seems to embrace aspects of world-rejection and world-affirmation. The tens of thousands of followers in the West do not see themselves as members of a religion, but the adherents of a system of teachings that extol the goal of enjoying life to the full' (Hunt, 2003: 116–17).

3 The views of dissatisfied ex-students of Prem Rawat can be found on http://www. ex-premie.org.

4 This would appear to be an example of moral panic defined as 'a widespread fear, most often an irrational one, that someone or something is a threat to the values, safety, and interests of a community or society at large' (Crossman, 2018). See also Victor (2015: 692–701).

5 Arya Samaj (Sanskrit: 'Society of Nobles') is an activist reform movement of modern Hinduism, founded in 1875 by Dayananda Sarasvati, whose aim was to re-establish the Vedas, the earliest Hindu scriptures, as revealed truth. The Arya Samaj is opposed to worship of *murti*s (images), animal sacrifice, shraddha (rituals on behalf of ancestors), basing caste upon birth rather than upon merit, untouchability, child marriage, pilgrimages, priestly craft and temple offerings. It upholds the infallibility of the Vedas, the doctrines of karma (the accumulated effect of past deeds) and samsara (the process of death and rebirth), the sanctity of the cow, the importance of the samskaras (individual sacraments) and the efficacy of Vedic oblations to the fire ('Arya Samaj: Religious Sect: India').

6 Kabir (1440–1518) is described in the entry to the online *Encyclopaedia Britannica* as an 'iconoclastic Indian poet-saint revered by Hindus, Muslims, and Sikhs'. It is his iconoclasm and total conviction that God is immanent within the living human being that makes him attractive to Prem Rawat. The article goes on to state, 'Although Kabir is often depicted in modern times as a harmonizer of Hindu and Muslim belief and practice, it would be more accurate to say that he was equally critical of both, often conceiving them as parallel to one another in their misguided ways. In his view, the mindless, repetitious, prideful habit of declaiming scripture could be visited alike on the sacred Hindu texts, the Vedas, or the Islamic holy book, the Qur'ān; the religious authorities doing so could be Brahmans or *qāḍī*s (judges); meaningless rites of initiation could focus either on the sacred thread or on circumcision. What really counted, for Kabir, was utter fidelity to the one deathless truth of life.' Kabir's principal media of communication were songs called *pada*s and rhymed couplets (*doha*s) sometimes called 'words' (*shabda*s) or 'witnesses' (*sakhi*s) written in the vernacular (https://www.britannica.com/biography/Kabir-Indian-mystic-and-poet).

7 The original Radhasoami lineage is continued at Dayalbagh in Agra. Dayalbagh was founded by Anand Swarup, a householder who established the financial security of the movement through the creation of small industries (Juergensmeyer, 1987: 333). On the other hand, Swarupanand Ji was a *sannyasi*. As well as the confusion of the names, there is also an Agra connection. Swarupanand Ji was sent by his master, Advaitanand Ji, to sit in solitary meditation at Nangla Padi in Agra. Swarupanand Ji passed thirteen years in this way before being called back to Teri in the NW Frontier district to rejoin his master. The time frames between the two

would have been similar. Anand Swarup founded Dayalbagh around 1910. It is not possible to ascertain the exact dates that Swarupanand Ji was in Agra but he was visited between 13 October 1915 and 8 June 1916 by his master, Advaitanand ji also known as Shri Paramhans Dyal Ji (Sri Swami Sar Shabdanand Ji, 1998: 41–8).

8 The Radhasoami (Satsang Beas) initiates are taught five 'names of God' along with other aids to inner focus. This is not the same as the four techniques described as Knowledge taught by Prem Rawat and the masters who came before him. In fact, there is anecdotal evidence from an eye witness that Prem Rawat's father, Shri Hans ji Maharaj, criticized Sant Kirpal Singh, the leader of the Radhasoamis, at Satsang Beas at a conference of world religions held in Delhi in 1958 concerning the issue of the 'Name of God'. Shri Hans ji Maharaj pointed out that Guru Nanak and Kabir spoke of one eternal and unspoken Name not five mantras or names. The Agra branch of Radhasoami disagrees with Satsang Beas in regard to practice and maintains that 'Radhasoami' is the proper name of God. For a detailed exposition of Radhasoami practice, read Chapter 4 of Juergensmeyer (1991).

9 Ramakrishna (1836–1886) was arguably the foremost Hindu religious leader of influencing the twentieth century and founder of a school of religious thought that became the Ramakrishna Order. In 1852, poverty forced Ramakrishna and his elder brother, Ramkumar, to leave their village to seek employment in Calcutta. There they became priests in a temple dedicated to the goddess Kali. In 1856, Ramkumar died. Ramakrishna, now alone, prayed for a vision of Kali-Ma (Kali the Mother). Soon after his first vision, Ramakrishna commenced on a series of sadhanas (spiritual disciplines) in the various religious traditions. After each of these sadhanas, Ramakrishna claimed to have had the same experience of *brahman*, the supreme power, or ultimate reality, of the universe. Seeing God in everything and everyone, he believed that all paths led to the same goal. That all religions could be seen as different paths to the same divine source or, even better, that this divine source revealed itself in traditional Hindu categories was liberating news for many Hindus. A small band of disciples, most of them Western-educated, including Swami Vivekananda, gathered around Ramakrishna in the early 1880s, drawn by the appeal of his message. Notably, Ramakrishna's teachings are preserved in Mahendranath Gupta's five-volume Bengali classic *Sri Sri Ramakrishna Kathamrita* (1902–32; *The Nectar-Speech of the Twice-Blessed Ramakrishna*), best known to English readers as *The Gospel of Ramakrishna*, based on conversations with Ramakrishna from 1882 to 1886. Moreover, his disciple and successor, Narendranath Datta (d.1902), became the world-travelling Swami Vivekananda and helped establish the Ramakrishna Order, whose teachings, texts and rituals identified Ramakrishna as a new avatar ('incarnation') of God. The headquarters of the mission is in Belur Math, a monastery near Kolkata. The Ramakrishna Order also played an important role in the spread of Hindu ideas and

practices in the West, particularly in the United States (https://www.britannica.com/biography/Ramakrishna).

10   Shankaracharya or Adi Shankara (788–820) was an Indian philosopher and theologian who expounded the doctrine of Advaita Vedanta. He is believed to have renounced the world at a very young age. Shankaracharya amalgamated the ideologies of ancient 'Advaita Vedanta' and also explained the basic ideas of Upanishads. He advocated the oldest concept of Hinduism which explains the identification of the soul (atman) with the Supreme Soul (Nirguna Brahman). Though he is best known for popularizing 'Advaita Vedanta', one of Shankaracharya's most important works is his efforts to synthesize the six subsects of Hinduism, that is, the worship of six supreme deities. Shankaracharya explained the existence of one Supreme Being (Brahman) and that the six supreme deities are part of one divine power. He also founded the 'Dasnami Sampradaya', which institutionalized monastic life. While Shankaracharya was a firm believer in ancient Hinduism, he condemned the 'Mimamsa school of Hinduism' which was purely based on ritual practices (https://www.culturalindia.net/indian-religions/shankaracharya.html).

11   Dasnami means the ten names and refers to the ten orders in which the Shaivite (the sect which worships Shiva) anchorites are commonly classified. Sadhu is a generic term for a religious mendicant. Shankaracharya is attributed with organizing Hindu monasticism. He divided the Hindu monks into ten sects called 'Dasnami' and organized them under four heads with the headquarters at Dwaraka in the west, Jagannatha Puri in the east, Rameswaram in the south and Badrikashrama in the north. These became the four sacred 'Dhams' or 'Holy Places' of the Hindus. He also enumerated other details of the order of Hindu monks grouped under these headings for their identity. Although there are today a number of Hindu monastic sects, the most authentic are the ten established by Acharya Shankaracharya. The Dasnamis worship Lord Siva or Lord Vishnu and meditate on Nirguna Brahman (Sarkar, 2018).

12   http://www.Prem Rawat.org has now been succeeded by https://www.premrawat.com/ which is more in line with his current representation of his work over the last six decades. It has no reference to a religious or spiritual heritage in the past. A detailed analysis of Prem Rawat's antecedents can be found in Geaves (2006b). See pp. 63–7 for the account of the lineage of Advaita Mat.

13   This does not seem to be denied even by the most vociferous of the Prem Rawat's opponents (e.g., see www.prem-rawat-bio.org/lineage.html). My own investigations of the lineage were carried out among the religious descendants of Swarupanand Ji at the shrine site in Nangli Sahib, Uttar Pradesh, and published as Geaves (2007). At the time of writing, there were still living mahatmas of Swarupanand Ji who remembered Hans Ji Maharaj.

14 It is not possible to trace the lineage further back than Anand Puri with any degree of accuracy, although Dasnami records would indicate the traditional lineage and show who initiated Anand Puri into their order; however, they would not show if he was initiated into the four techniques known as Knowledge by another guru met on his travels. The name Anand Puri (also known as Satchitanand Puri) suggests a Dasnami sadhu of a similar background to Totapuri but an interview with Atmaramanand Ji, the last surviving *sannyasi* follower of Swarupanand Ji, at his ashram in Radore in 2002 brought forth a clear statement that there was no connection between Anand Puri and Totapuri. This was also reinforced by a visit to the samadhi of Totapuri at the shrine centre of Baba Raj Puri near Ladhana in Punjab. However, the visit clarified that although Tota Puri belonged to one of the Dasnami *akharas* not connected with Anand Puri, the lineage of Advait Mat is associated with the traditional but legendary lineages of the Dasnamis through Shankarcharya. Atmaramanand mentioned legendary or historic figures such as Shiva, Vasishta, Sukhdeva and Shankarcharya as the seed gurus of each *yuga*, the descent then came down through the traditional Shankarcharya lineages culminating in the Puri order of *sadhu* renunciates (Geaves 2007).

15 Certainly by the time of Swarupanand Ji, a universalism was implicit in the teachings. People of all faiths were initiated and the teachings were promoted to all of India's religious communities. In a meeting with a group of Muslim peasants, Swarapanand Ji stated, 'A *faqir* has no particular religion: he is common to all. Wherever I go there will be no dearth of devotees, as I belong to all, and all belong to me' (Sar Shabdanand, 1998: 215–16).

16 This may not have been straightforward. The divisions that emerged in the family in the 1970s may have their origins in doubts concerning Prem Rawat's succession by some senior disciples and members of the family. Prem Rawat had already captured the hearts of his father's devotees in a public speech soon after the funeral, while the family and senior followers were meeting to discuss the succession. They were presented with a *fait accompli* and arrived at a compromise of a leadership under the 'holy family' until Prem Rawat was of age.

5 Festivals and music: Counterculture's religiosity?

1 The term 'psychedelic' is derived from the ancient Greek words *psychē* (ψυχή, 'soul') and *dēloun* (δηλοῦν, 'to make visible, to reveal' (https://web.archive.org/web/20040205200722/; http://www.etymonline.com:80/).

2 A Renaissance fair, Renaissance faire or Renaissance festival is an outdoor weekend gathering, open to the public, which recreates a historical setting usually Elizabethan. Some are permanent theme parks, while others are short-term events

in a fairground, winery or other large public or private spaces. Renaissance fairs usually include costumed entertainers or fair-goers, musical and theatrical acts, art and handicrafts for sale and festival food. Some offer campgrounds for those who wish to stay more than one day (Thomas et al., 1987).

3 Donovan's second album *Fairytale* released in 1965 contained the track 'Sunny Goodge Street'. The track describes the beat lifestyle in the area with the following lines:

> On the firefly platform on sunny Goodge Street
> Violent hash-smoker shook a chocolate machine
> Bobbed in an eating scene.
> Smashing into neon streets in their stillness
> Smearing their eyes on the crazy Kali goddess
> Listenin' to sounds of Mingus mellow fantastic. (https://www.azlyrics.com/lyrics/donovan/sunnygoodgestreet.html)

4 The Aldermaston marches were anti-nuclear weapons demonstrations in the 1950s and 1960s, taking place on Easter weekend between the Atomic Weapons Research Establishment at Aldermaston in Berkshire, England, and London, over a distance of 52 miles. At their peak in the early 1960s, they attracted tens of thousands of people and were the highlight of the Campaign for Nuclear Disarmament (CND) calendar (Minnion and Bolsover, 1983).

5 Use of the term 'hippie' did not become widespread in the mass media until early 1967, after *San Francisco Chronicle* columnist Herb Caen began to use the term; see 'Take a Hippie to Lunch Today', *San Francisco Chronicle*, 20 January 1967, p. 37; *San Francisco Chronicle*, 18 January 1967 column, p. 27.

6 'The attendance at the third Pop Festival at … Isle of Wight, England on 30 Aug 1970 was claimed by its promoters, Fiery Creations, to be 400,000' (Russell 1987: 91).

7 Probably coined from the 1932 horror film of the same name and considered too shocking to release. The characters were played by people who worked as carnival sideshow performers and had real deformities. In the film, the physically deformed 'freaks' are inherently trusting and honourable people, while the real monsters are two of the 'normal' members of the circus. The famous chant, 'We accept her, one of us' would enshrine many counterculture values (Skal and Savada 1995: 42–9, 78–9; Wolf, 2007).

6 The significance of Glastonbury

1 The poem is published in English as Robert (de Boron) (1990). *Joseph of Arimathea: A Romance of the Grail* (London: Rudolf Steiner Press). An account of the work can be found in Le Gentil (1959).

2 A flowering sprig is sent to the British Monarch every Christmas. The original tree has been propagated several times, with one tree growing at Glastonbury Abbey and another in the churchyard of the Church of St John (Rahtz and Watts, 2003: 59–61).

3 Fortune presented the Arthurian myths as racial memories that had been passed down from Atlantis, having been brought to Britain by Atlantean settlers after the cataclysm that destroyed their island. It also set forward a threefold system of training: that of Arthur and his Round Table Fellowship, that of Merlin and the Faery Woman and that of Guinevere and the Forces of Love (Knight, 2000: 264).

4 Nicholas R. Mann is the author of books on geomancy, mythology, the Celtic tradition, sacred geometry and, most recently, Glastonbury (Mann and Glasson, 2001, 2005, 2007).

5 Many of Geoffrey Ashe's historical books are centred on factual analysis of the Arthurian legend and the archaeological past of King Arthur, beginning with his *King Arthur's Avalon: The Story of Glastonbury* in 1957. Ashe's book *Camelot and the Vision of Albion* was often cited by Paul Weller as a major influence on The Jam's 1980 album *Sound Affects* (Irvin and McLear, 2007: 457).

7 Prem Rawat at Glastonbury: Occulture and Easternization?

1 Conversations with Carol Waters, November 2018.
2 Conversations with Suzy Witten, Los Angeles, July 2018.
3 Conversations with Charles Cameron, Roseville, California, August 2018.
4 Conversations with Suzy Witten, Los Angeles, July 2018.
5 Conversations with Carol Waters, November 2018.
6 Conversations with Ricardo and Lothar, Rainbow Gypsies, Pasadena, California, July 2018.

8 The aftermath of Glastonbury Fayre: Prem Rawat and counterculture

1 Rennie Davis was well known as a peace activist on the Underground circuit. He was one of the main organizers of the National Mobilization Committee to End the War in Vietnam and took a prominent part in the protests at the 1968 Democratic National Convention in Chicago. Davis was beaten into a concussion by Chicago police officers in spite of his pacifism. Along with seven other defendants, Abbie Hoffman, Jerry Rubin, David Dellinger, Tom Hayden, John Froines, Lee Weiner and Bobby Seale,

Davis was brought trial charged with conspiracy, inciting to riot and other charges related to nonviolent and violent protests that took place in Chicago (Schultz, 2009).

2 Conversation with Ricardo and Lothar, Rainbow Gypsies, Pasadena, August 2018.

9 Counterculture, occulture and Easternization revisited

1 Eaton's approach to Indian religions is discussed by Suthren-Hirst, Jacqueline and John Zavos (2005, March), 'Riding a Tiger? South Asia and the Problem of "Religion"', *Contemporary South Asia* 14 (1), 11–12.

2 Personal recollections of the author from his time living with Charnanand in London in 1970.

Bibliography

Aagaard, Johannes (1980), 'Who Is Who in Guruism?' *Update: A Quarterly Journal on New Religious Movements* IV (3).

Abrahams, Ian (2004), *Hawkwind: Sonic Assassins*. London: SAF.

Adriel, Jean (1947), *Avatar: The Life Story of the Perfect Master, Meher Baba*. Santa Barbara, CA: J. F. Rowney Press.

Anderson, Iain (2007), *This Is Our Music: Free Jazz, the Sixties, and American Culture*. Pennsylvania: University of Pennsylvania Press.

Anderson, T. H. (1995), *The Movement and the Sixties: Protest in America from Greensboro to Wounded Knee*. Oxford: Oxford University Press.

Apter, Joan (1996), *Divine Times*, Special Edition.

Armstrong, David (1981), *A Trumpet to Arms: Alternative Media in America*. Los Angeles: J. P. Tarcher.

Ashdown, Paul (2010), *The Lord Was at Glastonbury*. Butleigh: Squeeze Press.

Aubrey, Crispin, and John Shearlaw (eds) (2004), *Glastonbury Festival Tales*. London: Ebury Press.

Awakener Magazine (1963), 'The East-West Gathering', 9 (1–2).

Baba, Meher (1966), *God in a Pill? Meher Baba on L.S.D. and the High Roads*. California: Sufism Reoriented.

Baba, Meher (1987), *Discourses*, 7th edn. Myrtle Beach, SC: Sheriar Foundation.

Baba, Meher (1997), *God Speaks*. California: Sufism Reoriented.

Bailey, John (2013a), *Glastonbury: The Complete Story of the Festival*. Wellington: Halsgrove.

Bailey, John (ed.) (2013b), 'Andrew Kerr Remembers the 1971 Festival', *Glastonbury: The Complete Story of the Festival*, ed. Andrew Kerr. Wellington: Halsgrove.

Bainbridge, William Sims (1997), *The Sociology of Religious Movements*. London: Routledge.

Ballard, Roger (1996), 'Panth, Kismet, Dharm te Qaum: Continuity and Change in Four Dimensions of Punjabi Religion', in *Globalisation and the Region: Explanations in Punjabi Identity*, Pritam Singh and Shinder Thandi, ed. Coventry: University of Coventry.

Bangs, Lester, Reny Brown, John Burks, et al. (1970), 'The Rolling Stones' Disaster at Altamont: Let It Bleed', *Rolling Stone*, 21 January.

Baring-Gould, S. (1899), *A Book of the West: Being an Introduction to Devon and Cornwall*. London: Methuen.

Beauquier, Susan Ratcliffe (1996), 'Welcome to London', *Divine Times*, 17 July.

Bennett, J. G. (1974), *Witness: The Story of a Search (Autobiography)*. Tucson, AZ: Omen Press.

Bogdanov, V., C. Woodstra and S. T. Erlewine (eds) (2003), *All Music Guide to the Blues: The Definitive Guide to the Blues*, 3rd edn. Milwaukee: Backbeat.

Booth, Martin (2004), *Cannabis: A History*. New York: St. Martin's Press.

Bowman, Marion (2003–4), 'Taking Stories Seriously: Vernacular Religion, Contemporary Spirituality and the Myth of Jesus in Glastonbury', *Temenos*, 39–40, 125–42.

Bowman, Marion (2005), 'Ancient Avalon, New Jerusalem, Heart Chakra of Planet Earth: Localisation and Globalisation in Glastonbury', *Numen*, 52 (2), 157–90.

Bowman, Marion (2006) 'The Holy Thorn Ceremony: Revival, Rivalry and Civil Religion in Glastonbury', *Folklore* 117 (2), 123–40.

Bowman, Marion (2007a), 'A tale of Two Celticities: Sacred Springs, Legendary Landscape and Celtic Revival in Bath', *Australian Religious Studies Review*, Special Issue on 'Tradition as a Resource: Invention, Innovation, Inheritance', ed. Michael Hill, 20 (1), 95–117.

Bowman, Marion (2007b), 'Arthur and Bridget in Avalon: Celtic Myth, Vernacular Religion and Contemporary Spirituality in Glastonbury *Fabula*', *Journal of Folktale Studies*, 48 (1/2), 1–17.

Bowman, Marion (2008), 'Going with the Flow: Contemporary Pilgrimage in Glastonbury', in *Shrines and Pilgrimage in the Modern World: New Itineraries into the Sacred*, Peter Jan Margy, ed. Amsterdam: Amsterdam University Press, 241–80.

Bowman, Marion (2009a), 'Learning from Experience: The Value of Analysing Avalon', *Religion*, 39 (2), 161–8.

Bowman, Marion (2009b), 'From Glastonbury to Hungary: Contemporary Integrative Spirituality and Vernacular Religion in Context', in *Passageways: From Hungarian Ethnography to European Ethnology and Sociocultural Anthropology*, Gábor Vargyas, ed. Budapest: Department of European Ethnology and Cultural Anthropology, The University of Pécs – L'Harmattan Publishing House, 195–221.

Bowman, Marion (2011), 'Understanding Glastonbury as a Site of Consumption', in *Religion, Media and Culture: A Reader*, Gordon Lynch, Jolyon Mitchell and Anna Strhan, eds. London: Routledge, 11–22.

Bowman, Marion (2015a), 'Christianity, Plurality and Vernacular Religion in Early Twentieth Century Glastonbury: A Sign of Things to Come?', in *Christianity and Religious Plurality*, Studies in Church History, 51, Charlotte Methuen, Andrew Spicer and John Wolffe, eds. Woodbridge: Boydell & Brewer, 302–21.

Bowman, Marion (2015b), ' "Helping Glastonbury to Come into Its Own": Practical Spirituality, Materiality, and Community Cohesion in Glastonbury', in *Practical Spiritualities in a Media Age*, Curtis C. Coats and Monica M. Emerich, eds. London and New York: Bloomsbury Academic, 51–65.

Braybrooke, Marcus (1992), *Pilgrimage of Hope: One Hundred Years of Global Interfaith Dialogue*. London: SCM Press.

Brecher, Edward M., et al. (1972), 'How LSD Was Popularized', Consumer Reports/ Drug Library.

Briggs, Katharine (1978), 'Morgan le Fay', in *Encyclopedia of Fairies: Hobgoblins, Brownies, Boogies, and Other Supernatural Creatures*, Katherine Briggs, ed. New York: Pantheon.

Brody, Richard (2015), 'What Died at Altamont', *New Yorker*, March 11.

Bromley, David G., and Shupe Anson (1981a), *Strange Gods: The Great American Cult Scare*. Boston, MA: Beacon Press.

Bromley, David G., and Shupe Anson (1981b), 'Apostates and Atrocity Stories: Some Parameters in the Dynamics of Deprogramming', in *The Social Impact of New Religious Movements*, B. R. Wilson, ed. Barrytown, NY: Rose of Sharon Press, 179–215.

Bromley, David G., and Shupe Anson (1994), *Anti-Cult Movements in Cross-Cultural Perspective*. New York: Garland.

Bromley, David G., and Larry D. Shinn (1989), *Krishna Consciousness in the West*. Lewisburg, PA: Bucknell University Press.

Bromley, David G. (2007), *Teaching New Religious Movements (Aar Teaching Religious Studies Series)*. Atlanta, GA: American Academy of Religion.

Bromwich, Rachel (ed.) (2017), *Trioedd Ynys Prydein*. Cardiff: University of Wales Press.

Brooks, Charles R. (1992), *The Hare Krishnas in India* (reprint edn.). Delhi: Motilal Banarsidass.

Brown, Tony (1997), *Jimi Hendrix: The Final Days*. London: Omnibus Press.

Burrows, Robert (1986), 'Americans Get Religion in the New Age: Anything Is Permissible when Everything Is God', *Christianity Today*, 6 May.

Cameron, Charles, and Rennie Davies (1973), *Who Is Guru Maharaj Ji?* New York: Bantam.

Carley, James P., and David Townsend (2009), *Chronicle of Glastonbury Abbey: An Edition, Translation and Study of John of Glastonbury's Cronica sive Antiquitates*. Woodbridge: Boydell Press.

Castaneda, Carlos (1998), *The Teachings of Don Juan: A Yaqui Way of Knowledge*. Berkeley: University of California Press.

Chandler, Russell (1988), *Understanding the New Age*. London: Word Publishing.

Chapman, Robert (2010), 'Distorted View – See through Baby Blue', in *Syd Barrett: A Very Irregular Head*, Robert Chapman, ed. London: Faber.

Charnanand (1996), 'They Were Called "hippies", I Called Them "happies"', *Divine Times*, Special Edition, 17 July.

Chinmoy (2000), *Sri Chinmoy Answers, Part 23*. New York: Agni.

Chryssides, George (1991), *The Advent of Sun Myung Moon: The Origins, Beliefs and Practices of the Unification Church*. London: Palgrave.

Chryssides, George (2012), 'The New Age', in *The Cambridge Companion to New Religious Movements*, Olav Hammer and Mikael Rothstein, eds. Cambridge: Cambridge University Press.

Chryssides, George, and Benjamin Zeller (2014), 'Introduction', in *The Bloomsbury Companion to New Religious Movements*, George Chryssides and Benjamin Zeller, eds. London: Bloomsbury.

Chryssides, George D., and Margaret Z. Wilkins (2006), *A Reader in New Religious Movements*. London: Continuum.

Chryssides, George D., and Stephen E. Gregg (2018), *The Insider/Outsider Debate: New Perspectives in the Study of Religion*. Bristol: Equinox.

Clarke, David, and Andy Roberts (2007), *Flying Saucers: A Social History of UFOlogy*. Wymeswold: Alternative Albion.

Clarke, Michael (1982), *The Politics of Pop Festivals*. London: Junction.

Cohen, Allen (1991), *The San Francisco Oracle: The Psychedelic Newspaper of the Haight-Ashbury (1966–1968)*. Berkeley, CA: Regent Press.

Collier, Sophie (1978), *Soul Rush: The Odyssey of a Young Woman of the '70s*. New York: Morrow.

Corrywright, Dominic (2004), 'Network Spirituality: The Schumacher-Resurgence-Kumar Nexus', *Journal of Contemporary Religion*, 19 (3), 311–27.

Cowley, Susan Cheever, Martin Kasindorf and Laurie Lisle (1975), 'Sikhdom, U.S.A.', *Newsweek*, 21 April.

Cox, Harvey (1977), *Turning East*. London: Simon & Schuster.

Crimble, Thomas (2004), *Glastonbury Festival Tales*. Edited by Crispin Aubrey and John Shearlaw. London: Ebury Press.

Dasa Goswami, Satsvarupa (1981), *Srila Prabhupada Lilamrta, Volume 3: Only He Could Lead Them, San Francisco/India*, 1st edn. Los Angeles, CA: Bhaktivedanta Book Trust.

Dass, Ram (1971), *Be Here Now*. San Cristobal, NM: Lama Foundation.

Davis, Clive (2013), '8: Monterey Pop', in *The Soundtrack of My Life*. New York: Simon & Schuster.

Davis, Erik (2015), 'The Counterculture and the Occult', in *The Occult World*, Christopher Partridge, ed. London: Routledge.

de Boron, Robert (1990), *Joseph of Arimathea: A Romance of the Grail*. London: Rudolf Steiner Press.

De Penafieu, Bruno (1997), 'Gurdjieff', in *Gurdjieff: Essays and Reflections on the Man and His Teachings*, Jacob Needleman, George Baker and Mary Stein, eds. London: Bloomsbury.

Dobson, C. (1936), *Did Our Lord Visit Britain as They Say in Cornwall and Somerset?* Glastonbury: Avalon Press.

Dodin, Thierry, and Heinz Rather (eds) (2001), *Imagining Tibet: Perceptions, Projections and Fantasies*. Somerville: Wisdom.

Downton, James (1979), *Sacred Journeys: The Conversion of Young Americans to Divine Light Mission*. New York: Columbia University Press.

Dreyer, Thorne (1974), 'God Goes to the Astrodome', *Texas Monthly*, January.

Dua, Shyam (ed.) (2005), *The Luminous Life of Sri Chinmoy: An Authorised Biography*. Noida: Tiny Tot.

Dunlap, J. (1961), *Exploring Inner Space: Personal Experiences under LSD-25.* London: Scientific Book Club.

Dupertuis, Lucy (1986), 'How People Recognize Charisma: The Case of Darshan in Radhasoami and DLM', *Sociological Analysis*, 47 (2): 111–24.

Ellwood, Robert S. (1989), 'ISKCON and the Spirituality of the 60s', in *Krishna Consciousness in the West*, David G. Bromley and Larry D. Shinn, ed. Lewisburg, PA: Bucknell University Press.

Emick, Jennifer (2008). *The Everything Celtic Wisdom Book*. Avon, MA: Adams Media.

Farber, David (1992), 'The Counterculture and the Antiwar Movement', in *Give Peace a Chance: Exploring the Vietnam Antiwar Movement*, Melvin Small and William D. Hoover, eds. Syracuse: Syracuse University Press.

Farber, David (2013), 'Marc Benioff Explains Steve Jobs' Spirituality and Chides Apple'. CNET News, San Francisco, 10 September.

Farren, Mick (1972), *Watch Out Kids*. London: MacMillan.

Finch, Michael (2009), *Without the Guru*. United States: Babbling Brook Press.

Finch, Mike (1996), 'Adventures in Devon', *Divine Times*, Special Edition, 17 July.

Fitzgerald, T. (1990), 'Hinduism and the World Religion Fallacy', *Religion*, 20 (1): 101–18.

Forel, F. A. (1912), 'The Fata Morgana', *Procedures. Royal. Society*. Edinburgh 32, 175–82.

Foss, Daniel A., and Ralph W. Larkin (1976, Spring), 'From "The Gates of Eden" to "Day of the Locust": An Analysis of the Dissident Youth Movement of the 1960s and Its Heirs of the Early 1970s – the Post-Movement Groups', *Theory and Society*, 3 (1), 47–50.

Fountain, Nigel (1988), *Underground: The London Alternative Press 1966–74*. London: Comedia.

Frisk, Lisalotte (2013), 'Towards a New Paradigm of Constructing "Religion": New Age Data and Unbounded Categories', in *New Age Spirituality: Rethinking Religion*, Steven Sutcliffe and Ingvild Gilhus, eds. Durham: Acumen, 49–65.

Frost, William (1992), *What Is the New Age? Defining Third Millennium Consciousness*. Lampeter: Edwin Mellen Press.

Gablinger, Tamar (2010), *The Religious Melting Point: On Tolerance, Controversial Religions and the State*. Marburg: Tectum Verlag Marburg.

Geaves, R. A. (1998), 'The Borders between Religions: The Challenge to the World Religions' Approach to Religious Education', *British Journal of Religious Education*, 21 (1), 20–31.

Geaves, R. A. (2000), *Sufis of Britain: An exploration of Muslim identity*. Cardiff: Cardiff Academic Press.

Geaves, R. A. (2004a), 'From Divine Light Mission to Elan Vital and Beyond: An Exploration of Change and Adaptation', *Nova Religio*, 7 (3), 45–62.

Geaves, R. A. (2004b), 'Elan Vital', in *New Religions: A Guide: New Religious Movements, Sects and Alternative Spiritualities*, Christopher Partridge, ed. Oxford: Oxford University Press.

Geaves, R. A. (2005a), 'The Heart of Islam in the Indian subcontinent', in *The Intimate Other*, A. King and R. Stockton, eds. Hyderabad: Longman Oriental.

Geaves, R. A. (2005b), 'The Dangers of Essentialism: South Asian Communities in Britain and the "World Religions" Approach to the Study of Religion', *Contemporary South Asia*, 14 (1), 75–90.

Geaves, R. A. (2006a, April), 'Globalisation, Charisma, Innovation, and Tradition: An Exploration of the Transformations in the Organisational Vehicles for the Transmission of the Teachings of Maharaji', *Journal of Alternative Spirituality and New Age Studies*, 2.

Geaves, R. A. (2006b), 'From Guru Maharaj Ji to Prem Rawat: Paradigm Shifts over the Period of Forty Years as a "Master (1966–2006)"', in *New and Alternative Religions in the US*, Vol. 4 Asian Traditions, Eugene Gallagher and William Ashcroft, eds. Westport: Greenwood.

Geaves, R. A. (2006c), *Key Words in Hinduism*. London: Continuum.

Geaves, R. A. (2007), 'From Totapuri to Maharaji: Reflections on a (Lineage) Parampara', in *Indian Religions: Renaisance and Revival*, Anna King, ed. London: Equinox.

Geaves, R. A. (2009, January), 'Forget Transmitted Memory: The De-Traditionalized "Religion" of Prem Rawat', *Journal of Contemporary Religion*, 24 (1), 19–33.

Geaves, R. A. (2013), 'Hans Ji Maharaj and the Divya Sandesh Parishad', Handbook of Oriental Studies, Section 2, India, *Brill Encyclopedia of Hinduism*, J. Bronkhorst and A. Milinar, eds., Vol. 22: 5, Knut Jacobsen et al., eds., 470–5. Leiden: Brill.

Geaves, R. A. (2017), *Islam and Britain: Islamic Mission in an Age of Empire*. London: Bloomsbury.

Geaves, R. A. (2019), 'The "Death" Pangs of the Insider/Outsider Dichotomy in the Study of Religion', in *The Insider/Outsider Debate: New Perspectives in the Study of Religion*, G. Chryssides and Stephen Gregg, eds. Sheffield: Equinox.

Gerlach, Luther P. (2001), 'The Structure of Social Movements: Environmental Activism and Its Opponents', in *Networks and Netwars: The Future of Terror, Crime, and Militancy*, John Arquilla and David Ronfeldt, eds. Santa Monica, CA: RAND.

Germain, Eric (2008), 'The First Muslim Missions on a European Scale: Ahmadi-Lahori Networks in the Inter-War Period', in *Islam in Inter-War Europe*, Nathalie Clayer and Eric Germain, ed. London: Hurst.

Gilchrist, Roberta, and Cheryl Green (2016), *Glastonbury Abbey: Archaeological Investigations 1904–79*. London: Society of Antiquaries of London.

Gilhus, Ingvild (2013), ' "All over the Place": The Contribution of New Age to a Spatial Model of Religion', in *New Age Spirituality: Rethinking Religion*, Steven Sutcliffe and Ingvlid Gilhus, eds. Durham: Acumen, 35–49.

Girard, Gary (1996), 'Then the World Changed', *Divine Times*, Special Edition, 17 July.

Glyn, Richard (1999), 'Vivekananda and Essentialism', in *Swami Vivekananda and the Modernisation of Hinduism*, William Radice, ed. New Delhi; Oxford: Oxford University Press.

Gold, Daniel (1987), *The Lord as Guru: Hindi Sants in North Indian Tradition*.
New York: Oxford University Press.

Goldberg, Philip (2010), *American Veda: From Emerson and the Beatles to Yoga and Meditation*. New York: Harmony Books, Crown Publishing/Random House.

Gombrich, Richard, and Gananath Obeysekere (1988), *Buddhism Transformed: Religious Change in Sri Lanka*. Princeton, NJ: Princeton University Press

Goodspeed, Edgar J. (1956), *Modern Apocrypha*. Boston, MA: Beacon Press.

Goswami, Mukunda, and Mandira Dasi (2011), *Miracle on Second Avenue*. Badger, CA: Torchlight.

Grogan, Emmett (1990), *Ringolevio: A Life Played for Keeps*. New York: Citadel Press.

Gurdjieff, George (1963), *Meetings with Remarkable Men*. New York: E. P. Dutton.

Hale, Amy (2011), 'John Michell, Radical Traditionalism, and the Emerging Politics of the Pagan New Right', *The Pomegranate: The International Journal of Pagan Studies*, 13 (1), 77.

Hammer, Olav (2015), 'Theosophy', in *The Occult World*, Christopher Partridge, ed. London: Routledge, 250–9.

Hanegraaff, Wouter (1996), *New Age Religion and Western Culture: Esotericism in the Mirror of Secular Thought*. Leiden: Brill.

Hanegraaff, Wouter (2001). 'Prospects for the Globalization of the New Age: Spiritual Imperialism versus Cultural Diversity', in *New Age Religion and Globalization*, Mikael Rothstein, ed. Aarhus: Aarhus University Press.

Hartlaub, Peter, Sam Whiting (2017), 'Reliving the Human Be-In 50 Years Later', *San Francisco Chronicle*, January 13.

Haynes, Charles C. (1993), *Meher Baba, the Awakener*. N. Myrtle Beach, SC: Avatar Foundation.

Heelas, Paul (1996), *The New Age Movement*. Oxford: Blackwell.

Heelas, Paul (ed.) (2012), *Spirituality in the Modern World. Within Religious Tradition and Beyond*. London: Routledge.

Heelas, Paul, and Linda Woodhead (2004), *The Spiritual Revolution: Why Religion Is Giving Way to Spirituality (Religion and Spirituality in the Modern World)*. Oxford: Blackwell.

Hervieu-Léger, Danièle (2000), *Religion as a Chain of Memory*. Cambridge: Polity Press.

Hesse, Herman (1949), *The Glass Bead Game*. New York: Holt, Rinehart and Winston.

Hesse, Herman (1951), *Siddhartha*. New York: New Directions.

Hetherington, Kevin (1999), *New Age Travellers: Vanloads of Uproarious Humanity*. London: Continuum.

Hewison, Robert (1986), *Too Much: Art and Society in the Sixties, 1960–75*. London: Methuen.

Hexham, Irving (1983, March), 'The Freaks of Glastonbury: Conversion and Consolidation in an English Country Town', *Update*, 7 (1), 3–11.

Hinton, Brian (1995), *Message to Love: The Isle of Wight Festivals, 1968–70*. Chessington: Castle Communications.

Hobart, George Vere (1904), *Jim Hickey: A Story of the One-Night Stands*. New York: G. W. Dillingham.

Hopkins, Jerry (1970), *Festival! The Book of American Music Celebrations*. New York: Macmillan.

Houghton, Mick (2010), *Becoming Elektra: True Story of Jac Holzman's Visionary Record Label*. London: Jawbone Press.

Hunt, Stephen (2003), *Alternative Religions: A Sociological Introduction*. Aldershot: Ashgate.

Hutton, Ronald (1993), *The Pagan Religions of the Ancient British Isles: Their Nature and Legacy*. Oxford: Blackwell.

Hutton, Ronald (2013), *Pagan Britain*. New Haven, CT; London: Yale University Press.

Irvin, Jim, and Colin McLear (eds) (2007), 'The Mojo Collection – 4th Edition', in *The Jam: Sound Affects*. London: Canongate.

Isaacson, Walter (2001), *Steve Jobs: A Biography*. London: Simon & Schuster.

Ivakhiv, Adrian J. (2001), *Claiming Sacred Ground: Pilgrims and Politics at Glastonbury and Sedona*. Bloomington: Indiana University Press.

Jack, Alan (ed.) (1976), *New Age Dictionary*. Kanthaka Press, reprinted in 1990 by New York: Japan Publications.

Jackson, R. (1997), *Religious Education: An Interpretive Approach*. London: Hodder and Stoughton.

Jefferson, William (1976), *The Story of the Maharishi*. New York: Pocket.

Juergensmeyer, M. (1987), 'The Radhasoami Revival', in *The Sants: Studies in Devotional Literature*, K. Schomer and W. H. McLeod, eds. Delhi: Motilal Benarsidass.

Juergensmeyer, Mark (1991), *Radhasoami Reality: The Logic of a Modern Faith*. Princeton, NJ: Princeton University Press.

Kalchuri, Bhau (1986), *Meher Prabhu: Lord Meher, The Biography of the Avatar of the Age*. Myrtle Beach, CA: Manifestation.

Kaufman, W., and H. S. Macpherson (2005), *Britain and the Americas: Culture, Politics, and History*. Santa Barbara, CA: ABC-CLIO.

Kemp, Darren, and James Lewis (eds) (2007), *Handbook of the New Age*. Leiden: Brill.

Kent, Stephen (2001), *From Slogans to Mantras: Social Protest and Religious Conversion in the Late Vietnam Era*. Syracuse, NY: Syracuse University Press.

Kerouac, Jack (1957), *On the Road*. New York: Viking Press.

Kerouac, Jack (1958), *The Dharma Bums*. New York: Viking Press.

Kerr, Andrew (1996), 'A Pair of Anniversaries', *Divine Times*, 17 July.

Kerr, Andrew (2011), *Intolerably Hip: The Memoirs of Andrew Kerr*. Kirstead: Frontier Press.

King, Richard (1999), *Orientalism and Religion*. London: Routledge.

Knee, Sam (2017), *Memory of a Free Festival: The Golden Era of the British Underground Festival Scene*. London: Cicada.

Knight, Gareth (2000), *Dion Fortune and the Inner Light*. Loughborough: Thoth.

Knott, Kim (1986), *My Sweet Lord: The Hare Krishna Movement*. Newcastle: Newcastle Publishing Company.

Kozinn, Allan (2008), 'Meditation on the Man Who Saved the Beatles', *New York Times*, 7 February.

Krieger, Lisa M. (2017). 'Esalen's Survival Story: A Tale of Transformation', *Mercury News*, 21 July.

Kripal, Jeffrey (2007a), *Esalen: America and the Religion of No Religion*. Chicago, IL: University of Chicago Press.

Kripal, Jeffrey (2007b), 'Remembering Ourselves: On Some Countercultural Echoes of Contemporary Tantric Studies', *Religions of South Asia*, 1 (1), 11–28.

Kyle, Richard (1995), *The New Age Movement in American Culture*. Lanham, MD: University Press of America.

Lammers, Jos (2007), *Mescaline, Maharaj Ji and the Mojave Desert: Abandoned Roads*. Self-published.

Lang, Michael (2009), *The Road to Woodstock*. New York: HarperCollins.

Lans, Jan van der, and Fran Derks (1986, June), 'Premies versus Sannyasins', *Update: A Quarterly Journal on New Religious Movements* X (2).

Leary, Timothy, Richard Alpert and Ralph Metzner (2008), *The Psychedelic Experience: A Manual Based on the Tibetan Book of the Dead*. Harmondsworth: Penguin Modern Classics.

Lee, Peter (1996), 'A Heart Full of Love at Heathrow', *Divine Times* Special Edition. 17 July.

Le Gentil, Pierre (1959), 'The Work of Robert de Boron and the *Didot Perceval*', in *Arthurian Literature in the Middle Ages: A Collaborative History*, R. S. Loomis, ed. Oxford: Clarendon Press.

Lesh, Phil (2006), *Searching for the Sound: My Life with the Grateful Dead*. New York: Back Bay.

Lewis, Grover (1969, 18 December), 'Viewing the Remains of a Mean Saturday', *Village Voice*, XIV (62).

Lewis, H. D., and R. Slater (1966), *World Religions*. London: C. A. Watts.

Lewis, James (1992), 'Approaches to the Study of the New Age Movement', in *Perspectives on the New Age*, James Lewis and J. Gordon Melton, ed. New York: State University of New York Press.

Lewis, James, and Gordon J. Melton (1992), 'Introduction', in *Perspectives on the New Age*, James Lewis and J. Gordon Melton, eds. New York: State University of New York Press.

Lewis James, and Gordon J. Melton (eds) (1992), *Perspectives on the New Age*. New York: State University of New York Press.

Lindahl, Carl, John McNamara and John Lindow (2002), *Medieval Folklore: An Encyclopedia of Myths, Legends, Tales, Beliefs, and Customs*. Oxford: Oxford University Press.

Lopez, Donald (1996), 'The Image of Tibet of the Great Mystifiers', in *Imagining Tibet: Perceptions, Projections, and Fantasies*, Thierry Dodin and Heinz Rather, eds. Somerville: Wisdom.

Lopez, Donald S. Jr (1999), *Prisoners of Shangri-LA: Tibetan Buddhism and the West*. Chicago, IL: University of Chicago Press.

Lotfallah, Soliman (1993), 'Auroville: The Fulfillment of a Dream', *UNESCO Courier*, January.

Lovejoy, David (2005), *Between Dark and Dark*. New South Wales: Echo.

Lusher, Adam (2018), "Jonestown Massacre: How 918 People Followed a Cult Leader to Guyana, 'Drank the Kool-Aid' … and Died in a Single Day." *Independent*, February 28.

Lyttle, Mark Hamilton (2006), *America's Uncivil Wars: The Sixties Era from Elvis to the Fall of Richard Nixon*. Oxford: Oxford University Press.

MacDonald, Ian (1995, 2008), *A Revolution in the Head: The Beatles' Records and the 60s*. London: Pimlico.

Maharishi Mahesh Yogi (1986), *Thirty Years around the World: Dawn of the Age of Enlightenment*. Fairfield: Maharishi Vedic University Press.

Maltwood, K. E. (1934), *A Guide to Glastonbury's Temple of the Stars*. London: The Women's Printing Society.

Maltwood, K. E. (1937), *Air View Supplement to a Guide to Glastonbury's Temple of the Stars*. London: John M. Watkins.

Maltwood, K. E. (1944), *The Enchantments of Britain or King Arthur's Round Table of the Stars*. Victoria: Victoria Printing and Publishing.

Maltwood, K. E. (1946), *King Arthur's Round Table of the Zodiac*. Victoria: Victoria Printing and Publishing.

Mann, Nicholas (1986), *The Cauldron and the Grail*. Cheltenham: Triskele Publications.

Mann, Nicholas (1993), *Glastonbury Tor: A Guide to the History and Legends*. Cheltenham: Triskele Publications.

Mann, Nicholas (2004), *Energy Secrets of Glastonbury Tor*. Sutton Mallet: Green Magic

Mann, Nicholas (2001), *The Isle of Avalon: Sacred Mysteries of Arthur and Glastonbury*. Sutton Mallet: Green Magic.

Mann, Nicholas, and Philippa Glasson (2005), *Avalon's Red and White Springs: The Healing Waters of Glastonbury*. Sutton Mallet: Green Magic.

Mann, Nicholas, and Philippa Glasson (2007), *The Star Temple of Avalon: Glastonbury's Ancient Observatory Revealed*. Bridgewater: Temple.

Manning, Toby (2006), 'The Underground', in *The Rough Guide to Pink Floyd*. London: Rough Guides.

Mason, Paul (1994), *The Maharishi – The Biography of the Man Who Gave Transcendental Meditation to the World*. Dorset: Element.

Masters, Robert, and Jean Houston (1966), *The Varieties of Psychedelic Experience*. London: Turnstone.

Melton, Gordon J. (ed.) (1999), *The Encyclopaedic Handbook of Cults in America*, Garland Reference Library of Social Science (Vol. 797), Religious Information Systems Series, Vol. 7.

Melton, Gordon J. (2003), *Encyclopedia of American Religions*, 7th edn. Detroit, MI: Thomson.

McClory, Donald (1998), *Introduction to Hermann Hesse. Siddhartha*. London: Picador.

McCloud, Sean (2004), *Making the American Religious Fringe: Exotics, Subversives and Journalists, 1955–1993*. Chapel Hill: UNC Press.

McCutcheon, Russell T. (1998), The *Insider/Outsider Problem in the Study of Religion: A Reader* (Controversies in the Study of Religion). London: Continuum.

McGuire, Meredith B. (1981), *Religion: The Social Context*. Belmont, CA: Wadsworth.

McKay, George (2000), *Glastonbury: A Very English Fair*. London: Victor Gollancz.

McKay, George (2004), ' "Unsafe Things Like Youth and Jazz": Beaulieu Jazz Festivals (1956–61) and the Origins of Pop Festival Culture in Britain', in *Remembering Woodstock*, Andy Bennett, ed. Aldershot: Ashgate.

McKay, George (ed.) (2015), *The Pop Festival: History, Music, Media, Culture*. London: Bloomsbury.

Melton, Gordon J. (ed.) (1996), *Encyclopaedia of American Religions*, 5th edn. Detroit, MI: Gale Research.

"Midsummer Magic: To Go or Not to Go"(1996), *Divine Times* Special Edition, 17 July.

Minnion, John, and Philip Bolsover (eds) (1983), *The CND Story*. London: Alison and Busby.

Morgan, Ted (1973), 'Oz in the Astrodome', *New York Times Magazine*, 9 December, 38ff.

Muster, Nori Jean (1997), *Betrayal of the Spirit: My Life behind the Headlines of the Hare Krishna Movement* (reprint ed.). Urbana: University of Illinois Press.

Needleman, Jacob (1970a), *The New Religions*. New York: Doubleday.

Needleman, Jacob (1970b), 'Transcendental Meditation', in *The New Religions*. New York: Doubleday.

Nelson, Elizabeth (1989), *The British Counter-Culture 1966–1973: A Study of the Underground Press*. London: MacMillan.

O'Dea, Thomas (1961), "Five Dilemmas in the Institutionalization of Religion", *Journal for the Scientific Study of Religion*, 1 (1), 30–9.

Oldham, Andrew Loog (1965), 'Sleeve Notes', *The Rolling Stones, Now!*, Decca Records.

Ollivier, Debra (ed.) (2012), 'Esalen: 50 Years Ago, A "Crazy Place on a Godforsaken Road" Launched the New Age Movement', *The Huffington Post*, 25 May.

Olsen, Roger (1995), 'Eckankar: From Ancient Science of Soul Travel to New Age Religion', in *America's Alternative Religions*, Timothy Miller, ed. Albany: State University of New York Press.

O'Mahony, John (2008), 'A Hodgepodge of Hash, Yoga and LSD – Interview with Sitar Giant Ravi Shankar', *Guardian*, 3 June.

Owen, Alex (2004), *The Place of Enchantment*. Chicago, IL: University of Chicago Press.

Palmer, Spencer J., and Roger R. Keller (1990, 1997), 'Divine Light Mission', in *Religions of the World: A Latter Day Saints View*. Salt Lake City: Brigham Young University Press..

Parker, Martin, Valerie Fournier and Patrick Reedy (2007), *The Dictionary of Alternatives: Utopianism and Organization*. London: Zed.

Partridge, Christopher (2004), *The Re-Enchantment of the West: Alternative Spiritualities, Sacralization, Popular Culture and Occulture Volume 1*. London: T. & T. Clark.

Partridge, Christopher (2006), 'The Spiritual and the Revolutionary, Alternative Spirituality, British Free Festivals, and the Emergence of Rave Culture', *Culture and Religion* 7 (1), 41–60.

Partridge, Christopher (2015a), 'Introduction', in *The Occult World*, Christopher Partridge, ed. London: Routledge.

Partridge, Christopher (2015b), 'The Occult and Popular Music', in *The Occult World*, Christopher Partridge, ed. London: Routledge.

Partridge, Christopher (2017), 'Psychedelic Music', in *Religion and Popular Music*, Christopher Partridge and Marcus Moberg, eds. London: Bloomsbury, 294–305.

Partridge, Christopher (2018), *High Culture: Drugs, Mysticism, and the Pursuit of Transcendence in the Modern World*. Oxford: Oxford University Press.

Pearson, Joanne (2002), 'Introduction', in *Belief Beyond Boundaries: Wicca, Celtic Spirituality and the New Age*, Joanne Pearson, ed. Milton Keynes and Aldershot: Open University Press and Ashgate.

Pement, Eric (1988), '*Don't Touch That Dial: The New Age Practice of Channeling*', *Cornerstone Magazine*, November.

Perone, James E. (2001), *Songs of the Vietnam Conflict*. Westport, CT: Greenwood.

Perry, Charles (1988), *The Haight-Ashbury: A History*. New York: Vintage.

Petersen, William J. (1982), *Those Curious New Cults in the 80s*. Connecticut: Keats.

Pilarzyk, Thomas (1978, Autumn), 'The Origin, Development, and Decline of a Youth Culture Religion: An Application of Sectarianization Theory', *Review of Religious Research*, 20 (1), 23–43.

Pirsig, Robert (1974), *Zen and the Art of Motorcycle Maintenance*. New York: Bantam.

Popp-Baier, Ulrike (2010), 'From Religion to Spirituality – Megatrend in Contemporary Society or Methodological Artefact? A Contribution to the Secularization Debate from Psychology of Religion?', *Journal of Religion in Europe* 3 (1), 34–67.

Powys, John Cowper (1975), *A Glastonbury Romance*, 2nd edn. London: Picador.

Price, Dennis (2009), *The Missing Years of Jesus: The Greatest Story Never Told*. London: Hay House.

Puttick, Elizabeth (2000), 'The Human Potential Movement', in *Beyond New Age: Exploring Alternative Spirituality*, Steven Sutcliffe and Marion Bowman, eds. Edinburgh: Edinburgh University Press.

Rahtz, Philip, and Lorna Watts (2003), *Glastonbury Myth & Archaeology*. Stroud: Tempus.

Rawlinson, Andrew (1997), *The Book of Enlightened Masters: Wisdom Teachers in Eastern Traditions*. Chicago, IL: Open Court.

Ringrose, Kerren (1996), 'The Last Line of the Poem', *Divine Times*, 17 July.

Robbins, Thomas, and Benjamin Zablocki (2001), *Misunderstanding Cults: Searching for Objectivity in a Controversial Field*. Toronto and Buffalo: University of Toronto Press.

Rooney, Ben (2008). 'Maharishi Mahesh Yogi, Guru to Beatles, Dies'. *Telegraph*, 6 February, London.

Rooum, Donald (2008, Summer), 'Freedom, Freedom Press and Freedom Bookshop: A Short History of Freedom Press', *Information for Social Change* 27, 1–8.

Ross, Nancy Wilson (1958), 'Beat and Buddhist', *New York Times*, 5 October.

Rossman, Michael (1979), *New Age Blues. On the Politics of Consciousness*. New York: Dutton.

Roszak, Theodore (1969), *The Making of a Counterculture: Reflections on the Technocratic Society and Its Youthful Opposition*. New York: Doubleday.

Rudin, A. James, and Marcia R. Rudin (1974), *Prison or Paradise? The New Religious Cults*. Philadelphia, PA: Fortress Press.

Ruggles, Clive L. N. (2005), *Ancient Astronomy: An Encyclopaedia of Cosmologies and Myth*. Santa Barbara, CA: ABC-CLIO.

Russell, Alan (ed.) (1987), *The Guinness Book of Records*. London: Guinness World Records.

Russell, Peter (1977), *The T.M. Technique: An Introduction to Transcendental Meditation and the Teachings of Maharishi Mahesh Yogi*. London: Routledge.

Santelli, Robert (1980), *Aquarius Rising: The Rock Festival Years*. New York: Dell.

Sarkar, Jadunath (2018), *A History of the Dasnami Naga Sannyasis*. London: Taylor and Francis.

Sarlin, Bob (1973), *Turn It Up! (I Can't Hear the Words)*. London: Coronet.

Shiedlower, Jesse (2004), "Crying Wolof: Does the Word Hip Really Hail from a West African Language?" https://slate.com/news-and-politics/2004/12/the-real-history-of-hip.html, accessed 22 June 2019.

Schnabel, Paul (1982), *Tussen stigma en charisma: nieuwe religieuze bewegingen en geestelijke volksgezondheid* ('Between Stigma and Charisma: New Religious Movements and Mental Health'). Erasmus University Rotterdam, Faculty of Medicine, PhD thesis. Deventer: Van Loghum Slaterus.

Schomer, Karine, and W. H. McLeod (eds) (1987), *The Sants: Studies in a Devotional Tradition of India*. Delhi: Motilal Banarsidass.

Schultz, John (2009), *The Chicago Conspiracy Trial: Revised Edition*. Chicago, IL: University of Chicago Press.

Screeton, Paul (2010), *John Michell: From Atlantis to Avalon*. Avebury: Heart of Albion Press.

Seager, Richard (2009), *The World's Parliament of Religions: The East/West Encounter, Chicago, 1893 (Religion in North America)*. Indiana: Indiana University Press.

Shabdanand Ji, Sri Swami Sar (1998), *Shri Swarup Darshan*. New Delhi: Sar Shabd Mission.

Shannon, Bob (2009), *Turn It Up! American Radio Tales 1946–1996*. Washington, DC: Austrianmonk.

Shapiro, Harry (1988), *Waiting for the Man: The Story of Drugs and Popular Music*. London: Quartet.

Sharf, Robert (1995), 'Whose Zen: Zen Nationalism Revisited', in *Rude Awakenings: Zen, the Kyoto School, & the Question of Nationalism*, James W. Heisig and John C. Maraldo, eds. Honolulu: University of Hawai'i Press, 40–51.

Siegel, Roger (2004), *By His Example: The Wit and Wisdom of A. C. Bhaktivedanta Swami Prabhupada*. Badger, CA: Torchlight.

Singh, Sawan (1965), *Spiritual Gems*. Beas: Radhasoami Satsang Beas.

Singh, Trilochan, Jod Singh, Kapur Singh, et al. (trans.) (1973), *The Sacred Writings of the Sikhs*, 3rd edn. London: George Allen & Unwin.

Skal, David J., and Elias Savada (1995). 'Offend One and You Offend Them All: The Making of Tod Browning's *Freaks*', *Filmfax*, September–October.

Smith, A.W (1989) '"And Did Those Feet . . .?": The "Legend" of Christ's Visit to Britain.' *Folklore* 100 (1), 63–83.

Smith, David (2003), *Hinduism and Modernity*. Oxford: Blackwell.

Smith, John Z. (2003), 'Here, There and Anywhere,' in Prayer, Magic, and the Stars in the Ancient and Late Antique World, S. Noegel, J. Walker and B. Wheeler, eds. Pennsylvania: Pennsylvania State University, 21–36.

Snelling, John, and Mark Watts (eds) (1990), *The Modern Mystic: A New Collection of the Early Writings of Alan Watts*. Rockport: Element.

Spiro, Melford (1970), *Buddhism and Society: A Great Tradition and Its Vicissitudes*. Berkeley, CA: Berkeley University Press.

Srinivas, Aravamudan (2005), *Guru English: South Asian Religion in a Cosmopolitan Language*. Princeton, NJ: Princeton University Press.

Stanton, Scott (2003), *The Tombstone Tourist*. New York: Simon & Schuster.

Stewart, Tony (2003) 'Syncretism', in *South Asian Folklore: An Encyclopedia*, M. Mills, P. Claus and S. Diamond, eds. London: Routledge, 586–8.

Strachan, Gordon (1998), *Jesus the Master Builder: Druid Mysteries and the Dawn of Christianity*. Edinburgh: Floris.

Stone, C. J. (1999), *The Last of the Hippies*. London: Faber & Faber.

Stubbs, David (2003), *Voodoo Child: Jimi Hendrix, the Stories behind Every Song*. New York: Thunder's Mouth Press.

Sutcliffe, Steven (2000), 'A Colony of Seekers: Findhorn in the 1990s', *Journal of Contemporary Religion* 15 (2), 215–31.

Sutcliffe, Steven (2003), *Children of the New Age: A History of Spiritual Practices*. London: Routledge.

Sutcliffe, Steven (2013), 'New Age, World Religions and Elementary Forms', in *New Age Spirituality: Rethinking Religion*, Steven Sutcliffe and Ingvild Gilhus, eds. Durham: Acumen, 16–34.

Sutcliffe, Steven (2014), 'The New Age', in *The Bloomsbury Companion to New Religious Movements*, George Chryssides and Benjamin Zeller, eds. London: Bloomsbury.

Sutcliffe, Steven, and Ingvar Gilhus (2013a), 'Introduction', in *New Age Spirituality: Rethinking Religion*. Durham: Acumen, 1–16.

Sutcliffe, Steven, and Ingvild Gilhus (eds) (2013b), *New Age Spirituality: Rethinking Religion*. London: Routledge.

Suthren-Hirst, Jacqueline, and John Zavos (2005, March), 'Riding a Tiger? South Asia and the Problem of "Religion"', *Contemporary South Asia*, 14 (1), 3–20.

Suzuki, D. L. (1927), *Essays in Zen Buddhism: First Series*. New York: Grove Press.

Suzuki, D. L. (1933), *Essays in Zen Buddhism: Second Series*. New York: Samuel Weiser.

Suzuki, D. L. (1934a), *Essays in Zen Buddhism: Third Series*. Maine: Samuel Weiser.

Suzuki, D. L. (1934b), *An Introduction to Zen Buddhism*. Kyoto: Eastern Buddhist Society.

Suzuki, D. L. (1948), *An Introduction to Zen Buddhism* with Foreword by C. G. Jung. London: Rider & Company.

Suzuki, D. L. (1949a), *The Zen Doctrine of No-Mind*. London: Rider & Company.

Suzuki, D. L. (1949b), *Living by Zen*. London: Rider & Company.

Suzuki, D. L. (1957), *Mysticism: Christian and Buddhist: The Eastern and Western Way*. London: Macmillan.

Suzuki, D. L. (1959a), *The Training of the Zen Buddhist Monk*. New York: University Books.

Suzuki, D. L. (1959b), *Manual of Zen Buddhism*. London: Rider & Company.

Suzuki, D. L. (1959c), *Zen and Japanese Culture*. New York: Pantheon.

Sweers, B. (2005), *Electric Folk: The Changing Face of English Traditional Music*. Oxford: Oxford University Press.

Szatmary, David P. (1996), *Rockin' in Time: A Social History of Rock-and-Roll*, 3rd illustrated edn. Upper Saddle River, NJ: Prentice Hall.

Tacey, David (2003), *The Spirituality Revolution*. Australia: HarperCollins.

Thomas, Peter, Michael Kember and Richard J. Sneed (1987), *The Faire: Photographs and History of the Renaissance Pleasure Faire from 1963 Onwards*. Santa Cruz, CA: Good Book Press.

Tibballs, Geoff (2006), *The World's Greatest Hoaxes*. New York: Barnes & Noble.

Tingay, Kevin (2000), 'Madame Blavatsky's Children: Theosophy and Its Heirs', in *Beyond New Age: Exploring Alternative Spirituality*, Steven Sutcliffe and Marion Bowman, eds. Edinburgh: Edinburgh University Press, 37–50.

Tuedio, James A., and Stan Spector (2010), *Grateful Dead in Concert: Essays on Live Improvisation*. Jefferson, NC: McFarland.

Tunden, Professor (1970), *Satguru Shri Hans Ji Maharaj: Eternal Is He, Eternal Is His Knowledge*. Delhi: DLM.

van den Berg, Stephanie (2008). 'Beatles Guru Maharishi Mahesh Yogi Dies', *Sydney Morning Herald*, 5 February.

Vaudeville, C. (1987), 'Sant Mat: Santism as the Universal Path to Sanctity', in *The Sants: Studies in Devotional Literature*, K. Schomer and W. H. McLeod, eds. Delhi: Motilal Benarsidass.

Versluis, Arthur (2014), *American Gurus: From American Transcendentalism to New Age Religion*. Oxford: Oxford University Press.

Victor, Jeffrey (2015), 'Crime, Moral Panic and the Occult', in *The Occult World*, CristopherPartridge, ed. London: Routledge, 692–701.

von Hoffman, Nicholas (1968), *We Are the People Our Parents Warned Us Against*. New York: Fawcett.

Wallis, Roy (1984), *The Elementary Forms of the New Religious Life*. London; Boston, MA: Routledge and Kegan Paul.

Watkins, Alfred (1922), *Early British Trackways, Moats, Mounds, Camps and Sites*. London: Simpkin, Marshall, Hamilton, Kent.

Watson, J. L. (2009), *Initiations of the Aquarian Masters: The Theosophy of the Aquarian Gospel*. Colorado: Outskirts Press.

Watt, Mike (2007, August), 'Bath Festival, June 1969 & June 1970', *Classic Rock* 109. Future Publications.

Watts, Alan (1957), *The Way of Zen*. New York: Pantheon.

Watts, Alan (1961), *Psychotherapy East and West*. New York: Pantheon.

Weightman, S. (1978), *Hinduism in the Village Setting*. Milton Keynes: The Open University.

Weil, Andrew (2000), *Eating Well for Optimum Health*. New York: Random House.

White, Richard (1997), *King Arthur in Legend and History*. London: Dent.

Williamson, Lola (2010), *Transcendent in America: Hindu-Inspired Meditation Movements as New Religion*. New York: NY Press.

Wilson, Brian (1994), *Apostates and New Religious Movements*. Oxford: Oxford University Press.

Winter, Mark (1996), 'Midsummer Magic', *Divine Times*, Special Edition, 17 July.

Wolf, Mary Montgomery (2007), *'We Accept You, One of Us?': Punk Rock, Community, and Individualism in an Uncertain Era, 1974–1985*. Michigan: ProQuest.

Wolfe, Tom (1968), *Electric Kool Aid Acid Test*. New York: Farrar Straus Giroux.

Wolkin, Jan Mark, and Bill Keenom (2000), *Michael Bloomfield – If You Love These Blues: An Oral History*. San Francisco, CA: Backbeat.

Wright, Gary (2014), *Dream Weaver: A Memoir; Music, Meditation, and My Friendship with George Harrison*. New York: TarcherPerigee.

Yoganananda Paramahansa (1946), *Autobiography of a Yogi*, 1st edn. New York: The Philosophical Library.

York, Michael (1995), *The Emerging Network*. Lanham, MD: Rowman & Littlefield.

York, Michael (2006), 'New Age and Magic', in *Witchcraft and Magic: Contemporary North America*, Helen A. Barger, ed. Philadelphia, PA: University of Pennsylvania Press.

Zablocki, Benjamin (1980), *Alienation and Charisma: A Study of Contemporary American Communes*. New York: Free Press.

Ziolkowski, Theodore (1994), *Foreword to the Glass Bead Game*. London: Picador.

Websites (listed in order of appearance in the text)

Aston, Kate (2012), 'Insider and Outsider: An Anthropological Perspective', http://www.religiousstudiesproject.com/2012/02/24/katie-aston-insider-and-outsider-an-anthropological-perspective/, visited 23 February 2018.

INFORM, www.inform.ac.uk, visited 20 April 2018.

Learners, Dreamers and Dissenters, http://www.bl.uk/learning/histcitizen/21cc/counterculture/assaultonculture/provo/provo.html, British Library website, accessed 23 February 2018.

http://www.lobsangrampa.net/, accessed 25 April 2018.

Lowe, Nick, 'The Best of Glastonbury Moments', *Telegraph*, https://www.telegraph.co.uk/culture/music/3665988/The-best-of-Glastonbury-moments.html, visited 27 June 2019.

Gitlin, Todd, https://www.nytimes.com/2017/04/24/books/robert-pirsig-dead-wrote-zen-and-the-art-of-motorcycle-maintenance.html, visited 22 June 2019.

https://www.findhorn.org/about-us/, accessed 3 May 2018.

http://www.users.globalnet.co.uk/~pardos/GG.html, visited 2 May 2018.

http://eyewitnesstohistory.com/matahari.htm, visited 22 May 2018.

https://www.britannica.com/biography/Ruth-St-Denis, visited 2 May 2018.

www.vivekananda.net/PROSE/EastWest.html, accessed 24 May 2018.

Goldburg, Philip, 'Three Gurus Who Changed the Face of Spirituality in the West', https://www.huffingtonpost.com/philip-goldberg/three-gurus-who-rocked-ou_b_804186.html, visited 30 May 2018.

'The Rush of Gurus', *The Pluralism project*, http://pluralism.org/religions/hinduism/hinduism-in-america/the-rush-of-gurus/, Harvard University, visited 30 May 2018.

'The Auroville Charter: A New Vision of Power and Promise for People Choosing Another Way of Life', https://www.auroville.org/contents/1, accessed 31 May 2018.

'Census – Auroville population May 2018', https://www.auroville.org/contents/3329, accessed 31 May 2018.

http://www.dlshq.org/saints/siva.htm, visited 31 May 2018.

Crossman, Ashley (2018), 'Definition of Moral Panic Overview of the Theory and Notable Examples', https://www.thoughtco.com/moral-panic-3026420, visited 20 August 2018.

'Arya Samaj: Religious Sect: India', https://www.britannica.com/topic/Arya-Samaj,visited 20 August 2018.

https://www.britannica.com/biography/Kabir-Indian-mystic-and-poet, visited 20
    August 2018.

https://www.britannica.com/biography/Ramakrishna, accessed 20 August 2018.

https://www.culturalindia.net/indian-religions/shankaracharya.html, accessed 21
    August 2018.

http://www.gosavisamaj.com/articles/history/ visited 21 August 2018.

www.prem-rawat-bio.org/lineage.html, accessed 22 August 2018.

http://www.prem-rawat-bio.org/library/sg/sg.html#anchorpanoramic, visited on 22
    August 2018.

https://web.archive.org/web/20040205200722/http://www.etymonline.com:80/,
    accessed 20 September 2018.

Helms, Chet, 'About This eEvent...' *Summer of Love*. https://web.archive.org/
    web/20110228023419/http://www.summeroflove.org/event.html, accessed 20
    September 2018.

'Grateful Dead (Skull and Roses)', http://www.deaddisc.com/disc/Skull_And_Roses.
    htm, accessed 20 September 2018.

http://www.doorshistory.com/doors1965.html, last visited 10 September 2018.

https://www.azlyrics.com/lyrics/donovan/sunnygoodgestreet.html, visited 20
    September 2018.

'British Psychedelia', *Allmusic*, https://web.archive.org/web/20110101142207/
    http://www.allmusic.com/explore/essay/british-psychedelic-t684, visited 18
    September 2018.

Skip Stone, 'Hippies from A to Z' – Hippy Glossary, https://www.hipplanet.com/books/
    atoz/glossary.htm, accessed 18 September 2018.

https://en.wikipedia.org/wiki/Isle_of_Wight_Festival_1970, accessed 18
    September 2018.

'History of the Cambridge Folk Festival', https://www.cambridgelive.org.uk/folk-
    festival/history, accessed 27 June 2019.

Brennan, Matt (2006), 'Was Newport 1969 the Altamont of Jazz? The Role of Music
    Festivals in Shaping the Jazz-Rock Fusion Debate', University of Stirling, http://
    mattbrennan.ca/brennanLEEDS2006.pdf, accessed 24 September 2018.

http://www.postertrip.com/public/5577.cfm, accessed 28 September 2018.

https://www.univie.ac.at/Anglistik/easyrider/data/KeseyPrs.htm, accessed 28
    September 2018.

'Fantasy Fair and Magic Mountain Festival, Marin County History', https://web.archive.
    org/web/20090421002839/http://blogs.marinij.com/marinhistory/2008/09/fantasy_
    fair_magic_mountain_mu.html, accessed 1 October 2018.

'Steve Hoffman Music Forums, 1967 Fantasy Fair and Magic Mountain Music Festival',
http://forums.stevehoffman.tv/threads/1967-fantasy-fair-and-magic-mountain-music-
    festival.345009/ accessed 1 October 2018.

'The Hyde Park Free Concerts', http://www.ukrockfestivals.com/Hyde-park-Festivals.
    html, accessed 6 October 2018.

'Isle of Wight Festival History', http://www.bbc.co.uk/hampshire/content/
articles/2005/04/08/iowfestival_history_feature.shtml, accessed 6 October 2018.

'Isle of Wight Guru', https://www.isleofwightguru.co.uk/isle-of-wight-festival-history.
html, accessed 6 October 2018.

'The Archive: The Eleventh National Jazz and Blues Festival', http://ukrockfestivals.com/
reading-71.html, accessed 6 October 2018.

'Timeline: The History of the Reading Festival', http://www.fatreg.com/timeline.html,
accessed 5 October 2018.

http://news.bbc.co.uk/onthisday/hi/dates/stories/august/18/newsid_2760000/2760911.
stm, accessed 3 October 2018.

https://www.woodstock.com/lineup/, accessed 3 October 2018.

http://news.bbc.co.uk/onthisday/hi/dates/stories/august/18/newsid_2760000/2760911.
stm, accessed 3 October 2018.

https://www.history.com/this-day-in-history/woodstock-music-festival-concludes,
accessed 3 October 2018.

Mankin, Bill (2012), 'We Can All Join In: How Rock Festivals Helped Change America',
Like the Dew, http://likethedew.com/2012/03/04/we-can-all-join-in-how-rock-
festivals-helped-change-america/#.W7IUaGhKjIU, accessed 1 October 2018.

'Interview with Lou Adler by Tavis Smiley', https://web.archive.org/
web/20081227034529/http://www.pbs.org/kcet/tavissmiley/
archive/200706/20070604_adler.html, accessed 1 October 2018.

https://www.efestivals.co.uk/festivals/glastonbury/1970, accessed 9 October 2018.

https://www.somersetlive.co.uk/whats-on/music-nightlife/a-first-class-show-
remembering-19112, accessed 9 October 2018.

http://www.ukrockfestivals.com/phun-city-menu.html, accessed 9 October 2018.

McKay, George, 'The social and (counter)cultural 1960s in the USA, transatlantically',
http://www.academia.edu/196233/The_social_and_counter_cultural_1960s_in_the_
USA_transatlantically, accessed 10 October 2018.

Sutton, John William (trans.)(2001), 'Gerald of Wales: The Tomb of King Arthur', The
Camelot Project, University of Rochester, http://d.lib.rochester.edu/camelot/text/
gerald-of-wales-arthurs-tomb, accessed 14 October 2018.

Hare, John Bruno (17 June 2004), 'Early British Trackways, Moats, Mounds, Camps and
Sites by Alfred Watkins [1922]', http://www.sacred-texts.com/neu/eng/ebt/index.
htm, accessed 12 October 2018.

'Culhwch ac Olwen, part 2', translated by Lady Charlotte Guest, http://www.
ancienttexts.org/library/celtic/ctexts/culhwch2.html, accessed 18 October 2018.

'1968: Anti-Vietnam Demo Turns Violent', news.bbc.co.uk/onthisday/hi/dates/stories/
march/17/newsid_2818000/2818967.stm, accessed 24 October 2018.

Powis, Neville (2003), 'The Human Be-In and the Hippy Revolution', 22 January, https://
web.archive.org/web/20060421102203/http://www.radionetherlands.nl/features/
cultureandhistory/031221be-in.html, accessed 24 October 2018.

'Midsummer Night at Glastonbury: Guru Maharaj Ji Speaks at the Glastonbury Fair, June 21, 1971, England', http://www.prem-rawat-bio.org/dlm_pubs/pamphlets/satsangs/gmj_glaxobury.html, accessed 30 October 2018.

'The Daily Telegraph: Nick Lowe on Maharaji's Visit, 1971', cited in http://prem-rawat-reviewed.org/history.html#_ftn16, accessed 1 November 2018.

'Ananda Mettaya – the First to Bring the "Living Force" of Buddhism to Britain', https://vajratool.wordpress.com/2010/04/25/ananda-metteyya-the-first-to-bring-the-living-force-of-buddhism-to-britain/, accessed 20 November 2018.

Sheidlower, Jesse (8 December 2004), 'Crying Wolof: Does the Word Hip Really Hail from a West African language?', *Slate Magazine*, https://slate.com/news-and-politics/2004/12/the-real-history-of-hip.html, accessed 22 November 2018.

Gibson, Harry (1986), 'Harry the Hipster Autobiography – from Los Angeles to NYC, Fans, Attorneys, and Musicians Praise Him', *Hyzer Creek*, http://www.hyzercreek.com/harryautobio.htm, accessed 22 November 2018.

'About the Rainbow Gypsies', http://rainbowgypsies.com/#about, accessed 26 November 2018.

Nova Religio, http://nr.ucpress.edu/content/about-0, accessed 27 November 2018.

Erlewine, Michael, 'East-West Live – The Paul Butterfield Band', *Allmusic.com*, https://www.allmusic.com/album/east-west-live-mw0000184524, accessed 27 November 2018.

'Tiger Stripes: Identify Individual Tigers by Their Stripes and Markings', Bruce Kukule.com, posted 9 May 2013, http://brucekekule.com/photography_abroad/tiger-stripes-identify-individual-tigers-by-their-stripes-and-markings/, accessed 29 March 2019.

Index

Lightning Source UK Ltd.
Milton Keynes UK
UKHW020038221121
394373UK00004B/152

9 781350 265448